YOU ✝ CAN BE THE
ULTIMATE
ATHLETE

Integrating Your
WHOLE BEING as You
Train and Compete

Susan R. Germanson

ACW Press
Eugene, Oregon 97405

You Can Be the Ultimate Athlete!

Cover Design by Alpha Advertising
Interior design by Pine Hill Graphics
Artwork by Joe Doherty
Drawing on page 172 by Earl Keleny

Packaged by ACW Press
85334 Lorane Hwy
Eugene, Oregon 97405
www.acwpress.com
The views expressed or implied in this work do not necessarily reflect those of ACW Press. Ultimate design, content, and editorial accuracy of this work is the responsibility of the author(s).

Library of Congress Cataloging-in-Publication Data
(Provided by Cassidy Cataloguing Services, Inc.)

   Germanson, Susan R.

      You can be the ultimate athlete : integrating your whole being as you train
      and compete / Susan R. Germanson. -- 1st ed. -- Eugene, Ore. : ACW
      Press, 2004.

         p. ; cm.

      ISBN: 1-932124-19-5

         1. Athletes--Spiritual life. 2. Athletics--Religious aspects. 3. Physical
      education and training--Religious aspects. 4. Spiritual life. I. Title.

   BL625.9.A84 G47 2004
   204.4--dc22   0401

Printed in the United States of America.

This book is dedicated to Eric Applen. Eric was the most courageous student/athlete that I have ever had the privilege to know. Eric is an inspiration to all who knew him. His legacy lives on in this book and in our hearts. We love you, Eric.

1985 - 2002

A portion of the proceeds from this book will go to the Eric Nicolin Applen Memorial Fund which provides funding for families whose children have cancer.

Acknowledgments

I first and foremost want to thank God and His son Jesus Christ. I am so thankful for the faith that I have, because it always has been a source of strength for me. I also want to thank my incredible daughter and her best friend Kelly. In addition, I am so appreciative of having such wonderful parents and a caring family. Special thanks to Mary, Margarita, and Walter and Scott. My heart felt thanks go out to Paul, Sheila, and Marcia Wellstone for being such incredible public servants for the many people. As I was finishing this book, they passed away tragically. Their lives and their legacy will always live on. I am grateful to the many pastors who have touched my life and ignited my faith. A special thanks goes out to all of my student/athletes.

1 Corinthians 1:4 *"I always thank God for you because of his grace given you in Christ Jesus."*

Table of Contents

Eric Applen

Foreword

As we walk this journey of life, the first thing to remember when going after something that is difficult is to break everything down to a simple process.

My son, Eric, had Metastatic Osteogenic Sarcoma (bone cancer that had spread to his lungs). He was an athlete with very high goals. His simple approach to this difficult disease was to attack with *Faith*, *Hope* and *Courage*.

Faith:

Keep your faith in front of you. It will guide you and comfort you in times of difficulty and stress. It will strengthen your resolve when you are at your weakest point. It will lead you when you need to follow.

Hope:

Never give up hope. It is a mindset that drives the will to win and the positive attitude that fights negativity.

Courage:

Courage does not always roar.

"Sometimes courage is the quiet voice at the end of the day saying, I will try again tomorrow." Mary Anne Radmacher

Susan Germanson gives you the blueprint in this book to achieve great things, with a simple process.

Thanks to Susan for dedicating this book to Eric. He was a true Cancer Warrior, who lives daily with *Faith*, *Hope*, and *Courage*.

"It's not winning that counts—it's the will to win!"

Mark Applen

Pregame Show

his book is written for all types of athletes— beginning athletes or accomplished athletes with lots of experience. It doesn't matter what sport you play. This book will be very useful for you and your teammates. All of you will be encouraged to trust God in your sports and in your life. This can be done by letting go and allowing God to be in charge.

> Isaiah 48:17-18 *"This is what the Lord says—your Redeemer, the Holy One of Israel: 'I am the Lord your God, who teaches you what is best for you, who directs you in the way you should go. If only you had paid attention to my commands, your peace would have been like a river, your righteousness like the waves of the sea.'"*

"When I let God steer we really go places. When I steer, I go in circles."
Unknown

Unique features of this book.
1. You don't have to read it from cover to cover. Feel free to jump around.

2. There are personal notes and ideas at the end of each chapter to tailor the ideas in this book to your situation. These questions allow you to identify where you are, and help you figure out some solutions to improve your life.
3. Each chapter has Bible verses and quotes to enhance that chapter. The Bible verses come from the New International Version unless stated. Also all bolding in the verses is the author's emphasis.
4. It is a reader-friendly handbook for athletes to carry with them wherever they go. No other book is needed. Sure it would be great to have a Bible handy as you are reading this book, but it isn't necessary. This book travels very well.
5. This book takes a multidimensional approach to athletics. That is why it is titled *You Can Be the Ultimate Athlete*. It will help you to become a balanced, well-rounded athlete and person. It explores the six dimensions of man:

   a. physical
   b. emotional
   c. mental/intellectual
   d. occupational
   e. social
   f. spiritual

6. All of the stories in this book actually happened. Many times, the names have been changed for various reasons.
7. Proverbs 16:17 *"The highway of the upright avoids evil; he who guards his way guards his soul."* In this book there is a huge focus on *choice*. God has given us all free choice. You have control of your attitude and actions. *The ultimate responsibility is up to you!*

The following are warm-up Bible verses that will help you in preparing to read this book. Incorporate the book's wisdom into your life and choose to become God's ultimate athlete.

Colossians 3:23 *"Whatever you do, work at it with all your heart, as working for the Lord, not for men."*

Colossians 3:17 *"And whatever you do, whether in word or deed, do it all in the name of the Lord Jesus, giving thanks to God the Father through him."*

Proverbs 16:3 *"Commit to the Lord whatever you do, and your plans will succeed."*

Proverbs 19:21 *"Many are the plans in a man's heart, but it is the Lord's purpose that prevails."*

Psalm 19:1,5 *"The heavens declare the Glory of God; the skies proclaim the work of his hands...like a champion rejoicing to run his course."*

Titus 3:1-2 *"Remind the people to be subject to rulers and authorities, to be obedient, to be ready to do whatever is good, to slander no one, to be peaceable and considerate, and to show true humility toward all men."*

"Opportunity—you always miss 100% of the shots you don't take."

Unknown

"Skate to where the puck is going to be, not where it has been."

Wayne Gretzky

Ultimate Athletes...

...don't complain, no matter how tough it gets.

...will give their all, every day, because they have a healthy respect for themselves and their goals.

...will cooperate with coaches and other athletes, even if they don't agree with them, because of their common goals.

...put personality differences aside at practice, meets, and other team functions.

...don't engage in gossip about other teammates, especially if it is negative.

...maintain true humility at all times.

...will not bring their personal issues and problems to practice, meets, and other team functions.

...focus totally and completely on their sport during practice, meets, and other team functions.

...go on with their lives outside of practice, and do not eat, drink, and sleep their sport. Balance is the key!

...listen to their bodies, and stop training to avoid more injury.

...help coaches with various tasks voluntarily, and without complaining.

...stay psyched up and help others keep the mental and physical intensity going. They have the positive-positive mentality.

...don't socialize in practice.

...start working out on time, and without warnings from the coach.

...take charge of their flexibility and strength. They understand that their whole athletic career is dependent upon achieving their maximum flexibility and strength.

...are willing to give up some social life, because *sports* (especially at the elite level) and *sacrifice* go hand in hand.

...maintain their studies as a huge importance, without affecting their athletic performance.

...prioritize their lives as God (#1), family (#2), school (#3), sports (#4), social life and play (#5).

...realize that faith, discipline, hard work, positive attitude, dedication, and perseverance will help them not only in sports, but in life!

2 Corinthians 5:20 *"We are therefore Christ's ambassadors, as though God were making his appeal through us. We implore you on Christ's behalf: Be reconciled to God."*

Part One
WORKOUTS

Introduction to Workouts

A thletes spend most of their time at practice. Many athletes train at least twenty hours a week for a two-hour competition. Some athletes will practice up to forty hours a week and only compete once a month. It varies for the different sports, but the majority of an athlete's time is spent during workouts. All athletes need to take this time seriously. In addition to being time consuming, the workouts can be grueling. The utmost concentration is needed to perform well, and not make errors that could cause injuries. In addition each athlete needs to be prepared emotionally, mentally, physically, and spiritually to make the most out of each practice.

The following chapters will help you learn how you can be an ultimate athlete with respect to your workouts. Be prepared for just about anything to happen while you are training. It is very important that each athlete choose to stay positive, no matter what happens. Many challenges are ahead for you, but it is your choice to make matters *better* or *worse*.

Ultimate athletes never think about quitting. Notice the negative attitudes in the following verse.

Nehemiah 4:10 *"Meanwhile, the people in Judah said, 'The strength of the laborers is giving out, and there is so much rubble that we cannot rebuild the wall.'"*

Ultimate athletes always believe in themselves, even if they are not able to do a certain maneuver correctly. They will keep trying until they get it right. Yes, they might get frustrated in the process, but they don't give up.

Psalm 18:29 *"With your help I can advance against a troop; with my God I can scale a wall."*

Proverbs 23:18 *"There is surely a future hope for you, and your hope will not be cut off."*

In the following chapters, you will find that the majority of your success during workouts is up to you. It is imperative that you learn how to stay positive in all types of situations.

Warm-Up

"Train yourself to be godly. For physical training is of some value, but godliness has value for all things, holding promise for both the present life and the life to come."

I Timothy 4:7,8

Warm-up is one of the most important aspects in the life of an athlete. The human body is an incredible machine, but it needs to be taken care of properly. When buying a new car, one needs to go slowly, and drive in a certain way, until the car is ready to be used at highway speeds. It is same with the human body, but we need to warm up many different ways. Obviously one needs to prepare the body physically by stretching and doing low-level exercise to wake up the body and prevent injury. However, God has created us all as multidimensional beings. The following are the six dimensions: physical, mental/intellectual, emotional, spiritual, occupational, and social.

While warming up for practice, it is also very important to prepare oneself mentally, emotionally, and spiritually. Many practices are grueling, and the utmost concentration is needed. Therefore the mind, spirit, and emotions need to get ready to meet the new challenge. During the warm-up time one should:

Physically—Stretch and follow the warm-up instructions of the coach.

Mentally—Prepare your mind not only to focus on the tasks at hand, but to be a positive force during the tough times.

Emotionally—During practice and warm-up, one needs to temporarily forget about other worries and frustrations in life. This makes for a nice two to three-hour break from all the pain and hardship in life.

Spiritually—We have been given a spiritual dimension in our lives. We can choose to use this powerful force as a motivator in *every* situation.

Focusing is crucial in sports! Not only to perform well, but also to prevent injuries. Therefore, there needs to be a way that athletes can prepare themselves in a *consistent* manner. Each athlete must learn to put aside all other things in life during their workouts. Distractions are one of the biggest downfalls for athletes. Becoming still and quieting one's heart, soul, and mind can help tremendously with those distractions.

Psalm 37:7 *"Be still before the Lord and wait patiently for him..."*

Psalm 46:10 *"Be still and know that I am God."*

One idea is for the athlete to imagine that they are entering a special bubble every time they start practicing. This bubble is a place where most things aren't allowed. In this bubble, the athlete will put aside everything that doesn't have to do with their practice. So schoolwork, personal problems, social activities, negative attitudes... are not allowed to enter. In the bubble, the athlete must bring positive attitudes, helpful team-building ideas, and intense focus on all aspects of practice. After practice is over, each athlete will walk out of the bubble and can resume their lives again. Some athletes like to envision that God, Jesus Christ, or angels are in the bubble giving them the strength that they need. See chapter 2 on "Focus" for more information.

At times practices can become unbearable. In many sports the athlete has to constantly push his/her body to total muscle and mental fatigue. Many times this happens on a daily basis. It is tough to keep up these rigorous training demands all the time. One way that can be a constant source of power is to dedicate each practice as a prayer for someone. Each athlete can decide on the particular person during the warm-up. It could be for a group of people, a family member who is going to have surgery, a friend who is struggling, or for a particular cause. Your workout will have more meaning, becoming a special time for someone or something that needs prayer.

This is very powerful, because when the practices get tough we can focus on the *reason* for our workout. It reminds us that our reason for practicing is not only that we get stronger or faster, but that a certain prayer be heard by our God in heaven. It is amazing how many physical, emotional, mental, and spiritual reserves that the human body has to help us make it through a drill. Prayer puts a whole different perspective on your entire athletic life. Instead of being very "me" centered, your time and energy are also concentrated on helping others. This is a great way to stay in constant prayer. 1 Thessalonians 5:17 *"Pray continually." ("Pray without ceasing."* King James Version)

It is a good idea to unite as a team and say your team's workout oath. The following are oaths from one team.

Eleven and Under

I promise to:
…work very hard today.
…not goof around.
…listen to the coaches.
…not complain.
…be positive and dedicate my workout to someone.
…and to be the best I can be.

Twelve and older

I promise to:
…work very hard today
…listen to the coaches.
…not socialize.
…forget about my problems or exciting news.
…just focus on my sport/performance.
…be positive and to dedicate my workout to someone.
…and to become the best I can be.

*"The warm-up before a training or a game is of paramount importance in producing and maintaining high performance levels.
The different benefits are better playing performance, decreased risk of injury, and improved psychological preparation."*

www.soccerperformance.org

Personal Notes and Ideas

1. What is the best way for me to warm up:
   Physically

   Mentally

   Emotionally

   Spiritually

2. What are the "tough times" that I have to endure in practice?

3. What are some ideas that can help me to not only survive these "tough times," but to get the most out of them?

4. I want to dedicate some of my practices to the following people:

5. My oath for every practice will be:

6. What would Jesus do?

7. How do all the Bible verses in this chapter help me? Are there other verses that can help me be an ultimate athlete during my warm-up?

Focus

"Be still and know that I am God."

Psalm 46:10

Every sport requires a huge amount of concentration and focus. As mentioned in the "Warm-Up" chapter, we need to put ourselves in a situation where we can completely devote ourselves to the tasks at hand. One of the best ways to do this is to visualize the practice bubble. Yes, when you go to practice you need to pretend that you are going into a bubble, where most everything else is *not* allowed. There is so much going on in our lives that we need to quiet ourselves in order to get the most out of each practice. Be still and give yourself a break from all your daily stress. Don't bring personal problems, school, or work into the practice arena. Consider your practice time as a vacation from all the craziness of life. Not only do athletes need to focus completely to excel in their sport, but many sports are considered catastrophic. This means that you could get injured very seriously with just one mistake.

So what can come into the bubble? Obviously your athletic needs are one thing. Let your dedicated person come into the bubble, along with God and His angels. God can give us peace and the angels can be a source of assurance for us. The following verse can give us insight as to what we should bring into our bubble:

Philippians 4:8,9 *"...whatever is true, whatever is noble, whatever is right, whatever is pure, whatever is lovely, whatever is admirable—if anything is excellent or praiseworthy—think about such things."*

A typical problem that athletes have in practice is to socialize too much. Yes most of your teammates are your best friends, and you do have a lot to talk about. However, practice is *not* the place to do this. Your *talk* should be encouraging others to make their goals, team strategy, cheering ....Your actions should match your words. Read the following verses, because they should help you keep your socializing out of the practice arena.

Colossians 3:23 *"Whatever you do, work at it with all your heart, as working for the Lord, not for men."*

Philippians 3:12-14 *"Not that I have already obtained all this, or have already been made perfect, but I press on to take hold of that for which Christ Jesus took hold of me. Brothers, I do not consider myself yet to have taken hold of it. But one thing I do: **forgetting what is behind** and straining toward what is ahead, press on toward the goal to win the prize for which God has called me heavenward in Christ Jesus."*

One special note is that this bubble idea should work at least 95 percent of the time. There are times in life where we are rendered unconscious emotionally, spiritually, mentally, and physically. No one is immune to tragedy and the effects it has on their lives. Sometimes it will be nearly impossible to leave everything outside the bubble when you go to practice. During times like these, you need to go to practice and just do your best. If you feel that you might hurt yourself because you can't concentrate, maybe you shouldn't work out. Helping coach, encouraging, or spectating might be a good idea for that day. However, remember these times are for those excruciating tragedies, and not for the day-to-day inconveniences and frustrations that happen frequently.

> *"To play your best, you must keep your mind in the present moment and on the requirements of the task. You need to learn to forget about the results and focus on the process—one play at a time. Keep your mind focused on the present play, and if your mind wanders to results, let it go, and refocus on what you are doing at that moment."*
>
> Dr. Patrick J. Cohn, sports psychologist

Personal Notes and Ideas

1. What is my practice bubble like?

2. What good things should go into my bubble?

3. What are some things that come into my practice bubble that shouldn't be there?

4. What do I need to do to make sure that those distractions don't come with me to practice?

5. What is the best way that I can "still" myself so that I can concentrate and give it my all?

6. How can I help my teammates with their distractions and encourage them to use the bubble idea?

7. What would Jesus do?

8. How do all the Bible verses in this chapter help me? Are there other verses that can help me be an ultimate athlete when I focus?

Workout

"Make vows to the Lord your God and fulfill them."

Psalm 76:11

"When you make a vow to God, do not delay in fulfilling it. He has no pleasure in fools; fulfill your vow. It is better not to vow than to make a vow and not fulfill it."

Ecclesiastes 5:4-5

If you aim at nothing, you get just that. Nothing! Goals are important for athletes, and are very helpful in making a successful athlete. As mentioned previously in the "Warm-Up" chapter, make sure that you have chosen to dedicate your workout to someone. Also have some goals for that practice. For instance, you could try for a certain time, an amount of points, goals, baskets, new moves, or flips. Make yourself a vow that you will focus and try your best to achieve those goals. If for some reason you were not able to reach those goals, put them on the list for tomorrow.

The main ingredients in having an awesome workout are repetition, hard work, self-motivation, and a positive attitude.

Repetition is "the name of the game" for most sports. By doing something over and over and over again, that athletes achieve their goals. Fine tuning of a specific maneuver a necessity in sports. The only way to achieve that excellence is to do it a thousand times over. Yes, it can be tiring, and sometimes boring, but that is where hard work, self-motivation, and a positive attitude come into play.

Most athletes don't have a full understanding of what hard work really means. As a matter of fact, to work hard in practice is an understatement! Athletes need to push themselves incredibly hard physically, emotionally, mentally, and spiritually day in and day out. Some verses that can help us work hard are:

Proverbs 14:23 *"All hard work brings profit, but mere talk leads only to poverty."*

Luke 13:24 *"Make every effort to enter through the narrow door."*

Ephesians 5:15-16 *"Be very careful, then, how you live—not as unwise but as wise, making the most out of every opportunity."*

1 Timothy 4:7-8 *"Train yourself in godliness; for while the bodily training is of some value, godliness is of value in every way, as it holds promise for the present life and also for the life to come."*

Popular thought is that it is the coach who "makes or breaks" the season. Contrary to that though, it is the athlete who is the major factor in his/her success. Many athletes have excelled under coaches who are not that good. In addition, many athletes have not responded under some of the best coaches in the world. There is the old saying, "You can lead a horse to water, but you can't make him drink." Each athlete who is serious about competing needs to be in charge of their own *attitude* and *actions*. With respect to choices, the athlete should take the *credit* or the *blame*. It all comes down to the athlete. (However, we always should give God the glory for our successes.) Not enough can be said about self-motivation and a positive attitude. Each athlete should be doing his/her best whether the coach is watching or not.

Proverbs 6:6-8 *"Go to the ant...consider its ways and be wise! It has no commander, no overseer or ruler, yet it stores its provisions in summer and gathers its food at harvest."*

Psalm 18:29 *"With your help I can advance against any troop/run through a barricade; with my God I can scale a wall."*

Philippians 4:13 *"I can do everything through him who gives me strength."*

During a workout, make sure that you aren't just *trying*, but actually *training* all out to become your best.

> *"I have nothing to offer but blood, toil, tears, and sweat."*
>
> Winston Churchill

> *Enthusiasm and confidence are contagious...So is the lack of it!*
>
> Glen Mason, Head football coach, University of Minnesota

Personal Notes and Ideas

1. What are some of my goals for my workouts?

2. What repetitive drills are helpful to me? How can I stay motivated during those drills?

3. What does *hard work* really mean to me?

4. What does the following quote mean to me with respect to my *attitude* and *actions*? "Life is a do-it-yourself project, you can take the *credit* or the *blame*."

5. What are some great self-motivating ideas that will work for me?

6. How can I have a positive attitude, no matter what happens?

7. How can I encourage my teammates to have a positive attitude?

8. What would Jesus do?

9. How do all these Bible verses in this chapter help me? Are there other verses that can help me be an ultimate athlete with my workouts?

Stretching and Flexibility

"Don't you know that you yourselves are God's temple and that God's spirit lives in you? If anyone destroys God's temple, then God will destroy him; for God's temple is sacred, and you are that temple."

1 Corinthians 3:16-17

There is a great saying that goes like this: "Blessed are the flexible, because they will not be bent out of shape." There is a lot of truth to this statement, but not just in the physical sense. This also holds true both emotionally and spiritually. One of the main reasons for stretching in athletics is to avoid injury. However this important aspect usually gets short-changed by most athletes. Some don't make it a priority or say that they just don't have enough time. Let's look at Ecclesiastes chapter 3: *"There is a time for everything, and a season for every activity under heaven: a time to be born and a time to die, a time to weep and a time to laugh, a time to mourn and a time to dance..."* I would like to add that there is also a *time to stretch and work on your flexibility!*

Here are some solutions for those of you who do have busy schedules with school and other obligations. Stretching can be done while doing other activities. While you are stretching your legs, you can study, read a book, or write a letter. One of the best times to do full body stretching is when you watch TV. Instead of sitting on the couch for a half an hour, get down on the floor and stretch! You could also do some sit-ups and push-ups while watching television. For those of you who are not flexible at all, take heart. It can be done! During one month you must dedicate yourself to stretch every day for thirty minutes. Do this and you will be amazed at how your flexibility has improved. Make a vow or put a chart on the wall to check off each time you complete your thirty minutes. Be careful that you don't overdo it. Be patient and stick with it!

Psalm 76:11 *"Make vows to the Lord your God and fulfill them."*

Ecclesiastes 5:4-5 *"When you make a vow to God, do not delay in fulfilling it. He has no pleasure in fools; fulfill your vow. It is better not to vow than to make a vow and not fulfill it."*

In addition to physical stretching, continue to improve your emotional and spiritual flexibility so that they don't become injured either. Spiritually, we live in a diverse world. What is important to us may not be important to others. Moreover, other people will value different things more than we do. As Christians we are called to love one another. We must do that, no matter how different the other person is. We should also be ready to share our faith, in a gentle and respectful manner, with other people. This way they can have a chance to hear the Gospel and the source of our joy.

1 Peter 3:15 *"But in your hearts set apart Christ as Lord. Always be prepared to give an answer to everyone who asks you to give the reason for the hope that you have. But do this with gentleness and respect."*

Spiritually we need to realize that we live in a world of diverse cultures and religions. Even though our faith and religion are very important to us, we still need to coexist peacefully with others. We need to be inclusive of others and respect their heritage. A great

33

example of someone who was very inclusive was Jesus Christ. He hung out with everyone. However, when people were being abusive or crossing the line, He did let them know.

With respect to emotions, there are many different personalities that we interact with daily. We need to be patient and not overact in various situations. Most of the time, it is not worth it to lose your cool over a certain situation. However on the other hand, we are not doormats for people to walk over. At times we need to put up our boundaries and say "enough" in an assertive manner. One good way to know whether you should react or not is by asking yourself the following question, "A year from now, will this still frustrate me?" If it won't bother you, then think about being patient and tolerant. If it will still be a frustration a year later, then you need to stick up for yourself in a *dignified* manner.

As you ponder your flexibility in all areas of your life, think about this verse:

> 1 Timothy 4:15 *"Be diligent in these matters; give yourself wholly to them, so that everyone may see your progress."*

> *"If you want to recover quickly from annoying injury; put-a-stop to stiff, aching muscles; and radically improve your sporting performance; you need to stretch correctly."*
> Brad Walker—author of the *Stretching Handbook*

> *"Stretching is a must in any program for any level of athlete. Flexibility is essential for every athlete and should remain an important component of any fitness regime."*
> Ron Palmer—strength and conditioning coach

Personal Notes and Ideas

1. Where am I lacking in my flexibility?
   Physically

Mentally

Emotionally

Spiritually

2. What are some ideas to improve my flexibility?
Physically

Emotionally

Spiritually

3. What are the goals for my flexibility?
Physically

Emotionally

Spiritually

4. How can I encourage other teammates to be flexible too?

5. What would Jesus do?

6. How can the Bible verses in this chapter help me? Are there other verses that can help me be an ultimate athlete with my flexibility?

Strength and Conditioning

"Everyone who competes in the games goes into strict training. They do it to get a crown that will not last; but we do it to get a crown that will last forever."

1 Corinthians 9:25

The major goal in strength and conditioning is to get stronger physically. However, sports can be so grueling that the athlete needs to be strong in all areas of life. Therefore, we need to train ourselves with that in mind.

Physically—Each athlete should work on overall strength to boost performance and to prevent injuries.

Spiritually and emotionally—Time and time again we hear about the athlete that has overcome a personal crisis in the midst of his or her career. Sometimes these tragedies are during the biggest moments of athletic careers such as the Olympics, Nationals, or playoffs. Emotional and spiritual strength are imperative during these personal and athletic hardships. We need to tap into our faith and emotions on a *regular basis*, so that we don't become paralyzed in those areas. We live in a tough world, and there are no guarantees. Many times we can't control the *situation*, but we can control our *attitudes* and *actions*.

Intellectual/Occupational—Keeping a sharp mind is very important for all people. Many athletes are students too, so they need to do a balancing act with their studies and their sport. The intellectual and occupational areas will go together, because a student's main job is to graduate and get a degree. In most student/athlete's lives there isn't much time for being social. The workload is huge and time consuming. Therefore each person who chooses this life needs to understand that by sacrificing their social needs, they will be gaining through their sport.

Social—Yes, there isn't much time for a social life outside of work or school and sports. However, this can be approached two ways. Athletes can be frustrated that they can't do everything that they want to, or they can see their sports as their social life. It is very common for athletes to find their best friends in their sporting activities because they spend so much time together at practices, meets, travelling to meets, or team parties. Remember this when you have to give up a fun party due to an athletic commitment. On the other hand, beware that sports don't become your whole life. Balance is the key! You should make time for family and other friends so that you don't completely burn out on your sport.

Another important aspect regarding strength is to remember that each athlete must stay motivated. Day-to-day strength workouts can become tedious, boring, and painful. In order to get stronger, you need to push yourself to exhaustion. Hopefully the following verses will help you with your workouts. WARNING! It is imperative that athletes listen to their bodies. There is a difference between muscle fatigue and joint pain. Many athletes have been injured due to the Repetitive Motion Syndrome. They have pushed too hard while doing the same movement, and now they need to sit out due to stress injuries. Make sure your coach knows about your pain. Most teams have an athletic trainer, so take advantage of that too. Don't keep your pain to yourself, because it could be a potential injury!

Colossians 3:23-25 *"Whatever you do, work at it with all your heart, as working for the Lord, not for men, since you know that you will receive an inheritance from the Lord as a reward. It is the Lord Christ you are serving..."*

Galatians 6:4-5 *"Each one should test his own actions. Then he can take pride in himself, without comparing himself to somebody else, for each one should carry his own load."*

Ecclesiastes 5:4-5 *"When you make a vow to God, do not delay in fulfilling it. He has no pleasure in fools; fulfill your vow. It is better not to vow than to make a vow and not fulfill it."*

"Physical strength comes from training, lifting one more weight. Or in case of a gymnast, doing one more flip. But real courage and real strength comes from God."

Mary Lou Retton, Olympic Gold Medalist

"Without proper conditioning in all areas, you will fall short of your potential."

John Wooden, UCLA Head Basketball Coach

Personal Notes and Ideas

1. Where am I lacking in strength?

Physically—

Spiritually and emotionally—

Intellectually and occupationally—

Socially—

2. How can I strengthen myself in all of the areas of my life?

Physically—

Spiritually and emotionally—

Intellectually and occupationally—

Socially—

3. How can I encourage my teammates in their strength and conditioning?

4. What would Jesus do?

5. How can the Bible verses in this chapter help me? Are there other verses that help me be an ultimate athlete with my strength and conditioning?

Sore Muscles

"Endure hardship with us like a good soldier of Christ Jesus."

One big frustration with sports is sore muscles. It is not easy, or fun, to train with sore muscles. However, if we don't keep training hard, we will get out of shape. When athletes do a different style of workout, they may find "new muscles" the next day. Yes, you wake up the next day and a different part of your body is hurting. Then you say to yourself, "Ughh! I have to work out with this pain, too!" Here is some advice:

1. Sore muscles go with the territory.
2. Make sure that you get a good warm-up and have stretched that muscle adequately.
3. Remember that you have a buildup of lactic acid in the muscle and working out is the best thing for that muscle. In a couple of days you won't be sore, because your body/muscle will get used to that type of training. One of the worst things an athlete can do is to *not* work out, because they will have to start getting fit all over again.
4. Refer to the strength and conditioning chapter, which covers listening to your body.

5. Continue to remember the person to whom you are dedicating your practice.
6. Focus on your technique and not the pain. Instead of thinking about the aching muscles, have your mind set on polishing your technique. This will not only help you to become a fine-tuned athlete, but it can also prevent you from becoming injured due to lack of focus.

So the best advice is to learn to take care of and cope with sore muscles.

You can also put things into perspective. We are training our bodies to be physically fine-tuned, but remember that our pain is only temporary. Moreover, athletics is only one part of our complex lives. Read the following Bible verses:

Romans 8:17-18 *"Now if we are children, then we are heirs—heirs of God and co-heirs with Christ, if indeed we share in his sufferings in order that we may also share in his glory. I consider that our present sufferings are not worth comparing with the glory that will be revealed in us."*

1 Corinthians 9:24-27 *"Do you not know that in a race all the runners run, but only one gets the prize? Run in such a way as to get the prize. Everyone who competes in the games goes into strict training. They do it to get a crown that will not last; but we do it to get a crown that will last forever. Therefore I do not run like a man running aimlessly; I do not fight like a man beating the air. No, I beat my body and make it my slave so that after I have preached to others, I myself will not be disqualified for the prize."*

2 Corinthians 4:16-18 *"Therefore we do not lose heart. Though outwardly we are wasting away, yet inwardly we are being renewed day by day. For our light and momentary troubles are achieving for us an eternal glory that far outweighs them all. So we fix our eyes not on what is seen, but on what is unseen. For what is seen is temporary, but what is unseen is eternal."*

James 1:2-4 *"Consider it pure joy, my brothers whenever you face trials of many kinds, because you know that the testing of your faith develops perseverance. Perseverance must finish its work so that you may be mature and complete not lacking anything."*

Another way to put our physical pain into perspective is to look at how Jesus died. During that time period, being crucified was the cruelest, most painful, and torturous way to die. Crucified people didn't die instantly, but very slowly as their bodies gave out. Here is a play-by-play description of how Jesus died:

1. He was flogged. Flogging is similar to being hit with a whip. However these whips had rocks or pieces of metal on the end of the ropes. The torturers would aim for the top, dig the pieces in, and then pull down to the low back. By doing this most of the skin on the back was ripped off.
2. He also had to wear a crown of thorns. (And we complain about headaches!) It most likely had needles of sharp thorns one to two inches long.
3. His hands and feet were nailed to the cross.
4. They dropped the cross into the earth, so that the crucified body was jerked. By doing this, Jesus' shoulders were dislocated and He could not breathe.
5. In order to breathe, Jesus had to use His legs to push up in order to fill His lungs. Remember, the feet that He used had nails in them.
6. A sword pierced His side so that the blood and fluids would flow out of His body.
7. As time went on, the pain and fatigue overwhelmed Jesus to the point of total exhaustion. He ended up suffocating to death.

Research indicates that, in athletics, the mind tires before the body. Our bodies have more reserves than we could ever imagine. Knowing this and knowing how Jesus died can help us through our tough times. How was Jesus able to hang in there while He was on the cross? The emotional pain of His abandonment and His physical condition were just too unbearable. So Jesus needed to really depend on His other resources. His intellectual and spiritual dimensions had to work overtime. The only way Jesus could sacrifice His life and shed His blood to save us was to believe in what He had learned from His father while He was on earth. Therefore, He chose to listen to His intellectual and spiritual self so that He could finish the work that was destined for Him. Wow! That is a lot to imagine. But Jesus did it, and we can do it too!

> *"If you want God to move a mountain, you'd better bring a shovel."*
>
> Unknown

> *"Focus your mind on what is positive and working in your life, not on the defeats or what is causing you pain or tension."*
>
> Hans Selye

Personal Notes and Ideas

1. What muscles hurt the most? What can I do to fix the problem?

2. What are some positive mental things that I can do to take my mind off my tired muscles?

3. How can I help my teammates if they are struggling with sore muscles?

4. How can I put my sore muscles into perspective with how Jesus died for me?

5. What would Jesus do?

6. How do all the Bible verses in this chapter help me? Are there other verses that can help me with my sore muscles?

Boredom

*"Create in me a pure heart, O God, and renew
a steadfast spirit within me."*

Psalm 51:10

s previously mentioned in the workout chapter, repetition is the key to excellence. Obviously when we do the same thing over and over again, boredom can be a challenge, if not a frustration. During this time a positive attitude is a must! When one begins to complain, it can be destructive and contagious. Philippians 2:14 *"Do everything without complaining or arguing."*

What can we do to keep ourselves from becoming too bored?

1. If it is a repetitive set (10 X 100 meters) then you can dedicate each 100 meters to someone as a prayer.
2. Sing some fun songs during the rest intervals or sing them as you are doing each set.
3. You can play the Guessing Game, known also as Twenty Questions. Have the coach think of a person, place, or thing. Various groups will try to guess what the coach has chosen. The groups should start with general questions and get more specific as they go. All questions need to be answered with yes or no. If it is no then everyone has to do the lap. If

it is answered yes, no one has to do the lap, and the next group gets to ask their question. Continue with the game with each group taking turns asking their yes or no questions.

At any time a group can raise their hands and go for the final answer. The group that guesses the specific person, place or thing correctly will get fewer laps than the rest of the groups. However if they guess wrong, they will get ten penalty laps more than the other groups. Continue playing until some group guesses the final answer correctly. The beauty of this game is that instead of thinking about your sore muscles, lack of breath, or boredom, your mind is set on trying to figure out what the coach has chosen.

4. Think of some good, *clean* jokes that can keep the humor going. Laughter is the best medicine for almost anything.

5. If it is a matter of doing the same maneuver, flip, trick, dive, or basket many times over, try to see how many that you can nail (do correctly) out of ten. Challenge yourself to beat your old record.

6. Keep your focus on your personal goals and also on the *person* to whom you dedicated your practice.

7. Be patient and optimistic that these drills will help you to achieve your goals. Proverbs 19:11 *"A man's wisdom gives him patience…"*

Hebrews 12:1-3 *"Therefore, since we are surrounded by such a great cloud of witnesses, let us throw off everything that hinders and the sin that so easily entangles, and let us run with perseverance the race marked out for us. Let us fix our eyes on Jesus, the author and perfector of our faith, who for the joy set before him endured the cross, scorning its shame, and sat down at the right hand of the throne of God. Consider him who endured such opposition from sinful men, so that you will not grow weary and lose heart."*

"A day without laughter is a day wasted."
Charlie Chaplin

> *"Humor is a proof of faith, proof that everything is going to be all right with God."*
> Charles M. Schulz (creator of the Peanuts comics)

Personal Notes and Ideas

1. What are the parts of my practices that are boring to me?

2. What can I do to make the most of those boring times?

3. How can I be a positive motivator for the team during those times?

4. How can I encourage my teammates to be positive motivators?

5. What would Jesus do?

6. How do all the Bible verses in this chapter help me? Are there other verses that can help me be an ultimate athlete with respect to boredom?

Breaking Training

> "Stop listening to instruction, my son, and you will stray from the words of knowledge."
>
> Proverbs 19:27

> "You were running a good race. Who cut in on you and kept you from obeying the truth?"
>
> Galatians 5:7

People

1. Samson—He was a very strong champion many times over. However he chose to "break his training" with God. He became a selfish, shallow, and violent person who liked to blame others. He was motivated by lust, vengeance, power and hatred and ended up losing his eyes, strength, dignity, and life due to his poor choices. Read Judges chapters 14-16.

2. Judas—Judas chose to follow Jesus, but then he chose to abandon, abuse, deceive, and betray his good friends. He was not only a traitor to Jesus, but to God, the other disciples, and people of faith.

Not only did he stop what was good, but he made matters worse for a lot of people.

All of Psalm 106 is about people making poor choices (especially verses 6,13,25,39,43).

6 *We have sinned, even as our fathers did; we have done wrong and acted wickedly.*

13 *But they soon forgot what he had done and did not wait for his counsel.*

25 *They grumbled in their tents and did not obey the Lord.*

39 *They defiled themselves by what they did; by their deeds they prostituted themselves.*

43 *Many times he delivered them, but they were bent on rebellion and they wasted away in their sin.*

There are many ways of breaking training:

- Skipping practice or faking an illness.
- Messing around at practice, not doing all the work, getting in the way of others...
- Drugs/alcohol/smoking/poor nutrition
- Becoming academically ineligible.
- Totally giving up on God and faith.
- Abusing teammates by being an negative force (emotionally) on the team.

Some of these actions are abusive to your teammates and coaches. All of these actions are self-destructive. See more on self abuse in chapter 39, "Abusive Situations." Check out the arrows of choice!

Self-Destructive verses:

Proverbs 11:17 "*A kind man benefits himself, but a cruel man brings trouble on himself.*"

Proverbs 26:27 *"If a man digs a pit, he will fall into it; if a man rolls a stone, it will roll back on him."*

Proverbs 14:1 *"The wise woman builds her house, but with her own hands the foolish one tears hers down."*

Psalm 30:9 *"What gain is there in my destruction, in my going down into the pit? Will the dust praise you? Will it proclaim your faithfulness?"*

There is hope, because people can turn their lives around. Look at the life of Paul. He used to persecute the followers of Jesus, and then he became one of the biggest disciples. Read Acts chapters 7:54–8:3 and 9:1-31. Judas did accept responsibility for his actions too. Matthew 27:3,4 *"When Judas, who had betrayed him, saw that Jesus was condemned, he was seized with remorse and returned the thirty silver coins to the chief priests and the elders. 'I have sinned,' he said, 'for I have betrayed innocent blood.'"*

Verses of advice and hope:

Proverbs 25:26 *"Like a muddied spring or a polluted well is a righteous man who gives way to the wicked."* If others are breaking training, don't follow along. Don't yield to peer pressure.

Isaiah 52:2 *"Shake off your dust; rise up, sit enthroned, O Jerusalem. Free yourself from the chains on your neck, O captive Daughter of Zion."* This basically says get your act together!

Isaiah 49:23 *"… those who hope in me will not be disappointed."*

Isaiah 66:13 *"As a mother comforts her child, so will I comfort you; and you will be comforted over Jerusalem."* No matter what you have done, God is there to help you fix your life and to comfort you.

Solutions for breaking training: Admit to yourself, teammates, coaches, and God that you have made a serious mistake.

Psalm 119:67 *"Before I was afflicted I went astray, but now I obey your word."*

Malachi 3:6 *"Return to me and I will return to you."*

Read all of Psalm 51.

Personal Notes and Ideas

1. What have I done to break training and what can I do to fix the problem?
   against myself

   against my teammates and coaches

2. Who can help me with this problem?

3. How can I help my teammates if they are breaking training?

4. What can we learn from Judas, Paul, and Samson?

5. What would Jesus do?

6. How do all the Bible verses in this chapter help me? Are there other verses that can help me with breaking training?

Other self-abuse verses:

Proverbs 28:10
Proverbs 29:6
Proverbs 8:36
Psalm 7:15,16
Proverbs 22:3

"Breaking training is an easy thing to fall into, and unfortunately it is contagious. Be aware of the various temptations that can trap you."
Joe Thiel, collegiate athlete and coach

Part Two
COMPETITION

Introduction to Competition

*"The horse is made ready for the day of battle,
but victory rests with the Lord."*

Proverbs 21:31

ompetition is the main event for all athletes. The reason that they make tremendous sacrifices, work their bodies to complete exhaustion, and invest huge amounts of money and time is primarily to be able to compete. Athletes want to jump the highest, have a great shooting percentage or superb batting average, or perform a special maneuver to perfection in order to win the gold. The big event can bring nervous excitement and volatile emotions. A lot is at stake and one small mistake can cost the athlete tremendously. Philippians 4:6 *"Do not be anxious about anything, but in everything, by prayer and petition, with thanksgiving, present your requests to God."*

It is very important that athletes prepare themselves correctly so that they will be able to perform in an *excellent* manner. Notice I didn't say in a "perfect" manner. No one is perfect, and striving for perfection isn't a healthy goal. It should be every athlete's goal to strive for excellence. *This is being the best that you can be at that particular time!* To aim at perfection is very harmful to athletes, because perfection is not attainable. Striving for perfection makes athletes feel inferior and frustrated with themselves.

In addition to the physical act of competition, the athlete needs to look at the big picture. Most are role models whether they like it or not. People are watching their every move, making self-control essential during the competition. There are tons of reasons that athletic events become very emotional. Sports bring out the very *best* or the very *worst* in us. During competition you will experience all kind of emotions from the fantastic exhilaration of winning to the devastating feelings of loss and tragedy. To avoid any embarrassing moments, each athlete needs to prepare themselves in *all areas* of their life for *each* competition. With respect to being a good example and role model refer to Colossians 3:8: *"But now you must rid yourselves of all such things as these: anger, rage, malice, slander, and filthy language from your lips."*

Being a good sport is a must! No matter what the situation, athletes will be tested to the max as to how they will respond. Sports are like life. You have your ups and downs, fairness and unfairness, cheaters and clean players. The list of what can happen during competition is endless. However, "an ounce of prevention is worth a pound of cure." You need to consider all the various situations you might experience, and have a plan to act in an appropriate manner. The following chapters will help you to prepare for your competitions.

"You are responsible for the effort, not the outcome, God is in charge of the outcome."
Mary Jo Copeland, founder of Sharing and Caring Hands

Pre-Competition

> *"Don't you know that you yourselves are God's temple and that God's Spirit lives in you? If anyone destroys God's temple, God will destroy him; for God's temple is sacred, and you are that temple."*
>
> 1 Corinthians 3:16-17

With respect to pre-competition there are two trains of thought. First, there are the *couple of days* leading up to the competition. Next, there are the *couple of hours* before you begin competing. Both are very important and need to be taken seriously.

Taking care of ourselves is of utmost importance for everyone, whether we are athletes or not! 1 Corinthians 10:31 *"So whether you eat or drink or whatever you do, do it for the glory of God."* Think of your life as a car. If you run it to the ground, don't do any maintenance, don't change the oil, or put in the wrong kind of gas, the car will break down. It is the same with our bodies, our emotions, our faith… these areas need constant attention. This should be done on a regular basis.

A. The days leading up to a competition. We should be very vigilant with ourselves, especially for a major competition. Some of the important things to do are:

- Eat right
- Get sleep
- Don't do anything that is physically draining except for your workout. (Example: water ski, haul dirt, lift heavy wood....)
- Stay spiritually focused and spend time with God.
- Do lots of mental/visual imagery for your event.

B. During the hours before the competition. The most important thing is to put yourself in the right frame of mind, body, spirit, and emotions. No matter what the situation is, do your best to stay positive. It may be hard work, but stay positive! Build up yourself, your teammates, and your coaches through encouraging, positive statements. Remember that one bad apple can spoil the whole bunch! Don't be that bad apple. Instead be the positive energy force for you and your team.

> Ephesians. 4:29 *"Do not let any unwholesome talk come out of your mouths, but only what is helpful for building others up according to their needs, that it may benefit those who listen."*

As far as your physical warm-up, do what is best for you and follow the coach's advice. With respect to calming oneself, and becoming still in your heart, soul, and mind, one needs to have a plan. One plan that has worked for many athletes is to imagine that the only person in the stands is God. Psalm 37:7 *"Be still before the Lord and wait patiently for him; do not fret when men succeed in their ways..."* Whether your audience is large or small, just focus on the fact that God is the only one sitting there. The neat thing about this is that *God loves us* whether we perform well or not. This should take away the pressure that you might be experiencing. Focusing on God will help you to see the whole picture of life. It won't be the end of the world whether you win or lose. More on this idea is found in chapter 16, "Pressure to Perform."

"When I am warming up I put a cross behind the mound. I always walk over to the cross before I face every batter. That's a comforting feeling for me to be out there and to have that peace of mind that I'm playing for an audience of One. So I can handle whatever the result is."

Andy Benes, pitcher for St. Louis Cardinals

Personal Notes and Ideas

1. What is the best way for me to get ready in the days before my competition?

2. What is the best way for me to prepare myself just before competition?

3. How can I stay positive no matter what happens?

4. How will it help me to visualize that God is the only one in the stands?

5. How can I be helpful to my coach and teammates during pre-competition?

6. How can I encourage my teammates to take care of themselves before the meet?

7. What would Jesus do?

8. How do the Bible verses in this chapter help me? Are there other verses that could help me be an ultimate athlete during pre-competition?

Traveling

"Have I not commanded you? Be strong and courageous. Do not be terrified; do not be discouraged, for the Lord your God will be with you wherever you go."

Joshua 1:9

raveling plays a big part in competition. In order to compete, one group needs to travel to the competition site. Car, bus, train, or plane are the most common modes of transportation. Some trips are long and some are short. Even though it can be exciting to go to a new city, traveling isn't always easy. There can be flight delays, long boring rides, and bad hotels or accommodations. However traveling is necessary, and four things come to mind.

I. Safety

Most athletes are excited about their upcoming sports event, but they do need to travel safely. This means allowing the driver to concentrate. Moving around on the bus, screaming and shouting, throwing things—all are distractions to the driver. Doing team cheers is a great idea, but getting out of control is asking for an accident to happen.

Along with safety comes the fear factor. Some people are afraid of flying. Since the terrorist attacks on the United States, more people have become nervous about flying. Please read Luke 21:9-19. It talks about the dangers of wartime. However it also encourages us that we will not be hurt, and to use this time as a testimony. Many verses in the Bible can give you peace as you are in the air. These verses encourage us to not be fearful.

> Psalm 46:1-2, 10 *"God is our refuge and strength, an ever-present help in trouble. Therefore we will not fear, though the earth give way and the mountains fall into the heart of the sea, 'Be still, and know that I am God; I will be exalted among the nations, I will be exalted in the earth.'"*

> Proverbs 24:19-20 *"Do not fret because of evil men or be envious of the wicked, for the evil man has no future hope, and the lamp of the wicked will be snuffed out."*

> Psalm 34:7 *"The angel of the Lord encamps around those who fear him, and he delivers them."*

2. Long trips

Many times the trips we take to competition can be long. Yes, it can get boring at times, but choose to make this time a positive experience. This time could be used for team bonding. Get to know the other people on your team. Play some games, do some cheers, or think of some team-building topics that you can share. You can also do some team strategizing and get emotionally, mentally, and spiritually ready for your competition.

> Hebrews 10:25 *"Let us not give up meeting together, as some are in the habit of doing, but let us encourage one another…"*

3. Representing your team, school, nation, God…

Don't forget that when traveling you are representing your team and possibly your school, your country and God. Many unwritten rules have been adapted by the athletic community. Therefore athletes should be on their best behavior and dress appropriately.

Unfortunately many judge a book by its cover—first impressions are critical. Be proud of the team you represent! Wear nice clothes or team outfits when traveling. Instead of grumbling about the clothes that you have to wear, use those clothes as a way to psych up for competition. At one high school, the girls had to wear dresses on the days of competition. At first this was an awful idea to the girls. However, they found that more people realized when they were having their competitions, due to the dresses. Students and staff all day long were wishing them good luck!

Many athletes are not only representing their teams, but also God and Jesus Christ. So athletes should follow the lead of Jesus. He was humble, considerate, and caring

> 2 Corinthians 5:20 *"We are therefore Christ's ambassadors, as though God was making his appeal through us."*

Your actions and your talk should also be positive, because people are watching. The key word is "appropriate." Don't do anything that would cause embarrassment or harm to yourself or your team.

4. Hints for traveling:

Leave early! Plan for some kind of delay, whether it be snow, bad traffic, or a car accident. No athlete needs the stress of having a short warm-up. If something does happen, remember that you are in control of your *attitudes* and *actions*. Think positive in your situation, and act accordingly.

Fly early! There are plane delays all the time. Don't fly the day before your competition. Many athletes have missed out on competing nationally due to flight problems. You need to fly two days before your competition date. Then if there is a problem, you have another twenty-four hours to get on another plane. Also carry on your athletic equipment, because luggage gets lost easily. So plan ahead and carry on the necessities. Put your other things in a suitcase that you will check in at the counter.

Here is a special psalm for you, especially when you travel to competitions.

Psalm 121 *"I lift up my eyes to the hills—where does my help come from? My help comes from the Lord, the Maker of heaven and earth. He will not let your foot slip—he who watches over you will not slumber; indeed, he who watches over Israel will neither slumber nor sleep. The Lord watches over you—the Lord is your shade at your right hand; the sun will not harm you by day, nor the moon by night. The Lord will keep you from all harm—he will watch over your life; the Lord will watch over your coming and going both now and forevermore."*

"Courage is not the absence of fear. It is the presence of fear and the will to go on."
Unknown

Personal Notes and Ideas

1. What can I do to make sure that my team travels safely?

2. How can I remain calm when traveling?

3. What are some ideas for long trips with my team?

4. What can I do to encourage myself and my team to dress and act appropriately when traveling?

5. What can I do to make sure that I leave early for all of my competitions?

6. What would Jesus do?

7. How do the Bible verses in this chapter help me? Are there other verses that can help me be an ultimate athlete when I travel?

Preparation

"Love the Lord your God with all your heart and with all your soul and with all your mind and with all your strength."

Mark 12:30

1. Mental Preparation

Colossians 3:2 *"Set your minds on things above, not on earthly things."*

Romans 12:2 *"Do not conform any longer to the pattern of this world, but be transformed by the renewing of your mind. Then you will be able to test and approve what God's will is—his good, pleasing and perfect will."*

Jim Morris was a very talented baseball player who could pitch ninety-five miles an hour. He definitely had the physical skill, but his mental focus was holding him back from becoming a superstar. "My biggest problem wasn't my arm; it was my head. I didn't face batters with the belief that I would dominate them. I did it with the fear of screwing up." Morris worked very hard on his mental game. He learned that when he threw a home-run pitch, not to focus on that last pitch. He finally was able to combine his great physical ability with mental toughness. "Either maturity or God's grace allowed me to immediately forget the homer and retire the next six batters in two innings by throwing ninety-eight-mile-an-hour fastballs and a vicious slider." The following ideas will help you achieve mental toughness:

A. Positive mental imaging

1. The weeks prior to a big competition:

It is important to do visual imagery. Every day you should be in a quiet and relaxed position. Visualize traveling to the competition, arriving at the venue, meeting the other team, warming up, the event itself… Have your coach get a description of the competition site if you have never been there before. Be mentally ready for your big day!

2. When you are at the competition:

a. You need to go into your bubble. Forget about your social life, studies, the next meet, or friendship problems. Only the things that you allow into your practice bubble can be present in your competition bubble. Remember some sports are catastrophic and need complete focus to avoid injury. For more information on your bubble, refer to chapter 2 about "Focus."

b. Visualize that God is the only one in the stands. No one else is there, and God loves you no matter what happens. This should take the majority of the pressure off so that you can perform well. See chapter 9 on "Pre-competition."

c. Remember that your attitude is your choice. Refer chapter 36 on "Attitude" to refresh your memory about choosing to be *negative*, *kind of positive*, and *totally positive*. For instance, you could be at a competition and feel very tired. However it is your choice whether you say:

> I am tired.
> I'll try not to be tired.
> I have energy!

3. Biofeedback

Biofeedback is a powerful source of preparation for all athletes. Biofeedback uses the mind to positively visualize your life and control your body. This is done by listening to tapes, relaxing the mind, body, and spirit so that one can get refocused again. "Athletes who wish to excel find biofeedback an excellent addition to their training. There is instant feedback of their overall development to improve their mental, physical, spiritual, social, and emotional skills as an athlete." Dr. Lilli Ann Jeffrey-Smith, Founder of the Biofeedback Training & Treatment Center, INC.

B. Positive mental image verses

Philippians 4:13 *"I can do everything through him who gives me strength."* (This is a fantastic verse and is filled with great motivation for all athletes. However, don't abuse this verse by thinking you can do anything that *you* want to. Remember, God's will is always better than whatever future we could imagine. Ephesians 1:11 *"In him we were also chosen, having been predestined according to the plan of him who works out everything in conformity with the purpose of his will."*)

Matthew 19:26 *"Jesus looked at them and said, 'With man this is impossible, but with God all things are possible.'"*

Job 23:10 *"But he knows the way that I take; when he has tested me, I will come forth as gold."*

Psalm 18:29 *"With your help I can advance against a troop; with my God I can scale a wall."*

C. Negative mental image verses

Psalm 53:1,3,5 *"The fool says in his heart, 'There is no God.' They are corrupt, and their ways are vile; there is no one who does good. Everyone has turned away, they have together become corrupt; there is no one who does good, not even one. There they were, overwhelmed with dread, where there was nothing to dread. God scattered the bones of those who attacked you; you put them to shame, for God despised them."*

Psalm 69:20 *"Scorn has broken my heart and has left me helpless; I looked for sympathy, but there was none, for comforters, but I found none."*

2. Emotional Preparation

Philippians 4:8 *"Finally, brothers, whatever is true, whatever is noble, whatever is pure whatever is lovely, whatever is admirable—if anything is excellent or praiseworthy—think about such things."*

Galatians 5:22 *"But the fruit of the Spirit is love, joy, peace, patience, kindness, goodness, faithfulness."*

Romans 12:12 *"Be joyful in hope, patient in affliction, faithful in prayer."*

You can use your emotions to your advantage during competition. Refer to the story about Becky in chapter 46 on "Tragedies." Dedicating each meet to a certain person or specific cause can be very powerful. Use your emotions positively in order to push you forward rather than backward. One caution in doing this is that the results may not come out the way you want. It still is a possibility that you could lose the game, make mistakes during your routine, or have a slower race. However, you will be satisfied with *how* you chose to compete. You were performing your heart out for your good friend!

As the author was putting the finishing touches on this book, her student, and a dear friend of the Champlin Park football team, died of cancer. Eric had courageously battled bone cancer for eighteen months. He was a talented athlete who would have been on the football team that year. It was his senior year, and he had played sports with his buddies for a long time. During his lifetime, Eric touched many people's lives and was voted Homecoming King that same year. Eric was an inspiration to all who knew him. Eric went to be with the Lord during the playoffs. It just so happened that the funeral was in the morning and the semi-finals for the state championship were that evening. The athletes, classmates, and staff at the school were all devastated. However, the athletes decided to dedicate that game to Eric. Wow, that night they played out of their minds! They won the game for Eric and were off to the state championship game!

The Champlin Park fans were screaming Eric's name over and over again. These athletes will never forget that game. Yes, they won the game, but more importantly, they'll never forget how they played their hearts out for Eric.

3. Spiritual Preparation
A. Prayer

As previously mentioned, you can *emotionally* dedicate your competitions to other people or causes. In addition you can *spiritually* dedicate your meet, games, or matches as prayer for others. By doing so, your time competing is more meaningful. This way you will not be self-centered but others-centered. Your motivation for playing is to participate and offer this time as a blessing or prayer for someone else. By looking at the big picture of life, the outcome of the competition is not as important. God gave us our bodies so let's give God the glory! Your only goal is to give the glory to God. God is in charge of the results.

> 1 John 5:14,15 *"This is the confidence we have in approaching God: that if we ask anything **according to his will**, he hears us. And if we know that he hears us—whatever we ask—we know that we have what we asked of him."*

> 2 Corinthians 9:13-15 *"Because of the service by which you have proved yourselves, men will praise God for the obedience that accompanies your confession of the gospel of Christ, and for your generosity in sharing with them and with everyone else. And in their prayers for you their hearts will go out to you, because of the surpassing grace God has given you. Thanks be to God for his indescribable gift!"*

> 1 Peter 4:11 *"Speak and do with God's strength so all things praise him."*

> Ephesians 1:3 *"Praise be to the God and Father of our Lord Jesus Christ, who has blessed us in the heavenly realms with every spiritual blessing in Christ."*

B. Scripture

Take time to read and memorize the Bible verses. You can use them as your guide in life and in sports.

> Romans 10:17 *"Consequently, faith comes from hearing the message, and the message is heard through the word of Christ..."* (Read your favorite scripture before you compete.)

> Joshua 1:8 *"Do not let this book of the Law depart from your mouth; meditate on it day and night, so that you may be careful to do everything written in it. Then you will be prosperous and successful."*

> Proverbs 6:22 *"When you walk, they will guide you; when you sleep, they will watch over you; when you awake, they will speak to you."* (They refers to the verses in the Bible.)

> Proverbs 4:4-6 *"He taught me and said, 'Lay hold of my words with all your heart; keep my commands and you will live. Get wisdom, get understanding; do not forget my words or swerve from them. Do not forsake wisdom, and she will protect you; love her, and she will watch over you.'"*

Don't forget to put on the full armor of God. (Read Ephesians 6:11-18 in chapter 49 on "Spiritual Warfare.")

4. Physical

Remember that you have trained, brainstormed, practiced, and memorized for this event. Just let your body do what it does best. At that particular moment you are as ready as you are going to be. So, go for it! God has made an incredible human machine that is far more complex and wonderful than any high-tech computer.

> Psalm 18:31-36 *"For who is God besides the Lord? And who is the Rock except our God? It is God who arms me with strength and makes my way perfect. He makes my feet like the feet of a deer; he enables me to stand on the heights. He trains my hands for battle; my arms can bend a bow of bronze. You*

give me your shield of victory, and your right hand sustains me; you stoop down to make me great. You broaden the path beneath me, so that my ankles do not turn."

Psalm 139:14 *"I praise you because I am fearfully and wonderfully made; your works are wonderful, I know that full well."*

Proverbs 21:31 *"The horse is made ready for the day of battle, but victory rests with the Lord."*

Emotional:

"Only a life worth living, is when it is lived for others."

Albert Einstein

"I think that if you dedicate a game to a friend that has passed on, it will never be a disappointment if you played as hard and well as you could."

Melissa Budde, high school volleyball MVP

Spiritual:

"Prayer is not an old woman's idle amusement. Properly understood and applied, it is the most potent instrument of action."

Mahatma Gandhi

Mental:

"Optimists see the donut and pessimists see the donut hole."

Unknown

"I tell my coaches that I don't want to hear one negative word in our practice room. Let's catch somebody doing something good and positively reinforce that."

Mike Denney, University of Nebraska wrestling coach

"Teams usually beat themselves by mental mistakes or just blunders."

Herman Edwards, NY Jets coach

Physical:

"Physical preparation is an essential aspect of peak performance training, because it is your power base. One can visualize the best performance, but they must physically prepare for that opportunity. Otherwise the visual image is just a dream."

Debbie Kiefink M.Ed, Certified Strength and Conditioning Specialist

Emotional, physical, mental, spiritual...

According to Adrienne Johnson, guard for the Orlando Magic, this is her game day ritual, "I start my day with prayer. This gives me perspective on the day. It's game preparation from there, looking over scouting reports, focusing on what my assignment may be for the night. Eat a good meal, get in a good nap, and see myself performing to the best of my ability..."

Personal Notes and Ideas

1. What is the best way for me to get prepared:

    Physically

    Mentally

    Emotionally

Spiritually

2. How can I stay positive and strong during the tough times in a competition?
Physically

Mentally

Emotionally

Spiritually

3. I want to dedicate my competitions to the following people:

4. What is my favorite verse that I can memorize and use at each competition?

5. How can I encourage my teammates to prepare themselves physically, mentally, emotionally and spiritually?

6. What would Jesus do?

7. How do all the Bible verses in this chapter help me? Are there other verses that can help me with my preparation for competition?

Game Time

"The horse is made ready for battle, but the victory rests with the Lord."

Proverbs 21:31

You are ready! You have practiced many hours, prepared mentally, prayed to God, have had enough sleep.... Just go for it! If for some reason you have not been able to do everything that you wanted to do—you have an injury, didn't sleep well...*make* yourself ready! Your mind is a powerful controller. If you say you are tired, then you will be tired. Sometimes you really have to talk yourself into being ready for competition due to various circumstances. But it can be done! Continue to focus on the *positive* and what you *have*, rather than the *negative* and what might be *missing*.

1. Most importantly, don't forget to pray and get yourself focused spiritually.
2. If you are nervous or apprehensive, read Proverbs 3:25-26: *"Have no fear of sudden disaster or of ruin that overtakes the wicked, for the Lord is your confidence and will keep your foot from being snared."*

3. Remember in chapter 9 about pre-competition that God is the only one in the stands.
4. Make sure that you are not praying to win, but that you are praying to do your *best* and to *glorify* God. 1 Corinthians 10:31 *"...whatever you do, do it all for the glory of God."*
5. The victory is the Lord's. Remember Proverbs 21:31, at the beginning of this chapter.
6. And if you don't win, don't your best, or don't perform up to other's expectations, you can still glorify God! So you are in a win-win situation.

A multitude of things can happen in competition. One of the most common emotions is *anger*, because so many things can go wrong. You may make a mistake, your teammates might falter, the referees can make a bad call, you could get disqualified or race very slowly. However all anger needs to be kept under control. It is almost for certain that some kind of anger will happen during a competition. Get rid of anger and forgive!

Proverbs 29:11 *"A fool gives full vent to his anger, but a wise man keeps himself under control."*

Ephesians 4:31-32 *"Get rid of all bitterness, rage and anger, brawling and slander, along with every form of malice. Be kind and compassionate to one another, forgiving each other, just as in Christ God forgave you."*

So, knowledge is power! All athletes must learn how to control their anger. Set up possible situations and do some role playing. Have an appropriate response for each situation. Doing this leaves no excuse for not keeping your emotions under control. Practice five different situations each week. If you run out of ideas, repeat some old situations. After brainstorming the situation and your response, spend some time visualizing this happening and your positive response. (Make sure that you are not visualizing the mistake, but focusing on the *response* to the mistake.) If something happens that is really terrible, make sure you process this anger with a teammate, friend, parent, or coach at a later time.

"Anger is only one letter short of danger."
Unknown

*"When angry, count to ten before you speak;
if very angry, count to one hundred."*
Thomas Jefferson

"Just play. Have fun. Enjoy the game."
Michael Jordan, NBA MVP

Personal Notes and Ideas

1. How can I prepare to be ready emotionally no matter what happens? Write down five situations that could make you angry, and your responses to them.

2. How can I be positive, and in control of my emotions, for myself, my teammates and my coaches?

3. What can I do to stay positive during game time when everything is going my way?

4. What can I do to stay positive during game time if I am experiencing some challenges?

5. How can I encourage my teammates to stay positive, and in control of their emotions, during game time?

6. What would Jesus do?

7. How do the Bible verses in this chapter help me? Are there other verses that can help me be an ultimate athlete during game time?

Play-Offs and Finals

"The end of all things is near. Therefore be clear minded and self-controlled so that you can pray."

1 Peter 4:7

Wow! You made it! This is what you have dreamed of for years. You have sweated, overcome tough situations, worked through muscle fatigue, battled with burnout, sacrificed your personal life...and the list goes on! It's almost too much to take in! The emotions that go along with achieving this goal are excitement, nervousness, disbelief, fear of failure, the incredible feelings of success. But the fact of the matter is that you have made it! You have qualified! This is a big reason to celebrate.

Since there is a lot at stake, it is crucial that you remember that *participation* is the key. All your hard work has paid off and now you have an opportunity of a lifetime. So enjoy yourself and don't become such a worrywart that you miss out on all the excitement. Your job is to relax, enjoy, and stay motivated, because you have coaches to sort out the details. Also you are physically fine-tuned, and are ready to go. Even though you might have an injury, you can keep yourself relaxed and motivated. No matter what, there isn't much more that you can do for yourself *physically* other than eat, sleep, and keep your muscles loose. Your competition is in a couple of days, so focus on your mental, emotional, and spiritual dimensions.

With all this excitement we need to do our best to stay "clear-minded" for many reasons. This is not easy, but it can be done. There is an old saying, "An ounce of prevention is worth a pound of cure." The following are ideas to help you "keep it together" as you train for this championship, and while you are competing.

Remember that *participation* is the key. You made it!

Do your best to be at *peace*. John 14:27 *"Peace I leave with you; my peace I give to you."* Anxiety does not help a person perform. Yes, you want to have your adrenaline pumping, and be emotionally, mentally, and spiritually excited to do your best. But don't be *anxious!* A cartoon with Ziggy sitting in a rocking chair says, "Worrying is like a rocking chair. It gives you something to do, but it doesn't get you any where."

Next you need to get into the positive mode! No matter what…you are ready! Proverbs 21:31 *"The horse is made ready for the day of battle, but victory rests with the Lord."* Talk yourself into being ready whether you feel like it or not. Then you need to spread that positive attitude among your teammates and coaches. It is not the time to be timid, self-centered, or out of control. 2 Timothy 1:7 *"For God did not give us a spirit of timidity, but a spirit of power, of love, and of self-discipline."* Instead of focusing on your fears and anxiety, program yourself to be positive. Most importantly make sure that your positive attitude is contagious, and continue to build up your team.

As mentioned in chapter 9, "Pre-competition," it is of utmost importance to remember that God is the only one in the stands. He is there for you and loves you no matter what.

> *"You need to play for God and God alone. Whatever else comes along is nice, but it doesn't really mean as much as having God say, 'Well done.'"*
>
> Tom Lehman, professional golfer

"In the pinnacle moment of your season, be it team playoffs or your last individual competition, it is key to remember the importance lies not within the outcome, but within the performance itself."

Joel Ward, decathlete and high school coach

Personal Notes and Ideas

1. Participation is the key! What do I need to do to make sure I remember that?

2. What can I do mentally and emotionally if I get nervous?

3. What Bible verses are the best for me if I am nervous?

4. What do I need to do so that I can be at peace?

5. How can I *be* and *stay* positive during the playoffs? The traveling, warm-up, watching other competitors, competing, and dealing with the results?

6. How can I encourage my teammates to be positive and not nervous?

7. What would Jesus do?

8. How do all the Bible verses in this chapter help me? Are there other verses that can help me be an ultimate athlete during the play-offs and finals?

Olympics

"So do not fear, for I am with you; do not be dismayed, for I am your God. I will strengthen you and help you; I will uphold you with my righteous right hand."

Isaiah 41:10

The number one goal for most athletes is to qualify for the Olympics. This competition tends to be more prestigious because it only comes every four years. The amount of sacrificing that athletes do to make it to the Olympics is huge. Arriving at the Olympic village brings so many emotions, ranging from excitement, disbelief, happiness, fear of the unknown, and anxiety about your competition. Don't let these emotions control you. Remember 1 Peter 5:7: *"Cast all your anxiety on him because he cares for you."* Please refer to the previous chapter on "Play-Offs and Finals," because all of that information is pertinent for the Olympics, too.

In the 2002 Winter Olympic Games, figure skater Sarah Hughes didn't have a good short program. Her chances of getting the gold medal were pretty small, but it could happen depending on how the other women skated. Sarah's chances were very slim, so she decided to just go out and have fun. Sarah didn't have the same pressure that the other three medal contenders had. She was very young, 16, and figured that she would have more chances. So she went out on the ice to have fun, and she ended up having the performance of her life! The other women made their mistakes due to all the pressure. Sarah ended up winning the gold medal! Afterwards she said, "I wasn't thinking of a gold medal, I went out to have fun and a great time. This is the Olympics. All I wanted to do is skate my best...I really thought there was no way in the world I would win. Realistically, there was this little window, but I didn't think I could win. I went out and just skated. Just skated. Of course it was a miracle. What are the chances of that happening?"

In addition to everything in the previous chapter, there are some other factors with respect to being in the Olympics. *Enjoy* the opportunity to meet athletes from all over the world. For most Olympics, you will be in another country with completely different surroundings. Embrace this special time to get to know a different culture. Obviously your athletic competition is one of your top priorities and you should focus on that. However, do take time to experience the beauty of the entire Olympics too.

The Olympic Creed

> *"The most important thing in the Olympic Games is not to win but to take part, just as the most important thing in life is not the triumph but the struggle. The essential thing is not to have conquered but to have fought well."*
>
> Baron De Coubertin, Father of the Modern Olympic Games

> *"The Olympic medal was an outstanding accomplishment for our team, but it really didn't change my inner life one bit. Only God could do that and He did!"*
>
> Steve Janaszak, goalie for USA 1980 Olympic Gold Medal Hockey Team

Personal Notes and Ideas

1. What does the Olympic creed mean to me?

2. How can I prepare to be ready emotionally no matter what happens? Write down five situations and your response to them.

3. How can I enjoy the Olympics and encourage my teammates to do so also?

4. How can I keep everything into perspective during the Olympics?

5. What have I learned from Sarah's attitude with respect to competing?

6. What would Jesus do?

7. How do the Bible verses in this chapter help me? Are there any other verses that can help me be an ultimate athlete before and during the Olympics?

Good Sport

"Set your mind on things above, not on earthly things."

Colossian 3:2

The main emphasis in all sports is to train hard and make big sacrifices in order to do well in a competition. Many times it is hard to control our emotions due to the extreme pressure that comes with athletic competition. Add to that freak accidents, tough luck, and bad judging… However one thing always remains the same. We are in control of our *attitudes* and *actions*! So let's take time to prepare ourselves for future situations.

The best advice for athletes is that there is more to life than just sports! At times we get so focused that we forget this important advice. We need to realize that, whether we win, lose, perform well, or make huge mistakes…life does go on! Memorize Colossians 3:2 so that it becomes a constant reminder for you. This will help you to be a good sport no matter what happens.

Here are some ways to be a good sport:

- Greet the opposing team and help them in any way. For instance, help them find the locker rooms, trainer's office, field…

- Congratulate the other team or player when they make a good play.
- Help someone who has fallen down, so they can get back on their feet again.
- Shake hands after the race.
- Stay calm and keep others calm.
- Encourage your teammates.
- Form a line at the end of the competition and shake hands with the other team.
- Add to the list…

Philippians 4:5 *"Let your gentleness be evident to all."*

Galatians 5:22-23 *"But the fruit of the Spirit is love, joy, peace. Patience, kindness, goodness, faithfulness, **gentleness**, and self-control."*

Philippians 4:8 *"Finally, brothers, whatever is true, whatever is noble, whatever is right, whatever is pure, whatever is lovely, whatever is admirable—if anything is excellent or praiseworthy—think about such things. Whatever you have learned or received or heard from me, or seen in me—put it into practice. And the God of Peace will be with you."*

On the negative side, here are ways of not being a good sport:

- Having a temper tantrum.
- Throwing some of your equipment. (tennis racket, helmet, swimming goggles, gymnastics hand grips, football, glove…)
- Swearing
- Yelling at teammates, opposing team, or referees
- Crying
- Cheating or playing dirty.
- Add to the list…

Proverbs 14:17 *"A quick-tempered man does foolish things, and a crafty man is hated."*

Proverbs 4:24 *"Put away perversity from your mouth; keep corrupt talk far from your lips."*

Psalm 15:3 *"and has no slander on his tongue, who does his neighbor no wrong, and casts no slur on his fellowman."*

It was a very important high school basketball game, and the emotions were running high. Obviously there were some bad calls, but one referee made a horrendous call. Most everyone in the gym exploded, because the call was ridiculous. The head coach was incredibly angry and was about to get a technical foul. Tanisha, his top player on the team, went over and gave him a bear hug to restrain him. She kept talking to him and holding onto him until he was calm. Tanisha was about the only one in the gym who kept her calm and kept her coach from getting a technical foul. He could have been kicked out of the game. Tanisha has proved that it can be done! Amidst all the emotion, adrenaline, heat of the moment, and intense competition, you can keep your cool and make good decisions.

> *"In order to be a good sport, you have to lose to prove it."*
>
> Unknown

Personal Notes and Ideas

1. My role as a good sport is very important. What can I do to make the season a success?

2. Specifically in my sport, what can I do to be a good sport to the opposing team, referees, and my teammates?

3. What should I not do? (I don't want to be a bad sport.)

4. There is more to life than sports. What other important things do I have in my life?

5. How can I encourage my teammates to be good sports?

6. What can I learn from Tanisha's attitude and actions?

7. Why is being a good sport important to God?

8. What would Jesus do?

9. How do the Bible verses in this chapter help me? Are there other verses that can help me be a good sport?

Pressure
to Perform

*"Such confidence as this is ours through
Christ before God. Not that we are competent
in ourselves to claim anything for ourselves,
but our competence comes from God."*
2 Corinthians 3:4-5

There are many reasons why athletes have incredible pressure to perform. They may be professionals, or college athletes with a big scholarship, or high school athletes with an overbearing coach. The conference title may be on the line, or a recruiter is coming to your game. As mentioned in the other chapters, it is not good to allow your anxiety to overtake you in *any* situation.

The key is to focus on the fact that God is in the stands. He is there, He is with us, and He loves us no matter what! Philippians 4:6-7 *"Do not be anxious about anything, but in everything by prayer and petition, with thanksgiving, present your requests to God. And the peace of God, which transcends all understanding, will guard your heart and your minds in Jesus Christ."*

It is also very important that you understand the difference between "perfection" and "excellence." No one in this world can be perfect. This is about the only impossibility that exists for us. (Other than that, it is not good to use the word *impossible!*) God,

Jesus, and the Holy Spirit are the only perfection that exists. Therefore, to aim for perfection will only result in frustration and self-concept problems. Don't set yourself up for failure. What we need to do is to strive for *excellence*. That is being the best that you can be in all situations. It is not being perfect. For instance, if you have a terrible cold, you might not perform as well as you want. But you can be *excellent*, and be the best you can be, for *that day, that time, and that situation!* By striving for excellence, we can strive to reach our goals, but not set ourselves up for frustration and depression. A verse that can help us strive for perfection is Psalm 18:29 *"With your help I can run through a barricade, with my God I can scale a wall."* As mentioned previously, a positive attitude is a must! You will probably read about this in every chapter of this book. Psalm 62:2 *"He alone is my rock and my salvation; he is my fortress, I will never be shaken."*

> *"When you've got God in your life, it's so much easier to deal with a lot of the pressures and situations because when the demands come down on you, it's so easy to just pray about it and let God worry about it."*
>
> Jeff Gordon, NASCAR Driver

> *"Those times of trial are good. They have allowed me to get back the proper perspective that my self-worth is not based on my performance."*
>
> Josh Davis, professional swimmer

> *"For so many of us, happiness is derived by how well we perform. So the message I try to convey is that we are unconditionally loved, and we are eternally accepted by God, regardless of our success or failures in business. Or in life."*
>
> Tom Lehman, professional golfer

"I have learned not to put so much pressure on myself for a certain result. Whatever happens, I come off the ice saying, 'Thank you, God for the talents and opportunities you've given me'"
Catriona LeMay Doan, gold medalist in speed skating at the Olympics

Personal Notes and Ideas

1. How can I prepare for the times when I have pressure to perform? Write down five situations and your response to them.

2. How can I be there for my teammates and coaches if we are all under pressure?

3. How can I stay positive and focused?

4. Who can I talk to if I need help about this pressure?

5. How can I encourage my teammates to stay positive and focused?

6. What would Jesus do?

7. How do the Bible verses in this chapter help me? Are there any other verses that can help me be an ultimate athlete when I have too much pressure to perform?

The Last
Thirty Seconds

"Though an army besiege me, my heart will not fear; though war break out against me, even then will I be confident."

Psalm 27:3

In all situations you need to keep your cool, no matter what happens! In athletics, the majority of the time, it is *not* the end of the world if something bad happens. Sure it is frustrating, but it is usually something that we can overcome. So in the last moments of your competition, do your best to keep everything in perspective. In doing so, you will be able to maintain the focus that you need to perform. Even if the competition is very close, you should also be able to stay calm and not let your anxiety over take you.

1 Corinthians 9:24-27 *"Do you not know that in a race all the runners run, but only one gets the prize? Run in such a way as to get the prize. Everyone who competes in the games goes into strict training. They do it to get a crown that will not last; but we do it to get a crown that will last forever. Therefore I do not run like a man running aimlessly; I do not fight like a man beating the air. No, I beat my body and make it my slave so*

that after I have preached to others, I myself will not be disqualified for the prize."

Luke 21:14 *"But make up your mind not to worry beforehand how you will defend yourselves."*

John 14:1 (Jesus Comforts His Disciples) *"Do not let your hearts be troubled. Trust in God; trust also in me."*

Another helpful hint is to momentarily pause and reflect that God is the only one in the stands. Refer to the chapter 9 about "Precompetition." This should help keep you from becoming nervous and allow your adrenaline to go to work for you. Prepare yourself for moments like these. Think of all the situations, find a positive response, and visualize it. Refer to chapter 12 about "Game Time."

Luke 24:36 *"While they were still talking about this, Jesus himself stood among them and said to them, 'Peace be with you.'"*

Stay positive and remember that your confidence comes from God.

2 Corinthians 3:4-5 *"Such confidence as this is ours through Christ before God. Not that we are competent in ourselves to claim anything for ourselves, but our competence comes from God."*

Psalm 71:5 *"For you have been my hope, O Sovereign Lord, my confidence since my youth."*

Psalm 118:6 *"The Lord is with me; I will not be afraid. What can man do to me?"*

Psalm 125:1 *"Those who trust in the Lord are like Mount Zion, which cannot be shaken but endures forever."*

These verses are not saying that you will win. You should not pray to win, but pray to play in an excellent way for God.

"I had struggled to that point with a lack of confidence and way too many feelings of anxiety. I just didn't trust in who I was as a golfer. I went to the seventy-second hole needing a birdie. It was the kind of shot where you need the ball to fade. That was a shot I really didn't have confidence in. I hit a nearly perfect fade and had a two-foot putt for a birdie. That was the turning point in my golf career at that point. I felt like all the anxiety and fear that had been on my shoulders for so many years just lifted away. It was as if God had given me another chance to learn my lesson. It was as if God were saying 'I gave you the ability, and I trust in you now. Now trust in yourself when you play golf.'"

Tom Lehman, professional golfer

"My faith has helped me believe there is always something better out there. God has given me the ability to be athletically competitive. It's great to go out and use it."

Tony Perez, national champion high school wrestler

Personal Notes and Ideas

1. How can I maintain control in the last moments of my competition ? Write five situations and your response to them.

2. How can I be there for my teammates and coaches during times like these?

3. My confidence is from God... The following verse helps me *the most* with confidence. (Memorize the verse and use it when you need it.)

4. How can I encourage my teammates to have confidence and maintain control during the final moments?

5. What would Jesus do?

6. Do the Bible verses in this chapter help me? Are there other verses that can help me be an ultimate athlete during the last moments of the competition?

Time-Out

"All Scripture is God-breathed and is useful for teaching, rebuking, correcting and training in righteousness, so that the man of God may be thoroughly equipped for every good work."

2 Timothy 3:16-17

 n this book you will find that the major emphasis of "Time-Out" is the studying of God's Word. "Time Off," which is found in the "Miscellaneous" section is mainly about prayer.

What:

Time-outs in all types of sporting events are crucial. Not only do the athletes need physical rest, but they also need to do some strategic planning for the rest of the competition. Time-outs are the same thing in life, but let's refer to them as "quiet times." During a quiet time, you can get the physical, spiritual, and emotional rest that you need. In addition, you can plan your strategy for the day and for the future. Quiet times consist of reading the Bible and praying to God. Ideally it is best for everyone to have this time with God daily.

Where:

Mark 1:35 *"Very early in the morning, while it was still dark, Jesus got up, left the house and went off to a solitary place, where he prayed."* It is very important that we find our own solitary place. A place where we can forget about our daily tasks and pressures, and focus on what God has to teach us. It may be your room, a library, a park, a beach… find a place where you are comfortable and won't be interrupted.

When:

Acts 17:11 *"Now the Bereans were of more noble character than the Thessalonians, for they received the message with great eagerness and examined the Scriptures **every day** to see if what Paul said was true."* It is in your best interests to take time out of each and every day. Could you imagine a soccer game without any time-outs? Time-outs/quiet times are very important and we need to keep them as one of our first priorities. In certain situations, you may not be able to study the Bible the way you want. Just spend extra time in prayer that day. Joshua 1:8 *"Do not let this Book of the Law depart from your mouth; meditate on it day and night, so that you may be careful to do everything written in it. Then you will be prosperous and successful."*

How:

John 14:16 *"And I will ask the Father, and he will give you another Counselor to be with you forever."* First of all we need to completely depend on God as we read the Bible. He will give us the insight we need while we are studying His word. The Counselor that helps us to understand the Scripture is the Holy Spirit. So just ask for the presence of God and His Holy Spirit as you read the Bible, and you will be amazed at all you can learn.

There are many ways to have a quiet time:

- Just sitting and reading the Bible is one way.
- You could get a special book that helps to explain a specific book in the Bible. This way you can do an in-depth study on a particular part in the Bible.
- If you have never read the Bible, start with the Gospels in the New Testaments (Matthew, Mark, Luke, and John). This way you can learn about Jesus and His life.

- Another option is to study a book of the Bible with other people. You can make up a schedule of daily reading, and then get together once a week to discuss it.
- Get a journal and take notes as you are reading. You can also write down your prayer requests for that day.

Why:

If you read Psalm 119 you will see why we need to read the Bible on a regular basis. It shows us that when there are hard times, we *can* make good choices by knowing the Word of God. Here are some of the verses. Make sure that you take time to read the entire Psalm someday. (All the bold font represents the good choices that we can make, and the solutions we have to help us in life.)

Psalm 119:9-11 *"How can a young man keep his way pure?*
By living according to your word.
I seek you with all my heart;
do not let me stray from your commands.
I have hidden your word in my heart
that I might not sin against you.

Psalm 119:25 *I am laid low in the dust;*
preserve my life according to your word.

Psalm 119:28-30 *My soul is weary with sorrow;*
strengthen me according to your word.
Keep me from deceitful ways;
be gracious to me through your law. [the word "law" refers to God's word]
I have chosen the way of truth;
I have set my heart on your laws.

Psalm 119:51-52 *The arrogant mock me without restraint,*
but I do not turn from your law.
I remember your ancient laws, O Lord ,
and I find comfort in them.

Psalm 119:89-92 *Your word, O Lord , is eternal;*
it stands firm in the heavens.

Your faithfulness continues through all generations;
you established the earth, and it endures.
Your laws endure to this day,
for all things serve you.
If your law had not been my delight,
I would have perished in my affliction.

Psalm 119:143-144 *Trouble and distress have come upon me,*
but your commands are my delight.
Your statutes are forever right;
give me understanding that I may live."

Quiet time helps us keep our lives in perspective. It calms us and reassures us when we are going through a hard time. There is plenty of advice to help us in our journey of life. Quiet time takes us away from the grind of life and offers us *hope*. The Bible is our Owners Manual for life. See chapter 57 on Explorers for a complete explanation of the Owners Manual. The word *Bible* stands for:

Basic
Instruction
Before
Leaving
Earth

Romans 15:4 *"For everything that was written in the past was written to teach us, so that through endurance and the encouragement of the Scriptures we might have hope."*

Colossians 3:16 *"Let the word of Christ dwell in you richly as you teach and admonish one another with all wisdom, and as you sing psalms, hymns and spiritual songs with gratitude in your hearts to God."*

Hebrews 4:10-11 *"For anyone who rests from his own work, just as God did from his. Let us, therefore, make every effort to enter that rest, so that no one will fall by following their example of disobedience."*

Hebrews 4:12 *"For the word of God is living and active. Sharper than any double-edged sword, it penetrates even to dividing soul and spirit, joints and marrow; it judges the thoughts and attitudes of the heart."*

"Take time to be holy."

Howard Finster

"The more time we spend with God in His Word, praying or learning about Him, the better we get to know and understand Him, and the more purpose we will feel in the word."

David Martin, Stanford University tennis player

"My keys to victory are intense physical and spiritual workouts. The spiritual is as important to tennis as the physical, and it is more important in life overall. I do a Bible study first thing in the morning and also at night. Throughout the day, I will pray—whenever— because the Lord is always there."

Michael Chang, pro tennis player

Personal Notes and Ideas

1. What is my ideal time-out/quiet time? (Describe it.)

2. Where is the best place to have my time-out/quiet time?

3. When is the best time to have my time-out/quiet time?

4. How can I use my time-outs/quiet times to help me as a person and as an athlete?

5. How can time-outs/quiet times help me to make good decisions?

6. How can I put into practice what I have learned from my time-outs/quiet times?

7. How can I encourage my teammates to have time-outs/quiet times?

8. What would Jesus do?

9. How do the Bible verses in this chapter help me? Are there any other verses that can help me be an ultimate athlete with my time-outs/quiet times?

10. Here are some more verses about quiet times:
    Proverbs 4:4-6
    Romans 10:17
    Proverbs 30:5
    Psalm 119:16
    Matthew 4:4
    Deuteronomy 8:3

Bad Luck

"In this you will greatly rejoice, though now for a little while you have had to suffer grief in all kinds of trials. They have come so that your faith—of greater worth than gold, which perishes even though refined by fire—may be proved genuine and may result in praise, glory and honor when Jesus Christ is revealed."
1 Peter 1:6-7

Sometimes things go our way, and sometimes they just don't. There is no rhyme or reason as to why it went the way it did. It just happened. Most of the time we cannot control the situation, but we can always control our *attitudes* and our *actions* to that particular situation. The situation happened, and it can't be reversed as much as we may want it to be. We can choose to use each situation to make us *bitter* or *better* people.

Jeanna and Janelle were training very hard for the state competition. They chose to join a private team and take private lessons so that they could be ready for the high school season. They paid for the lessons on their own, and when they weren't practicing or studying, they lifted weights and spent time stretching. Their sacrificing went above and beyond the call of duty for most high school athletes. On the big day, they were more than ready to go. They were psyched up to show their routine. Halfway through the routine, Jeanna blacked out. They had to stop the music and help Jeanna out of the pool. At that point everyone involved decided that it would not be wise for them to compete again due to Jeanna's fragile physical state. What a disappointment! All that time, money, sore muscles…down the drain. It was a freak incident and there was no explanation.

Of course the girls cried at home with their coach, because the thought of not being able to compete was unbearable. But also during that time the girls and their coach reflected on the good times that they had together. They thought about how close they all became as friends, and how much they had learned from each other. Then the tears turned to giggling. All three had realized that it isn't always the final results that matter, but what they have experienced in their quest for excellence. Jeanna and Janelle showed up for the next two days of competition. They wanted to cheer on their teammates even though they wouldn't be competing. It was tough for them, but they would never think of abandoning their team due to their misfortune.

How can our faith help us in these situations? Look at 2 Corinthians 5:6-7: *"Therefore we are always confident and know that as long as we are at home in the body we are away from the Lord. We live by faith, not by sight."* We are encouraged to dig deep and acknowledge that we are in a tough situation. We need to be honest and say that we don't like it. On the other hand, we have a God and a faith that can keep us going no matter what the situation looks like.

2 Timothy 4:5 *"But you keep your head in all situations, endure hardship, do the work as an evangelist…"* We are also commanded to hang in there when the going gets tough! We need to stay calm and do our best to make the situation *better* rather than *worse*. If you would like to read about a person that had a lot of "bad luck," refer to the book of Job in the Old Testament. Job felt all the emotions of his terrible situation, and he was honest about it. However he always stayed faithful to God.

When you are in pain, talk to someone who has been through it. Always remember that Jesus can be your support group! He is always there, 24/7. If your situation is tragic, you may need extra help to get you beyond this tragedy. Make sure that you get counsel from other people such as coaches, pastors, or psychologists.

Most importantly, with respect to a "bad luck" situation, we must *learn* from it. Don't become bitter, ignore the pain, deny the frustration, or wallow in your pity. Learn something! What can you learn that will make you a better person because of your situation? Proverbs 23:23 *"Buy the truth and do not sell it; get wisdom, discipline and understanding."* God doesn't promise life without hard times. However, God does promise to help you work through those hard times. He is always there with us. Sometimes life isn't fair, but God is always fair! After losing his only son, Bill Cosby made a special appearance on the show *Touched by an Angel*. These were his words: "God doesn't cause pain, He heals. God doesn't cause hate, He loves. God doesn't want bad things to happen, *they just happen!*"

"Don't pray for an easier life, but to be stronger."
John F. Kennedy

"Job was not so miserable in his sufferings, as happy in his patience."
Thomas Fuller

"If nothing seems to go my way today, this is my happiness: God is my Father and I am his child."
Basilea Schlink

Personal Notes and Ideas

1. How can I prepare to be ready emotionally no matter what happens? Write down five situations and your response to them.

2. How can I be there for my teammates and coaches if something bad happens to them during the competition?

3. What can I do that night, and in the following days, to help myself and my teammates?

4. As difficult as the situation may be, can I *find* some good in it? Or what can I do to find some good in each situation?

5. How can I encourage my teammates to be ready emotionally no matter what happens?

6. Who can I talk to if I need help?

7. What would Jesus do?

8. How do the Bible verses in this chapter help me? Are there any other verses that can help me be an ultimate athlete when I have bad luck?

Losing Big Time

"So keep up your courage, men, for I have faith in God that it will happen just as he told me."

Acts 27:25

"So do not fear, for I am with you; do not be dismayed, for I am your God. I will strengthen you and help you; I will uphold you with my righteous right hand."

Isaiah 41:10

These Bible verses are very helpful to people in many different situations in life. They are very helpful for people who are enduring a difficult time. One of the biggest frustrations for an athlete is competing and losing big time. It doesn't matter if it is a team or an individual sport. You are trying your hardest, but you are way behind. So you try harder, and sometimes you can perform worse. It can be demoralizing. During a time like this it is important that we don't allow ourselves to be dismayed and become depressed. We need to dig deep, tap into our courage, and keep our faith in God. Finally we need to keep praying and never give up. Being frustrated, sad, or angry are normal emotions for a situation like this. However giving up is not the best idea right now. On the other hand, the emotions we are experiencing cannot be ignored. These emotions need to be confronted and processed during an appropriate time.

One emotion that is not OK is worry. Worrying is telling God that he can't handle the situation. It is another way of saying that your problem is more powerful than God . Another word for *worry* is *fear*. Fear is the exact opposite of what is needed in situations like these. *Faith* is what we need in our lives—faith that God knows what He is doing and that He will take care of us. Faith doesn't mean that God will give us what we *want*, but what is *best* for us.

Proverbs 3:25-26 *"Have no fear of sudden disaster...for the Lord will be your confidence and keep your foot from being snared."*

Psalm 46:1-2 *"God is our refuge and strength, and ever-present help in trouble. Therefore we will not fear, though the earth give away and the mountains fall into the heart of the sea."*

Here are some verses for the times when we have tough opponents:

Psalm 56:3,4,11 *"When I am afraid, I will trust in you. In God whose word I praise, in God I trust; I will not be afraid. What can mortal man do? ...in God I trust; I will not be afraid. What can man do to me?"*

Psalm 27:1-3 *"The Lord is my light and my salvation—whom shall I fear? The Lord is the stronghold of my life—of whom shall I be afraid? When evil men advance against me to devour my flesh, when my enemies and my foes attack me, they will stumble and fall. Though an army besiege me, my heart will not fear; though war break out against me, even then will I be confident."*

The best thing about faith is that we can have hope in difficult circumstances. It is amazing how our faith can help us keep going when it looks like a hopeless situation. The beauty of sports is that during your athletic career you can transfer everything you are learning about God and use it in the future. Therefore, by learning more about your faith, you will have proper responses to situations in all areas of your life.

Proverbs 23:18 *"There is surely a future hope for you, and your hope will not be cut off."*

Matthew 19:26 *"Jesus looked at them and said, 'With man this is impossible, but with God all things are possible.'"*

> ## "Satisfaction lives in the effort not in the attainment."
> Gandhi

> ## "The only struggle lost is that which is abandoned."
> Las Madres from Argentina.

> ## "I know if I give 100 percent to Christ, then I've done all I can do. If I go out and things happen like they did last night [speaking of a 10-4 loss], I can still hold my head high."
> Mike Moore, pitcher for the Oakland A's

> ## "If I lose, I'll walk away and never feel bad...Because I did all I could, there was nothing more to do."
> Joe Frazier—World Heavyweight Boxing Champion

Personal Notes and Ideas

1. How can I prepare for the times when I am losing big time? Write down five situations and your response to them.

2. How can I be there for my teammates and coaches when we are losing big time?

3. What can I do that night, and in the following days, to help myself and my teammates after a big loss?

4. As difficult as the situation may be, can I find some good in it? Or what can I do to *find* some good in each situation?

5. How can I stay positive during the competition?

6. How can I encourage my teammates to stay positive?

7. What would Jesus do?

8. How do the Bible verses in this chapter help me? Are there any other verses that can help me be an ultimate athlete when I am losing big time?

Extra verse

2 Chronicles 20:1-26 *This is a great chapter that shows us how King Jehoshaphat reacted when he found out that an army, much larger than his, was coming to destroy Judah.*

Slump

"...always pray and not give up."

Luke 18:1

Your situation may be tough right now. You could be in a personal or a team slump. For some reason you and your team are not able to produce in your competitions. The frustration level is off the charts, and it is hard to keep going. Always remember that no matter the situation, it is your choice to give up or to keep going. Many people may choose to quit, or give less effort at practice, but no one can make you quit. It is totally *your* decision!

Nelson Mandela was in prison for twenty-six years just because he wanted freedom for all people in South Africa. Many of those years he spent doing hard labor in rock quarries. Even worse, he and his friends were put through intolerable conditions and isolation. One would think that after being imprisoned for so long, Mandela would have given up and tossed in the towel. However he and his friends chose to make the best of their time by sharpening their minds. They read books, talked politics, studied various subjects and Mandela wrote his autobiography, *The Long Walk to Freedom*. Moreover, they chose to work near the garbage dump whenever they could. They found the thrown away newspapers and read them, keeping up on what was happening in the world. During his slump, I am sure Mandela had many excruciating times and probably wanted to give up. But he didn't! He was freed from prison, won a Nobel Peace Prize, and became the president of his country.

Let's look at Noah's life. It was hard for Noah to listen to all the criticisms when he was building the ark. Then he needed to spend many days on the ark without seeing land. But Noah kept going and didn't let all the disappointments conquer him.

Here are words of encouragement from the Bible:

Hebrews 10:32-36 *"Remember those earlier days after you had received the light, when you stood your ground in a great contest in the face of suffering. Sometimes you were publicly exposed to insult and persecution; at other times you stood side by side with those who were so treated... So do not throw away your confidence; it will be richly rewarded. You need to persevere so that when you have done the will of God, you will receive what he has promised."*

2 Thessalonians 2:15-17 *"So then, brothers, stand firm and hold to the teachings we passed on to you, whether by word of mouth or by letter. May our Lord Jesus Christ himself and God our Father, who loved us and by his grace gave us eternal encouragement and good hope, encourage your hearts and strengthen you in every good deed and word."*

The most important thing is to not let yourself quit. Ultimate athletes can take it a step further. What lessons are to be learned in this situation? How can you become a better athlete and person because of this tough time? Proverbs 23:23 *"Buy the truth and do not sell it; get wisdom, discipline and understanding."*

There are many ways to fix the slump that you are experiencing:

- Use video tapes to watch yourself and learn.
- Talk with the coach and brainstorm new training ideas.
- Read books from experts on your sport.
- Bring in a national coach to help. Do a fundraiser to pay the expenses.
- Go to clinics and learn more about your sport.

• Be patient with yourself. Romans 8:25 *"But if we hope for what we do not yet have, we wait for it patiently."*

It never hurts to go back to the drawing board when something isn't working. Change isn't always easy, but it can be good. Remember the saying, "If the horse dies...dismount." In other words, if you are not getting results, then stop what you are doing and get a fresh start.

Believe it or not, there are more things that you can do during a slump. Stay positive! Even if you have to struggle to stay positive...do it! Read 2 Corinthians 4:7-11. By maintaining a totally positive attitude, you will be able to keep your hope for the future. Proverbs 23:18 *"There is surely a future hope for you, and your hope will not be cut off."*

Jackie Joyner Kersee has proven herself time and time again to be one of the best female athletes in the world. She has competed in many Olympics, and in the 1984 games she won three gold medals, two bronze, and one silver in track and field. She has had her share of ups and downs during her career. She has had to overcome many injuries and a death in the family as she was competing. "I didn't give up when it was difficult for me. I kept going. There are challengers in life. Don't let those challengers defeat you. Don't look at obstacle as excuses, but as a hurdle we have to get over."

"I find the great thing in this world is not so much where we stand, as the directions that we are going."

Oliver Wendell Holmes, Sr.

Personal Notes and Ideas

1. Being in a slump is very frustrating because...

2. How can I stay patient and encourage my teammates to do so also?

3. The following are five ways that my team and I can fix our situation:

4. How can I stay positive, and encourage my teammates to stay positive when we are in a slump?

5. What would Jesus do?

6. How do the Bible verses in this chapter help me? Are there other verses that can help me be an ultimate athlete when I am in a slump?

Mistakes

"Not that I have already obtained all this, or have already been made perfect, but I press on to take hold of that for which Christ Jesus took hold of me. Brothers, I do not consider myself yet to have taken hold of it. But one thing I do: Forgetting what is behind and straining toward what is ahead, I press on toward the goal to win the prize for which God has called me heavenward in Christ Jesus."

Philippians 3:12-14

t is very important that when making a mistake each athlete always remembers the difference between *perfection* and *excellence*. Refer to chapter 16, "Pressure to Perform," for more information. We all make mistakes, and this needs to be an accepted fact in society today!

Linda was a senior and team captain on the high school gymnastics team. Linda's team was at the region finals to see who would qualify for the state competition. She had a great chance of qualifying with her uneven bars routine. As she was performing her routine, she fell on a stunt that she had never missed before. She immediately mounted the bars and finished her routine. She saluted the judges and then went directly to the teammate who was about to perform. She said, "Come on Laura, I know you can do it. Nail your routine!" She continued to encourage the other athletes, knowing that she would *not* be going to the state competition. She chose not to cry during the rest of the meet. This is a fantastic example for all athletes to see.

Remember that you are representing many people. Each athlete needs to make sure they handle themselves with dignity in *all* situations. Your actions can damage your reputation along with your team, school, or nation. Moreover, if you choose to let people know about your faith, and you throw a fit during competition, you will be seen as a hypocrite. Of course it is tough when a mistake is made, because you feel that you have let yourself and your teammates down. Do your best to *not* throw your equipment, stomp off the field, hit someone, argue with the referee, burst in to tears, or isolate yourself from your teammates...because everyone's energy will be put into *consoling you* instead of *concentrating on the game.* Ecclesiastes 3:4 *"A time to weep, and a time to laugh, a time to mourn and a time to dance."* Yes, there is a time for everything. However, during the competition is not the time for crying, bad attitudes, and poor behavior.

So all athletes should stuff their feelings! Absolutely not! But there is a time and a place for everything. Have a plan! When you are at home that night, do something to process your pain and frustration. Write in your journal, cry, scream out loud, hit a pillow....Don't do any thing that hurts yourself, others, or any thing. God wants us to be honest with ourselves and Him.

In processing our frustration over mistakes, it is important that we confront the issue of forgiveness. Not only forgiving others, but forgiving ourselves. With respect to forgiveness, let's see what God has to say:

Matthew 6:14-15 *"For if you forgive men when they sin against you, your heavenly Father will also forgive you. But if you do not forgive men their sins, your Father will not forgive your sins."*

Proverbs 19:11 *"A man's wisdom gives him patience; it is to his glory to overlook an offense."*

Matthew 18:21-22 *"Then Peter came to Jesus and asked, 'Lord, how many times shall I forgive my brother when he sins against me? Up to seven times?' Jesus answered, 'I tell you, not seven times, but seventy-seven times.'"*

Proverbs 24:32 *"I applied my heart to what I observed and learned a lesson from what I saw."*

"An error doesn't become a mistake until you refuse to correct it."
Unknown

"Forget your mistakes, but remember what they taught you."
Dorothy Galyean

"No mistake that you have ever made is bigger than God's ability to fix it."
Unknown

"Be bold. If you're going to make an error, make a doozy, and don't be afraid to hit the ball."
Billy Jean King, professional tennis player

"If you have made mistakes, there is always another chance for you...you may have a fresh start any moment you choose. For this thing we call 'failure' is not the falling down, but the staying down."
Mary Pickford, actress

Personal Notes and Ideas

1. How can I prepare myself for my mistakes during competition? Write down five situations and your response to them. (Don't focus on the mistake, but your response to it.)

2. How can I be there for my teammates and coaches if someone else makes a mistake during the competition? Write down five situations and your response to them. (Don't focus on the mistake, but your response to it.)

3. If it is a huge mistake that costs the team the competition, what can I do that night, and in the following days, to help myself and my teammates?

4. As difficult as the situation may be, can I find some good in it? Or what can I do to find some good in each situation?

5. How can I stay positive in the midst of a mistake?

6. What can I learn from Linda's actions and attitude?

7. What would Jesus do?

8. How do the Bible verses in this chapter help me? Are there other verses that can help me be an ultimate athlete when I make a mistake?

Part Three
CHALLENGES

Introduction to Challenges

"Trust in the Lord with all your heart and lean not on your own understanding; in all your ways acknowledge him, and he will make your paths straight."

Proverbs 3:5-6

The rollercoaster of the sports world can be overwhelming. You are in for a long haul with lots of ups and downs along your winding journey. However, it is up to you to make it *work* or make it *worse!* The only thing constant in life is change! Change can be both good and bad. However, change in any form can be hard for people to accept, especially when it causes pain. As human beings, we get used to our lives the way they are. Then when something happens, and it upsets the balance of our lives, we have to adjust our daily routine. This is called stress! There is both good and bad stress in our lives, and we need to be ready to deal with it. Many times there isn't an explanation as to why things happen, but it is our choice to *give up* or *go on.*

> *"Life is change. We cannot direct the wind, but we can adjust the sails."*
> Unknown

1. During these times we can tap into our faith to help us overcome the challenges of life. Faith can be a great source of comfort. Time and time again we hear stories about how people have endured horrible tragedies. Many of these people have chosen to help others who are experiencing the same tragedy that they did.

2 Corinthians 1:3-5 *"Praise be to the God and Father of our Lord Jesus Christ, the Father of compassion and the God of all comfort, who comforts us in all our troubles, so that we can comfort those in any trouble with the comfort we ourselves have received from God. For just as the sufferings of Christ flow over into our lives, so also through Christ our comfort overflows when we can comfort others."*

2. Faith can also give us hope when it seems like everything is falling apart.

Psalm 71:5 *"For you have been my hope, O Sovereign Lord, my confidence since my youth."*

Proverbs 23:18 *"There is surely a future hope for you, and your hope will not be cut off."*

2 Corinthians 4:4-9 *"But we have this treasure in jars of clay to show that this all-surpassing power is from God and not from us. We are hard pressed on every side, but not crushed; perplexed, but not in despair; persecuted, but not abandoned; stuck down, but not destroyed."*

3. Faith helps us to see the whole picture of life when we are in the midst of pain. It helps us to move forward by giving us a vision of hope.

Philippians 3:13-14 *"Brothers, I do not consider myself yet to have taken hold of it. But one thing I do: Forgetting what is behind and straining toward what is ahead."*

Romans 8:18 *"I consider my present suffering are not worth comparing with the glory that will be revealed in us."*

Romans 8:28 *"And we know that in all things God works for good of those who love him, who have been called according to his purpose."*

Isaiah 49:23 *"...Then you will know that I am the Lord; those who hope in me will not be disappointed."*

> *"Challenges will always overwhelm you unless you are really grounded in Christ."*
> David Robinson, NBA Most Valuable Player

> *"I would rather live in a world where my life is surrounded by mystery than live in a world so small that my mind could comprehend it."*
> Harry Emerson Fosdick—Riverside Sermons

> *"If you're trying to achieve, there will be roadblocks. I've had them; everybody has had them. But obstacles don't have to stop you. If you run into a wall, don't turn around and give up. Figure out how to climb it, go through it, or work around it."*
> Michael Jordan, NBA Most Valuable Player

> *"Nothing in life is to be feared. It is only to be understood."*
> Madame Marie Curie, famous scientist

The following chapters about challenges are dedicated to all of those athletes who have courageously overcome their own personal challenges in a positive way.

Injuries

*"Be very careful how you live—not as
unwise but as wise, making the most of
every opportunity..."*

Ephesians 5:15-16

*"Not only so, but we also rejoice in our
sufferings, because we know that suffering
produces perseverance; perseverance,
character; and character, hope. And hope
does not disappoint us, because God has
poured out his love into our hearts by the
Holy Spirit, whom he has given us."*

Romans 5:3-5

njuries can be one of the most frustrating challenges for athletes.
Most injuries bring athletes to a complete stop. This is the opposite of what athletes want. They are like the Energizer Bunny and
want to keep going, and going...The athletes need to do many physical things to fix their bodies—icing, elevation, rest, surgery, or physical therapy. With their focus on healing their bodies, many athletes
forget to heal themselves emotionally and spiritually. There is more
to injuries than you think. Read the following examples:

Example 1:

Barry tore all the ligaments in his knee one month before the state championships. He will be out for six months. There are many ways that he can react, but let's focus on two different reactions.

Reaction #1

Barry gets frustrated with his injury and his terrible luck in missing the state championships. He decides that life isn't fair and chooses to wallow in his pity. After school he goes straight home, finishes his homework, and then watches TV. Barry has decided he will spend his time watching television until he is well again.

Reaction #2

Barry is definitely not thrilled with his injury, but he decides to go to every practice. He wants to help the coach any way he can. He also wants to help his teammates get psyched up for the big tournament. When Barry is not at practice or studying, he spends his time exercising the rest of his healthy body. Barry also does rehabilitation exercises with his bad knee so that he will get back to full strength as soon as possible. In addition, he makes sure he talks about his emotions and frustrations with various people. This way he is able to process his grief and go on. He also knows that he can help other athletes when they get injured, because he knows what it is like firsthand.

It is the same knee, in other words, the same problem. However, there are completely different *attitudes* and *actions*. Yes, everyone has a choice on how to feel and act. We may not like the choices, but we all have to make our *own* decisions. What do you need to do so that you can have a positive attitude and follow through with good actions?

Example 2:

During a national championship, Jim had a biking accident and broke his arm. "Throughout this ordeal, God helped me to realize a new source of strength in Him. He also helped me to realize the meaning behind my injury, that it was being used by God to develop and strengthen my character to be like that of His Son Jesus. God gave me the strength to endure the pain and setback of injury and to make a comeback less than three months later." Jim Quinn, world class triathlete

Want some advice?

OK

Here it is…Wait patiently!

Are you kidding?

No!

Romans 8:25 *"But if we hope for what we do not yet have, we wait for it patiently."*

You can make your situation worse or better depending on your attitude and your P.Q. (Patience Quotient: See chapter 25 on "Sitting Out") Here are some more verses to help you keep things in perspective:

1 Peter 1:6-7 *"In this you greatly rejoice, though now for a little while you may have had to suffer grief in all kinds of trials. These have come so that your faith—of greater worth than gold, which perishes even though refined by fire—may be proved genuine and may result in praise, glory and honor when Jesus Christ is revealed."*

Psalm 6:2 *"Be merciful to me, lord, for I am faint; O Lord, heal me, for my bones are in agony."*

2 Corinthians 1:3-7 *"Praise be to the God and Father of our Lord Jesus Christ, the Father of compassion and the God of all comfort, who comforts us in all our troubles, so that we can comfort those in any trouble with the comfort we ourselves have received from God. For just as the sufferings of Christ flow over into our lives, so also through Christ our comfort overflows. If we are distressed, it is for your comfort and salvation; if we are comforted, it is for your comfort, which produces in you patient endurance of the same sufferings we suffer. And our hope for you is firm, because we know that just as you share in our sufferings, so also you share in our comfort."*

> *"Patience is the ability to keep your motor idling when you feel like your gears are stripping."*
> Unknown

> *"God may not always come when we need Him, but He will always be on time."*
> Alex Haley, author of *Roots*

Personal Notes and Ideas

1. What are my frustrations about my situation/injuries?

2. Who can I talk to about my frustrations?

3. What are my limitations right now?

4. What can I do for myself, my team, my coach when I an injured?

5. What can I do for God?

6. How can my faith help me to overcome this situation?

7. My short and long term goals are:

8. What would Jesus do?

9. How can the Bible verses in this chapter help me? Are there other verses that can help me be an ultimate athlete with respect to injuries?

Extra verses
1 Peter 5:9
2 Corinthians 4:7-11

Pain

"To this you were called, because Christ suffered for you, leaving you an example, that you should follow in his steps."

1 Peter 2:21

The first thing that we need to do when we are in pain is to say "Ouch!" Yes, we need to be honest with ourselves and God. Whether we are in physical, emotional, or spiritual pain, we need to *acknowledge it*. This is the first step. When we don't say ouch, we are not being honest with ourselves, others, and God. In addition we will not be able to heal correctly, because we haven't *acknowledged* or *confronted* the pain. If you aim at nothing, you get just that. Nothing! So, be real, and say "Ouch!" What does the Bible say about pain?

Psalm 38:6-8 *"I am bowed down and brought very low; all day long I go about mourning. My back is filled with searing pain; there is no health in my body. I am feeble and utterly crushed; I groan in anguish of heart."*

Psalm 55:16-17 *"But I call to God and the Lord saves me. Evening, morning and noon I cry out in distress. And he hears my voice."*

Psalm 142:1,2 *"I cry aloud to the Lord; I lift up my voice to the Lord for mercy. I pour out my complaining before him, before him I tell my trouble."*

Psalm 69:29 *"I am in distress; may your salvation, O God, protect me."*

The Healing Process

Acknowledge the pain, but don't dwell on it. Instead, *focus* on the healing.

For every kind of pain, there is a healing process. If you cut your arm, it bleeds, forms a scab, the scab falls off, and then your skin grows back. If you break your leg, the bones calcify, the cast comes off, and then you go through therapy to strengthen the limb. It is the same with our hearts. In the process of emotional healing, three things take place:

1. You come to know YOURSELF better because you really have to dig down deep inside.
2. You come to know OTHERS better because they help you ease your pain.
3. You come to know your GOD better if you so choose. Your faith will need to work overtime during this time period. What does the Bible have to say about healing?

Psalm 147:3 *"He heals the brokenhearted and binds up their wounds."*

Psalm 71:20 *"Though you have made me see troubles, many and bitter, you will **restore** my life again."*

Isaiah 55:22 *"Cast your cares on the LORD and he will sustain you; he will never let the righteous fall."*

Grief

The grieving process is like an onion: we need to peel off one layer at a time. This step-by-step process can be very frustrating. Just when we think we have things figured out, another layer of pain is revealed. Therefore, we need to proceed with caution, do it one step at a time, and take baby steps.

People grieve differently. Allow people to grieve the way they need. You will need to intervene if they are doing something that is harmful to themselves or others.

Remember, your grief is your grief. Do what you need to do to process it, but don't do anything to endanger yourself or your loved ones. Honor your need for quiet times alone, but don't shut yourself off from the world. You need people and they need you. Don't let anyone tell you that you should be "over it," but do take their comment into consideration: Are you wallowing in a pity party?

There are times when grief is overwhelming. When we are grieving a horrible tragedy and the pain is intolerable, we need to be willing to overcome our emotions. At times it can be a real struggle, and this is when we need to be stubborn and say, "Even though this is so excruciatingly painful, I will survive. I will go on. I will become whole again. By the grace of God and with my faith working overtime…"

Matthew 26:37-38 *"Then Jesus went with his disciples to a place called Gethsemane, and he said to them, 'Sit here while I go over there and pray.' He took Peter and the two sons of Zebedee along with him, and he began to be sorrowful and troubled. Then he said to them, 'My soul is overwhelmed with sorrow to the point of death. Stay here and keep watch with me.'"*

Matt 14:13 (After John the Baptist was beheaded Jesus chose to grieve alone.) *"When Jesus heard what had happened, he withdrew by boat privately to a solitary place."*

Romans 12:15 *"Rejoice with those who rejoice; and mourn with those who mourn."*

Hebrews 5:7 *"During the days of Jesus' life on earth, he offered up prayers and petitions with loud cries and tears to the one who could save him from death…"*

John 11:35 *"Jesus wept."*

Matt 17:23 (Jesus was telling his disciples that he will be betrayed and crucified.) *"...and the disciples were filled with grief."*

In times of pain we need to saturate ourselves with God's promises. We may not understand what is happening, but we can trust in God. The toughest time to trust is when you are in so much excruciating pain that you can't see the end of the tunnel. However it is a choice! You can focus on your pain and make yourself miserable, or you can choose to plunge into the reality of your pain and start processing it. You need to surround yourself in God's love, because it won't be easy. Listening to Christian music, praying with friends, crying out to God, reading the Psalms, and receiving good honest Christian counseling are some of the ways that you can surround yourself in God's love.

God is always there for us because He says He is. We can be sure of this because God doesn't lie.

Hebrews 6:18 *"...it is impossible for God to lie."*

Hebrews 13:5-6 *"...because God has said, 'Never will I leave you; never will I forsake you.' So we say with confidence, 'The Lord is my helper, I will not be afraid. What can man do to me.'"*

What does the Bible say about trusting God?

2 Corinthians 5:7 *"We live by faith, not by sight."*

Joshua 23:14 *"Now I am about to go the way of all the earth. You know with all your heart and soul that not one of all the good promises the Lord your God gave you has failed. Every promise has been fulfilled; not one has failed."*

For more information about pain and healing, refer to the author's other book, *Ouch! Life Can Hurt, but Healing Is Your Choice!*

> *"One of the most important challenges of your life—to heal the wounds of your past so you don't continue to bleed."*
>
> Oprah

> *"If God sends us on stony paths, he provides strong shoes."*
>
> Corrie ten Boom, holocaust survivor and prevailer

Personal Notes and Ideas

1. How can I say "Ouch!" by acknowledging and confronting my pain?

2. What pain am I currently experiencing? What is the problem?

3. Who can help me deal with this pain?

4. What can I do to make the situation *better* instead of *worse*?

5. How can the power of prayer help me?

6. How can my faith help me in my situation?

7. How can I help my teammates if they are experiencing pain?

8. What would Jesus do?

9. How do the Bible verses in this chapter help me? Are there other verses that can help me be an ultimate athlete with respect to pain?

Extra verses

Titus 1:2
James 1:17
Hebrews 1:12
Psalm 102:25-27
Proverbs 3:5-6

Sitting Out

"Love is patient, love is kind. It does not envy...it is not self-seeking."

1 Corinthians 13:4-5

"But if we hope for what we do not yet have, we wait for it patiently."

Romans 8:25

Sitting out and watching is one of the toughest things an athlete has to do. Whether at practice or during competition, it can be very frustrating. As athletes, we want to play, compete, participate, and sitting out is the exact opposite. In situations like these, we need to focus on what can be gained from all of this. Hopefully, we will learn to be more patient. Most people are lacking in patience, because we live in a spoiled, push-button society. When we cannot get what we want immediately, we get impatient. We always say, "Why do I have to wait? How can this be?" Learning patience is never fun, but it can help us in the future when we will need to be patient again. If we choose, we can improve our Patience Quotient. It can also be called our P.Q., just like our I.Q. Our I.Q. measures how much intelligence we have, and our P.Q. measures the amount of patience we have. Each time you go through a frustrating experience

127

you can deposit more patience into your P.Q. account. Colossians 1:11 *"...being strengthened with all power according to his glorious might so that you may have great endurance and patience, and joyfully giving thanks to the Father..."*

Sally was an athlete who had to sit out many times due to various injuries. It was tough for her, but she did learn how to be patient. During her adult years, she was faced with more tragedies. She wasn't thrilled about her situation, but she was so glad that she had already learned patience through her athletics. This really helped her to cope when she was going through some very tough times. She thought, "Wow, I am so glad that I learned how to deal with my tragedies in sports, because I have what it takes to make it through anything now!"

1 Peter 1:6-7 *"In this you greatly rejoice, though now for a little while you may have had to suffer grief in all kinds of trials. These have come so that your faith—of greater worth than gold, which perishes even though refined by fire—may be proved genuine and may result in praise, glory and honor when Jesus Christ is revealed."*

As Christian athletes, what should our response be when we have to sit out. First and foremost, we need to be real about our pain. We shouldn't hide behind a spiritual mask and say that we are doing just fine. No, God wants us to be honest! We need to admit that we are frustrated. Then move forward with the power of God in our lives. We can pray, encourage others while they are competing, be cheerleaders for the team, help the coaches with statistics, and increase our P.Q. There are endless options of making lemonade out of the lemon we are experiencing. We have a future hope, and that is more important than any other athletic achievement.

Please remember that God is like a stoplight. He knows when it is good for us to stop and collect ourselves. He also knows when it is safe to go and proceed with our lives. During tough times we need to remember that God *does* have everything in control, and there is a reason for what is happening. We might not know what it is right away, but we will be sure to find out soon!

Proverbs 23:18 *"There is surely a future hope for you, and your hope will not be cut off."*

James 5:10-11 *"Brothers, as an example of patience in the face of suffering, take the prophets who spoke in the name of the Lord. As you know, we consider blessed those who have persevered. You have heard of Job's perseverance and have seen what the Lord finally brought about. The Lord is full of compassion and mercy."*

> *"Life is like a dance party. Sometimes you dance, sometimes you sit out, and you may even need to switch partners. But it is imperative that you never stop dancing! Never give up on yourself or your faith. These are two precious things that you can't live without."*
>
> The Author

Personal Notes and Ideas

1. What frustrates me the most about sitting out?

2. What can I learn from this situation?

3. How can I improve my patience quotient (P.Q.)?

4. How will my athletic frustrations and hardships help me with my life in the future?

5. How can my faith grow during these tough times?

6. How can I encourage my teammates if they have to sit out?

7. What would Jesus do?

8. How do the Bible verses in this chapter help me? Are there other verses that can help me be an ultimate athlete with respect to patience?

Sickness

*"Be merciful to me, Lord, for I am faint; O
Lord, heal me, for my bones are in agony."*
Psalm 6:2

We are all physical beings, and our health condition is constantly changing. We catch colds, have sore muscles, feel great, have headaches, get nauseated, are tired, have a lot of energy…. It would be great if we always felt good, but that is not reality. Most of the time we have to deal with minor health issues. However there are some times when we need to endure painful and serious injuries or even sickness.

Ana Maria had excruciating pain in her stomach and needed to go to the hospital. The doctors found that her colon was kinked and that she needed emergency colon surgery. This happened right in the middle of her competitive season. She figured that she would be able to make a comeback for the final competition. Three weeks after her surgery, she started having complications. Ana Maria had to go back to the hospital many times. She still did everything that she could to get ready for her competition. She walked every day and stretched her muscles so that she would be somewhat fit when she could train again. In between hospital visits, Ana Maria went to practice and did what she could. It was looking like she would make it back in time for the final competition. Unfortunately, the day before her meet Ana Maria had to be hospitalized again. It was a very sad situation because she couldn't compete.

However, Ana Maria has a very strong faith and a close relationship with Jesus Christ. Due to her mature faith she was able to put everything into perspective. Sure she was frustrated and sad because she couldn't compete. She trained very hard for six months (before her operation) just for this particular meet. But Ana Maria realized that she didn't have it all that bad:

- She had a wonderful family and supportive friends.
- God was with her all the time, and gave her the strength to make it through all the excruciating pain.
- She met other children in the hospital who had it a lot worse.
- Even though there were complications, her surgery went well. She wasn't dealing with a permanent situation. She would heal.
- She has also chosen to use her story to share her faith with others. Her faith in God is much more important to her than her athletics.

What does the Bible say about illness?

Jesus knows how important physical health is to us, because he spent a lot of time healing the sick.

Matthew 14:14 *"When Jesus landed and saw a large crowds, he had compassion on them and healed their sick."*

Therefore we can call out to Him in prayer.

Psalm 30:2 *"O Lord my God, I called to you for help and you healed me."*

Psalm 41:3 *"The Lord will* sustain him on his sickbed and restore him from his bed of illness."

We need to make sure that we are praying that *God's will* be done in our lives.

1 John 5:14-15 *"This is the confidence we have in approaching God: that if we ask anything according to **his will**, he hears us."*

Ephesians 1:11 *"In him we were also chosen, having been predestined according to the plan of him who works out everything in conformity with the purpose of **his will**."*

Make sure that we praise and thank Him and not take our good health for granted.

Psalm 103:2-3 *"Praise the Lord, O my soul, and forget not all his benefits—who forgives all your sins and heals all your diseases."*

We need to revere and honor God's name.

Malachi 4:2 *"But for you who revere my name, the sun of righteousness will rise up with healing in its wings."*

"In 1993 after struggling for 2 years with unexplained fatigue and injury, I suddenly collapsed during play at the Olympic sports festival. After being diagnosed with Chronic Fatigue Immune Dysfunction Syndrome (CFIDS), a year later I found myself physically and emotionally at the end of my rope. I had accepted Jesus Christ as my savior in high school, but the next ten years were lived on my own terms. Now for the first time in my life, I found I needed a strength I couldn't muster. In despair I gave my life back to Christ. My health struggles continued but Christ's inexplicable hope and peace were always for me. God never abandoned me, and then in 1996, he helped me achieve the impossible—an Olympic gold medal. Jesus had to take it all away, so he could give me back so much more."

Michelle Akers, U.S.A. women's soccer player.

Personal Notes and Ideas

1. When I was sick in the past, how did I handle it?

2. How would I change the way I reacted to my past illnesses?

3. What illness do I have now? What is the problem?

4. What can I do to make my situation better?

5. Write ideas and solutions (Exhaust all possibilities and create alternatives) See chapter 48 on "Prevailing."

6. How can I encourage my teammates when they are sick?

7. How can the power of prayer help me to persevere?

8. How can my faith help me in my situation?

9. What would Jesus do?

10. How do the Bible verses in this chapter help me? Are there other verses that can help me be an ultimate athlete with respect to being sick?

Drugs, Alcohol, Smoking

"Don't get drunk on wine...Instead be filled with the Spirit."

Ephesians 5:18

"The acts of the sinful nature are obvious: sexual immorality, ...hatred, discord, jealousy, fits of rage, selfish ambition...envy, drunkenness...I warn you, as I did before...that those who live like this will not inherit the kingdom of God."

Galatians 5:19-21

One would think that an athlete would *never* use drugs and alcohol, because they really harm the body. It is really amazing the number of athletes who decide to abuse substances like drugs, alcohol, and cigarettes. Whether you are an athlete or not, it just doesn't make sense to use, or abuse, these substances during your lifetime. However athletes should *never* try, use, or abuse these harmful things. Why would anyone train for hours daily, put their body though rigorous workouts, deal with sore muscles, rehabilitate injuries... just to ruin their bodies with dangerous chemicals? There is absolutely no benefit to the body. As an athlete you are trying to fine-tune your body, so don't start using any of these harmful substances. Let's see what the Bible has to say about this.

134

Romans 14:20 *"Don't destroy the work of God for the sake of food."* (Feel free to substitute the words *drugs, alcohol,* or *smoking,* in this sentence.)

1 Corinthians 3:16-17 *"Don't you know that you yourselves are God's temple and that God's Spirit lives in you? If any one destroys God's temple, God will destroy him; for God's temple is sacred, and you are that temple."*

1 Corinthians 6:19-20 *"Do you not know that your body is a temple of the Holy Spirit, who is in you, whom you have received from God? You are not your own; you were bought at a price. Therefore honor God with your body."*

Romans 12:1-2 *"Therefore I urge you, brothers, in view of God's mercy, to offer your bodies as a living sacrifice, holy and pleasing to God—this is your spiritual act of worship. Do not conform any longer to the pattern of this world, but be transformed by the renewing of your mind. Then you will be able to test and approve what God's will is—his good, pleasing and perfect will."*

Isaiah 5:11,12,22 *"Woe to those who rise early in the morning to run after their drinks, who stay up late at night till they are inflamed with wine. They have harps and lyres at their banquets, tambourines and flutes and wine, but they have no regard for the deeds of the Lord, no respect for the work of his hands. Woe to those who are heroes at drinking wine and champions at mixing drinks."*

Another reason to stay away from alcohol is that if you are younger than the legal age for drinking, you are breaking the law. Use of all drugs is breaking the law, and it is not worth the risk of getting a criminal record. Unfortunately there are many poor role models in professional sports. We hear, time and time again, about how a certain pro-athlete was picked up for drinking and driving, drug abuse… They now have criminal records and have lost a lot of respect.

135

Many people have turned their lives around and can serve as an example for us. Have you ever heard a former drug addict, an alcoholic, or a person with lung cancer say that they were glad they started using these chemicals? No they all say, "I wish that I never started, so don't start."

Proverbs 23:20,21,30-35 *"Do not join those who drink too much wine or gorge themselves on meat, for drunkards and gluttons become poor, and drowsiness clothes them in rags... Those who linger over wine, who go to sample bowls of mixed wine. Do not gaze at wine when it is red, when it sparkles in the cup, when it goes down smoothly! In the end it bites like a snake and poisons like a viper. Your eyes will see strange sights and your mind imagine confusing things. You will be like one sleeping on the high seas, lying on top of the rigging, 'They hit me,' you will say, 'but I'm not hurt! They beat me, but I don't feel it! When will I wake up so I can find another drink?"*

Proverbs 20:1 *"Wine is a mocker and beer a brawler; whoever is led astray by them is not wise."*

Unfortunately some of you have poor role models. Your parents, teammates, team captain, friends, or coaches may abuse chemicals. However, this does in *no way mean that you have to follow their example!* Remember no one can make you take anything that you don't want to take. They may pressure you, but the ultimate decision is up to *you* as to whether you start drinking, smoking, or taking drugs.

> *"When I got to Rochester, there was a big party where everyone was supposed to get drunk. I asked God to give me strength to say 'no.' I kept thinking of that verse 'be strong and courageous.' I was laughed at a lot, but I was glad I made a stand. I just want to be as close to Jesus as I can be. I want to live the way He wants me to and to be an example to people who don't know Him."*
> Kevin Haller, Assistant Captain of the Mighty Ducks pro hockey team

2 Corinthians 7:1 *"Since we have these promises, dear friends, let us purify ourselves from everything that contaminates body and spirit, perfecting holiness out of reverence for God."*

Daniel 1:8 *"But Daniel resolved not to defile himself with the royal food and wine, and he asked the chief official for permission not to defile himself this way."*

1 Peter 2:11 *"Dear friends, I urge you as aliens and strangers in this world to abstain from sinful desires which war against your soul."*

"I was addicted to drugs for eight years. I dabbled in marijuana, cocaine, and I drank a lot. When I met Jesus, I found out that trusting in Him is the best thing in life. I realized that the life that I lived before was artificial, like a mask. Through Jesus, I took off my mask and became a real person."
Jojo de Olivenca, world class surfer from Brazil

Personal Notes and Ideas

1. Why do people, including athletes, use dangerous chemicals?

2. How do dangerous chemicals hurt an athlete's body and performance?

3. What does the following statement mean to me? Using most chemicals is breaking the law.

4. List some athletes, both professional and amateur, who have ruined their athletic careers due to chemical use.

5. What are five reasons that I don't want to start taking dangerous chemicals.

6. I need to be prepared to say no to people who use chemicals. List three possible "no" statements.

7. How can my faith help me not abuse chemicals?

8. How can I encourage my teammates to not abuse chemicals?

9. What would Jesus do?

10. How do the Bible verses in this chapter help me? Are there other verses that can help me be an ultimate athlete with respect to chemical use?

Steroids

*"Don't you know that you yourselves are
God's temple and that God's Spirit lives in
you? If any one destroys God's temple, God
will destroy him; for God's temple is sacred,
and you are that temple."*

1 Corinthians 3:16-17

*"Do you not know that your body is a
temple of the Holy Spirit, who is in you,
whom you have received from God? You are
not your own; you were bought at a price.
Therefore honor God with your body."*

1 Corinthians 6:19-20

Nike has a great logo that they have used for years. "Just do
it." Let's change that logo just a little for our campaign
against the use of steroids or performance-enhancing
drugs. "Just *don't* do it."

The only reason to use these harmful chemicals is to make
oneself stronger and faster in order to be the best and win.
However, anyone who has won using steroids is *not* victorious.
They have cheated, and it is impossible for cheaters to win. They

139

might have the gold ribbon around their neck, but they are not the winners.

There is no other reason to use steroids, because they are very harmful to athletes in many ways:

1. The long-term effects from using steroids are hazardous to the body.
2. Once the truth is out, the fans and other athletes have no respect for the steroid users.
3. Medals are taken away, and the athletes are banned from competing for a length of time.

If you are using performance-enhancing drugs, you need to stop now! The most important judge in this world is God, and no one can hide anything from Him. You might be able to fool others, but you can't fool God.

Your coach may tell you to take steroids, or a teammate could be pressuring you, too. Confront them and let them know that you will never take these drugs. In addition, you should report your coach or teammate to a responsible third party. If the pressure is still there, or they are treating you poorly due to your good decision, find a new team. Performance-enhancing drugs are dangerous and should not be taken lightly.

Just remember that most, if not all, athletes who were caught using steroids are not happy with themselves in the long run. They have to deal with the public embarrassment, the loss of their medals, the stripping of their titles and records, and banishment from competition. It is safe to say that these athletes have never said, "I was glad that I did it."

Finally, let's see what God has to say about using steroids.

Romans 12:1 *"Therefore, **I urge you**, brothers, in view of God's mercy, to offer your bodies as living sacrifices, holy and pleasing to God—this is your spiritual act of worship,"*

1 Peter 2:11 *"Dear friends, **I urge you**, as aliens and strangers of this world, to abstain from sinful desires, which war against your soul."*

2 Corinthians 7:1 *"Since we have these promises, dear friends, let us purify ourselves from everything that contaminated body and spirit, perfecting holiness out of reverence for God."*

"As a Master's woman weightlifter, I can give two great reasons not to use steroids:
Steroids are drugs.
Drugs can kill!
I think as a champion; therefore I have become one. It takes perseverance, many hours in the gym, but most of all, God gives me the strength and it is my spiritual connection with God."

Mary Adams, champion weightlifter master's division

Personal Notes and Ideas

1. Why do athletes use these dangerous chemicals?

2. Is it worth the consequences to take these drugs?

3. Who can I turn to if I am being pressured to use these dangerous chemicals?

4. List some athletes, both professional and amateur, who have ruined their athletic careers due to steroid use.

5. What are five reasons that I don't want to take steroids.

6. I need to be prepared to say no to people who use steroids.

7. How can my faith help me not to use steroids?

8. How can I encourage my teammates to never get involved with performance-enhancing chemicals?

9. What would Jesus do?

10. How do the Bible verses in this chapter help me? Are there other verses that can help me be an ultimate athlete with respect to steroid use?

Eating Disorders

"But the Lord said to Samuel, 'Do not consider his appearance or his height...The Lord does not look at the things man looks at. Man looks at the outward appearance, but the Lord looks at the heart.'"

1 Samuel 16:7

"So whether you eat or drink or whatever you do, do it all for the glory of God."

1 Corinthians 10:31

Anorexia and bulimia are eating disorders that are very harmful to the body. These diseases can cause permanent damage to the body's organs as well as death. Moreover, they can cause horrible psychological scars that require intensive counseling to undo the damage that has been done. Most people think that these two dysfunctions are all about eating. However, that isn't always the case. They are more about self-esteem issues and control. When individuals feel helpless due to stress, one thing that they can control is their eating. They can't control the other things, but they find satisfaction in controlling their appearance. In addition, people who tend to be perfectionists have a greater chance of becoming anorexic or bulimic. For more information call the American Anorexia and Bulimia Association (201) 836-1800.

Mary placed in the top ten in an international race, and beat many of the world's best runners. She also set many national records. Mary was a straight A student in high school. About nine months later, at age eighteen, she tried to kill herself by swallowing pills. A year later Mary walked to the river and jumped off a train bridge. She fell thirty-five feet onto ice and was hurt very badly. Eighteen months later, after five operations, she found herself paralyzed from the neck down. "I didn't want to jump into the river, but if I did turn back, it would be only to return to my room and resume those terrible thoughts." These terrible thoughts were all about food. She suffered from anorexia nervosa and bulimia. She wanted to be a serious runner, and to look like one too. She fit the profile, having the desire to please, being competitive, and being a perfectionist.

According to Dr. James Peterson, the director of sports medicine for the Women's Sports Foundation, "Fad dieting, an obsession with ever-greater thinness, bingeing and purging, and erratic eating habits are widespread in women's sports, especially where excess body weight is a drag on performance." "Obligatory runner's syndrome" is when athletes, both men and women, want to increase mileage and decrease body fat for better performance. According to Tracy Sundlun, one of Mary's coaches, "Virtually all serious runners force themselves into illness, injury, or weakness at some point because of weight loss."

Mary says, "There is a weight consciousness among runners, but I was already extremely sensitive to it." Mary limited herself to thousand calories a day and increased the intensity and duration of her workouts each day. For instance, she would wake up at 6:00 A.M. do a hundred sit-ups with a ten-pound weight on her chest, run five miles, and then have a piece of toast and a half grapefruit for breakfast. She fell to eighty-nine pounds and was too weak to run in competition. She received psychiatric treatment, but continued her unhealthy ways. This led to her suicidal thoughts.

When Mary was in the hospital she said, "When I saw that the Lord had given me a chance to live, I switched my values around. Knowing that the Lord accepted me for who I was helped me heal. It is O.K. to strive, but don't let it become your identity and reason for happiness. Even if you don't win all the time, you should be able to be joyful."

Here are some helpful hints for those suffering with anorexia or bulimia, and for their families too:

- Early detection and immediate action.
- Realization that their overall health is much more important than any competition or career.
- Look in the yellow pages or surf the Internet for more information about eating disorders and for a professional who can help.
- Stay by their side and work on their self-concept. Continual presence in their lives is imperative.
- Psychological/psychiatric help
- Support groups
- Youth pastor or minister
- Prayer warriors
- Have fun and laugh. Laughter is the best medicine!
- Work on the "perfection" issue. See chapter 16 about "Pressure to Perform," which expands on perfection vs. excellence.

Here is God's wisdom about eating and our bodies:

1 Corinthians 3:16 *"Don't you know that you yourselves are God's temple and that God's Spirit lives in you?"*

1 Corinthians 6:19-20 *"Do you not know that your body is a temple of the Holy Spirit, who is in you, whom you have received from God? You are not your own; you were bought at a price. Therefore honor God with your body."*

Proverbs 25:16 *"If you find honey, eat just enough—too much of it, and you will vomit."*

Galatians 6:4 *"Each one should test his own actions. Then he can take pride in himself, without comparing himself to somebody else."*

Galatians 2:6 *"God does not judge by external appearance."*

> *"Eating disorders are a serious public health concern affecting up to 8 million Americans, young and old, and, contrary to popular perception they cut across boundaries of race, color, and socioeconomic status."*
> David Herzog, M.D., president of the Eating Disorders Coalition for Research, Policy & Action

Personal Notes and Ideas

1. Do I have an eating disorder?

2. Is there anyone on my team who has an eating disorder?

3. How do eating disorders hurt an athlete's body and performance?

4. What does God have to say about eating and drinking?

5. What can we learn from Mary's story?

6. Here are five reasons why I don't want to have an eating disorder:

7. How can I help my teammates or myself if we have, or are prone, to eating disorders.

8. How can my faith help me if I am anorexic or bulimic?

9. What would Jesus do?

10. How do the Bible verses in this chapter help me? Are there any other verses that can help me be an ultimate athlete with respect to eating disorders.

More verses

1 Corinthians 6:12-13
Romans 14:20-21
Isaiah 55:2

Temptations

"And lead us not into temptation, but deliver us from the evil one."

Matthew 6:13

"Therefore, since we are surrounded by such a great cloud of witnesses, let us throw off everything that hinders and the sin that so easily entangles, and let us run with perseverance the race marked out for us."

Hebrews 12:1

The famous saying is, "It is not my fault, they made me do it." "They" can be other people, and sometimes "they" means the devil. This statement is just a shifting of blame—people not taking responsibility for their actions. Unfortunately this happens more often than not. We are embarrassed to say, "I was wrong, or it was my fault." It is funny how people are quick to take the *credit*, but very slow to take the *blame*. We need to see ourselves as targets for temptations because we are human beings.

James 1:13-15 *"When tempted, no one should say; 'God is tempting me.' For God cannot be tempted by evil, not does he tempt anyone; but each one is tempted when, by his own evil desire, he is dragged away and enticed. Then, after desire has conceived, it gives birth to sin; and sin, when it is full-grown, gives birth to death."*

Knowledge is power, and just knowing that we are susceptible to temptation is the first step. The second step is to admit when we have been tempted and have chosen incorrectly.

Is temptation real? Of course it is! We have all been tempted many times, and even Jesus was tempted three times in the desert. How did Jesus resist the temptation? Luke 4:1-13. *"Jesus, full of the Holy Spirit in the desert, was tempted by the devil...The devil said to him, 'If you are the Son of God, tell this stone to become bread.' Jesus answered, 'It is written: Man does not live on bread alone'...and he said to him, 'I will give you all the authority and splendor, for it has been given to me, and I can give it to anyone I want to. So if you worship me, it will all be yours.' Jesus answered, 'It is written: Worship the Lord you God and serve him only'...'If you are the Son of God,' he said, 'throw yourself down from here'...Jesus answered, 'It says: Do not put the Lord your God to the test.'"* Notice when Jesus was tempted three times, He used Scripture to get rid of Satan. Therefore we can do the same thing!

Hebrews 2:18 *"Because he himself suffered when he was tempted, he is able to help those who are being tempted."*

Psalm 119:11 *"I have hidden your word in my heart that I might not sin against you."*

Psalm 37:31 *"The law of his God is in his heart; his feet do not slip."*

We need to not only be on the *defense* with respect to temptation, but go on the *offense*. We must realize that if we have chosen to follow God, we are new creations in Christ.

Romans 12:2 *"Do not conform any longer to the pattern of this world, but be transformed by the renewing of your mind."*

2 Corinthians 5:17 *"Therefore, if anyone is in Christ, he is a new creation; the old has gone, the new has come!"*

Specifically, what are some temptations with sports?

- Eating too much or not eating the right foods for our training regimen.
- Making short cuts and not finishing everything in the workout....
- Cheating to make yourself look better, in order to get the starting position.
- Lying about making a bad choice.
- Sabotaging competitors with cheap physical or verbal shots.
- Taking drugs, steroids, alcohol... because it is the "cool" thing to do.
- Stretching the truth, or exaggerating, when talking to recruiters.
- Being dishonest when calling shots in or out, in sports like tennis, volleyball, soccer...
- add to the list.

"We are responsible for what we do, no matter how we feel."

Unknown

Personal Notes and Ideas

1. How do I feel when I am tempted and make a bad choice?

2. How do I feel when I am tempted and make a good choice?

3. What are the temptations in my sport?

4. What can I learn from my mistakes and my successes?

5. How can my relationship with Jesus Christ help me when I am tempted?

6. I want to be on the offense with temptations. What is my plan?

7. How can I encourage my teammates to not be the victims of temptation?

8. What would Jesus do?

9. How do all the Bible verses in this chapter help me? Are there other verses that can help me be an ultimate athlete with respect to temptations?

Cheating

"Ill gotten treasures are of no value, but right-eousness delivers from death."

Proverbs 10:2

Remember the golden rule, "Cheaters never win, and winners never cheat!" Even if you cross the finish line first and have the medal around your neck...you cheated. You didn't win! No matter how big or small the lie is, it is still a lie. There is a lot of pressure in sports to win. It comes from coaches, parents, media, recruiters, and even ourselves. Some athletes become so determined to win that they will do anything in order to reign on the victory stand. It may be the person that you would least expect who is cheating. Don't cheat, because it isn't worth it. If you choose to lie, someday the truth will come out. If you are able to hide the secret forever, you will live the rest of your life as a lie. Would you like your tombstone to say, "Here lies a cheater"? Take the time to make things right with yourself, your family, your friends, and God.

Even if others are doing it, don't! You have your own God-given dignity. (I am not talking about pride.) And you are the only one that can protect that dignity. No one can make you think or act a certain way. They will pressure you like crazy, but the ultimate decision ends with you.

Here are some situations that may tempt you to cheat:

• Needing to get that scholarship.
• Making it on a professional team and needing the money.
• Qualifying for another competition or championship.
• Wanting to make first string.
• Winning a game or event.

Here are ways that athletes have cheated:

• Taking performance-enhancing substances.
• Lying about their performance.
• Sabotaging competitor's food or drink.
• Taking cheap shots in a game.

Reasons why we should never cheat:

• Because we want to become more like God/Jesus.
   Hebrews 6:18 *"...it is impossible for God to lie."*
• Because we will displease God and be punished.
   Isaiah 29:15 *"Woe to you who go to great depths to hide their plans from the Lord, who do their work in darkness and think, 'Who sees us? Who will know?'"*

When we enter Heaven, we will have to give an account for everything that we did.

Hebrews 4:13 *"Nothing in all creation is hidden from God's sight. Everything is uncovered and laid bare before the eyes of him to whom we must give an account."*

Here is an example in the Bible where there was cheating and lying. In Acts 5:1-4 Ananias and his wife Sapphira sold a piece of property. They were going to give all the money to the apostles, but they decided to keep some of the money for themselves. Peter knew that Ananias was lying to them when they brought the money. Peter challenged them by saying, *"What made you think of doing such a thing? You have not lied to men but to God."* After Peter said that, both Ananias and Sapphira fell down and died.

This is what the Bible says about cheating/lying:

1 Peter 2:11 *"...abstain against sinful desires, which war against our souls."*

Proverbs 21:6 *"A fortune made by a lying tongue is like fleeting vapor and a deadly snare."*

Colossians 3:25 *"Any one who does wrong will be repaid for his wrong, and there is no favoritism."*

I Corinthians 10:12-13 *"So, if you think you are standing firm, be careful that you don't fall! No temptation has seized you except what is common to man. And God is faithful; he will not let you be tempted beyond what you can bear. But when you are tempted, he will also provide a way out so that you can stand up under it."*

2 Timothy 2:5 *"Similarly, if anyone competes as an athlete, he does not receive the victor's crown unless he competes according to the rules."*

This is what the Bible says about honesty:

Romans 9:1 *"I speak the truth in Christ. I am not lying, my conscience confirms it in the Holy Spirit."*

2 Corinthians 8:21 *"For we are taking pains to do what is right, not only in the eyes of the Lord but also in the eyes of man."*

1 Peter 2:12 *"Live such good lives among the pagans that, though they accuse you of doing wrong, they may see your good deeds and glorify God on the day he visits us."*

"Do nothing which, after being done, leads you to tell a lie."

Unknown

"*A liar needs a good memory.*"

Quintilian

A lie may take care of the present, but it won't help you in the future."

Unknown

Personal Notes and Ideas

1. How do I define cheating and lying?

2. How do I feel about cheating/lying?

3. How could I let cheating/lying destroy me?

4. What can I learn from my previous mistakes of cheating/lying?

5. Who can I talk to about cheating/lying?

6. How can I encourage my teammates to not cheat/lie?

7. What would Jesus do?

8. How do all the Bible verses in this chapter help me? Are there other verses that can help me be an ultimate athlete with respect to cheating/lying?

Extra verses

Luke 8:15
Philippians 4:8-9

Cheating Athletes or Coaches

"Do not repay evil with evil or insult with insult, but with blessing because to this you were called so that you may inherit a blessing."
1 Peter 3:9

"Do not be quickly provoked in your spirit, for anger resides in the lap of fools."
Ecclesiastes 7:9

ocus! No matter what happens don't forget about your focus. Why are you competing? What is your goal? What things are crucial for you to remember while you are still competing? Don't allow anything to have a *chance* to change your focus. That is one of the main reasons that opposing athletes and coaches choose to cheat, play dirty, and commit fouls. They are hoping that you will start thinking about *their actions* instead of what *you are supposed to do*. They want to shake you up, frustrate you, and make you become flustered. Knowing this is power! Prepare yourself for these cheating, unethical players and coaches, both mentally and emotionally. Don't give them the satisfaction of seeing you become frazzled. Keep your focus, because no one can change it except you. Keep talking positively to yourself and your teammates so that you can continue doing what you came to do. Don't take your mind off your game, because that's what they want.

Now let's take a Christian perspective on this:

Romans 12:17-22 *"Do not repay anyone evil for evil. Be careful to do what is right in the eyes of everybody. If it is possible, as far as it depends on you, live at peace with everyone. Do not take revenge, my friends, but leave room for God's wrath, for it is written: 'It is mine to avenge; I will repay,' says the Lord. On the contrary; 'If your enemy is hungry, feed him; if he is thirsty, give him something to drink. In doing this, you will heap burning coals on his head.' Do not overcome be evil, overcome evil with good."*

Show the other team that you won't lower yourself to their level. You have more dignity than that. They are expecting revenge. However, when you don't avenge yourselves, and choose to keep your focus, you will accomplish many things:

1. A chance to show that you take good sportsmanship seriously.
2. You can show people that your faith helps you stay calm and make the right decisions.
3. The other team won't know what to when you don't retaliate!

> *"The best way of avenging yourself is not to become like the wrong doer."*
> Marcus Aurelius

Personal Notes and Ideas

1. How do I feel when others cheat?

2. How can I keep my focus no matter what happens?

3. Write down five ways that others could cheat in my sport and my solutions for maintaining my focus.

4. Have I retaliated against cheaters? If so, what can I learn from my mistakes?

5. How can I encourage my teammates to not retaliate but keep their focus?

6. What would Jesus do?

7. How do all the Bible verses in this chapter help me? Are there other verses that can help me be an ultimate athlete with respect to when others cheat?

Choices

*"Make every effort to enter through narrow
door."*

Luke 13:24

*"LORD, who may dwell in your sanctuary?
Who may live on your holy hill? ...who keeps
his oath, even when it hurts."*

Psalm 15:1,4

Just say, "No"! Learning to say no can be very hard at times,
especially when peer pressure is strong.

1 Peter 2:11 *"...abstain from sinful desires, which war against
your soul."*

Titus 2:12 *"It teaches us to say 'no' to ungodliness and worldly
passions, and to live self-controlled, upright and godly lives in
this present age."*

1 Corinthians 10:23 *"Everything is permissible, but not
everything is beneficial."*

Psalm 106:3 *"Blessed are those who maintain justice, who constantly do what is right."*

2 Timothy 2:22 *"Flee the evil desires of youth, and pursue righteousness, faith, love and peace, along with those who call on the Lord out of a pure heart."*

There are consequences with your choices and also sometimes from the choices of other people. 1 Corinthians 4:20-21 *"For the kingdom of God is not a matter of talk but of power. What do you prefer? Shall I come to you with a whip, or in love and with a gentle spirit."* These verses are telling us that we will be held accountable for our choices to God. Do we want God to punish us for our bad decisions, or be loving and gentle with us because of our good decisions.

"In truth, my poor choices were based on a desperate need to find someone or something that could meet my deepest needs. However, instead of filling my void, I kept finding myself in situations that seemed to only intensify the emptiness in my heart. I realized that I needed to set my hopes in God."
LaVonna Martin Floreal, 1992 Olympic silver medalist.

Bad Choices

1 Corinthians 15:33 *"Do not be misled: 'Bad company corrupts good character.'"*

Galatians 2:13 *"The other Jews joined him in his hypocrisy, so that by their hypocrisy even Barnabas was led astray."*

James 1:27 *"Religion that God our Father accepts as pure and faultless is this: to look after orphans and widows in their distress and to keep oneself from being polluted by the world."*

God has given us many gifts. The most important gift is that He sacrificed His own Son, Jesus Christ, so that we could have eternal life. The second most important is the gift of *choice*. God doesn't *make* us do anything or feel a certain way. He leaves that up to us. Therefore *we* are in charge of our own *attitudes* and *actions*. No one can ever make us feel the way we do. For the most part, no one can control our actions either. In extenuating circumstances, people may act contrary to their own wishes. For instance, in the Holocaust, many of the Jewish people did not want to board the trains that went to concentration camps. Many of them did so because they had guns at their backs. However, most of use are in control of our actions 100 percent of the time. So don't start playing the Blame Game. Just accept responsibility for your attitudes and actions.

People don't always make good decisions. Most of us know what is the right thing to do, but don't always do it. James 4:17 *"Anyone, then, who knows the good he ought to do and doesn't do it, sins."* The response to James 4:17 is Ephesians 5:17 *"Therefore do not be foolish, but understand what the Lord's will is."* Here are some great solution verses to help you with your choices:

Solution Verses

Psalm 32:8-9 *"I will instruct you and teach you in the way you should go; I will counsel you and watch over you. Do not be like the horse or the mule, which have no understanding, but must be controlled by bit and bridle or they will not come to you."*

Proverbs 4:13-15 *"Hold on to instruction, do not let it go; guard it well for it is your life. Do not set foot on the path of the wicked or walk in the ways of evil men. Avoid it, do not travel on it; turn from it and go on your way."*

James 1:5 *"If any of you lacks wisdom, he should ask God, who gives generously to all without finding fault, and it will be given to him."*

1 Thessalonians 5:21-22 *"Test everything. Hold on to the good. Avoid every kind of evil."*

Even when we are in pain we are still held accountable for the choices we make. If you are experiencing tough times, don't make any decisions on your own. You can't think or see very clearly due to your pain. This doesn't mean that you are stupid or a weak person. You are in a crisis and need to be very careful because of the strong emotions that you are experiencing.

Psalm 119:28 *"My soul is weary with sorrow; strengthen me according to your word."*

> *"We are responsible for our own life. No other person is, or ever can be."*
>
> Oprah

> *"Always do the right. This will gratify and astonish the rest."*
>
> Mark Twain

> *"You can be the problem or you can be the solution."*
>
> The Author

> *"The greater part of our happiness or misery depends on our dispositions and not on our circumstances."*
>
> Martha Washington, First Lady

Personal Notes and Ideas

1. How do the choices I make affect my life and the lives of others?

2. Have I made bad choices before? If so, how did I feel?

3. My bad choices were totally my responsibility, because of my poor decisions. Why did I make those bad choices?

4. What can I do to make better decisions in the future? Write down five ideas or solutions (Exhaust all possibilities and create alternatives. See chapter 48 on "Prevailing.")

5. Who can I go to for help?

6. How can the power of prayer help me to make better decisions?

7. How can my faith help me in my next situation?

8. What Bible verse would be a good one for me to memorize? (This is the verse that you will need to remember when you are about to make a choice.)

9. How can I encourage my teammates to make good choices?

10. What would Jesus do?

11. How do the Bible verses in this chapter help me? Are there other verses that can help me be an ultimate athlete with respect to choices?

Extra verses
James 2:12
Psalm 119:24,105
1 Thessalonians 2:12

Laziness

"Never be lacking in zeal, but keep your spiritual fervor, serving the Lord."

Romans 12:11

Laziness has no place in the world of athletics. Sports take a lot of time, dedication, hard work, and perseverance—emotionally, physically, spiritually, and mentally. If you want to be lazy, find another pastime or hobby. This advice is not only for your own good, but also for the sake of the team. Choosing to be lazy takes up valuable time and resources from the team. Much worse, you could be getting in the way of some hard-working athletes. Nothing can be more frustrating than having a lazy athlete ruin your training schedule or practice.

> Hebrews 6:12 *"We don't want you to become lazy, but to imitate those who through faith and patience inherit what has been promised."*

Laziness can become contagious and infectious to the team. Some athletes, who are followers, may choose to do what the lazy athlete is doing. This athlete may be very popular, so the followers are thinking that slacking off is the cool thing to do. It is very simple.

If you are not there to be a contributing teammate, then why are you out for sports? If you are burned out and just can't push it any longer...choose to move on with your life. Burnout is real in the world of athletics and it is completely understandable. Refer to chapter 35 on "Burnout." However choosing to stay on the team and being lazy is not OK. Remember that the chain is as strong as the weakest link. No one should want to be the weakest link *by choice.* If you work hard and are the weakest link, don't worry. You may be the slowest one in your relay. But if you weren't available, there wouldn't be a relay, or it would be much slower with another person.

There are many ways to slack off at practice. For instance runners can go by a water fountain and splash water on their faces and T-shirts. It looks like they are working hard and are sweating a lot. This is just one of many ways to fool the coaches and teammates. Just remember, you will never be able to fool God. Let's see what the Bible has to say about laziness.

Philippians 2:14 *"Do everything without complaining or arguing, so that you may become blameless and pure, children of God without fault..."* (Please remember that complaining is one type of laziness.)

Proverbs 18:9 *"One who is slack in work is brother to the one who destroys."*

Proverbs 6:6-8 *"Go to the ant, you sluggard; consider its ways and be wise! It has no commander, no overseer or ruler, yet it stores its provisions in summer and gathers its food at harvest."*

2 Thessalonians 3:6-13 *"In the name of the Lord Jesus Christ, we command you brothers to keep away from every brother who is idle and does not live according to the teaching you received from us. For you yourselves know how you ought to follow our example. We were not idle when we were with you, nor did we eat anyone's food without paying for it. On the contrary, we worked night and day, laboring and toiling so that we would not be a burden to any of you. We did this...in*

order to make ourselves a model for you to follow…And as for you, brothers, never tire of doing what is right."

2 Corinthians 8:17 *"For Titus not only welcomed our appeal, but he is coming to you with much enthusiasm and **on his own initiative.**"*

2 Corinthians 9:2 "I know your eagerness to help, and I have been boasting about it to the Macedonians…and your enthusiasm has stirred most of them to action."

"Game shape is easy to lose and hard to get back. But you just wake up every day and make a decision to work hard."
Mia Hamm, U.S. women's soccer team

"Sooner or later, Charlie Brown, There's one thing you're going to have to learn. You reap what you sow! You get out of life exactly what you put into it. No more and no less."
(Violet talking to Charlie Brown) Charles M. Schulz

"You must work and do good, not be lazy…if you wish to earn happiness. Laziness may appear attractive, but work gives satisfaction."
Anne Frank

Personal Notes and Ideas
1. How do I feel about laziness?

2. How could I let laziness destroy myself and my team?

3. What are ways that I can slack off in my sport? Write them down and vow to never do those lazy tactics.

4. Do I complain? If so, how can I stop doing that?

5. How can I encourage my teammates to not be lazy?

6. What would Jesus do?

7. How do all the Bible verses in this chapter help me? Are there other verses that can help me be an ultimate athlete with respect to laziness?

Other verses for you to look up in the Bible

Proverbs 12:27   1 Timothy 6:1
Proverbs 19:15   2 Corinthians 8:11
Proverbs 21:25   Ephesians 5: 15
Proverbs 13:4

Burnout

> *"Come to me, all who are weary and burdened, and I will give you rest. Take my yoke upon you and learn form me, for I am gentle and humble in heart, and you will find rest for your souls. For my yoke is easy and my burden is light."*
>
> Matt 11:28-30

itting the wall. That is when athletes just can't keep going anymore, especially with respect to marathons. All types of athletes experience this emotion. "The grind" is just getting too tough. Day after day, and sometimes up to seven hours a day for serious athletes. For other athletes it is a combination of balancing school with sports, work, family time...It just gets to be too much and they need a break. For some athletes it is the constant pushing your body to the limit. It is dealing with the muscle burn, sore muscles, injuries due to overtraining...on a daily basis. It could be waking up at four in the morning and driving a long way to get to practice. Have you ever felt that way? If you have, you are absolutely normal! Burnout is *real* in athletics.

Isaiah 41:10 *"So do not fear, for I am with you; Do not be dismayed, for I am your God. I will strengthen you and help you; I will uphold you with my righteous right hand."*

Psalm 119:139, 140 *"My zeal wears me out, for my enemies ignore your words. Your promises have been thoroughly tested, and your servant loves them."*

Then there is mental and emotional burnout. This is when your body may be willing, but your mind cannot keep going. The amount of mental and emotional concentration that an athlete needs is tremendous. All times in your athletic career, you will need an mental and emotional break more than a physical one. It just gets to be too much!

Isaiah 40:30-31 *"Even youths grow tired and weary, and young men stumble and fall; but those who hope in the Lord will renew your strength"*

Psalm 51:10 *"Create in me a pure heart, O God, and renew a steadfast spirit within me."*

Solutions:
- Get advice from your coach, or a former coach.
- Talk with other athletes who have dealt with burnout and have conquered it.
- Talk with your pastor or youth group leader.
- Share your frustrations with friends or family. Definitely talk about it. Don't keep this to yourself.
- You might need two or three days off. Taking a couple days off in the whole scheme of things is nothing! Go do something completely different. Maybe take a break from competing, but continue to work out.

If it gets to the point that you are starting to hate your sport, then you will need to do some serious soul searching. You may need to leave your sport and move on with life. You are not on this earth to be miserable. But think once, twice, three times before you do hang up the towel.

One day Jane couldn't handle going to practice. She had been competing since the age of eight and now was a junior in college. Jane was a hard worker and never gave up in practice. Her coach knew this too. So her coach told Jane that she couldn't come to practice and needed to do something that she has always wanted to do. Jane wanted to go to a special dance class that was being offered that day. So Jane left practice, went to the dance class, had a wonderful time, and was all recharged to return to practice the next day. That was all that she needed. She finished the season in top form.

Galatians 6:9-10 *"Let us not become weary in doing good, for at the proper we will reap a harvest if we do not give up. Therefore, as we have opportunity, let us do good to all people..."*

"Motivation is a constant battle. It's easy to quit and hard to keep going...but you have to just push yourself through it."

Mia Hamm, U.S.A. women's soccer star

Personal Notes and Ideas

1. Have I experienced burnout? If so, what did I do about it?

2. Am I currently experiencing burnout?

3. What is the problem?

4. What can I do to make the situation better? Write down five solutions. (Exhaust all possibilities and create alternatives! See chapter 48 on "Prevailing.")

5. Who can help me with my burnout?

6. How can the power of prayer help me with my burnout?

7. How can my faith help me in my situation?

8. How can I encourage my teammates if they are experiencing burnout?

9. What would Jesus do?

10. How do the Bible verses in this chapter help me? Are there other verses that can help me to be an ultimate athlete with respect to burnout?

Attitude

"A man's spirit sustains him in sickness, but a crushed spirit who can bear?"

Proverbs 18:14

God has given each person free choice. This free choice has to do with our *attitudes* and *actions*. No one can make us feel the way we do, therefore we are totally in charge of our attitudes. For the most part, no one can control our actions either. The only time when our actions can be controlled is in rare circumstances, such as the Holocaust, slavery, South African Apartheid... The people didn't have a choice as to getting on trains, standing in various lines, or being tortured or killed. They had to follow the physical orders. However, as tough as it was, they all had a choice regarding their attitude. This proves that though we may not be able to control the situation, we can control all of our attitudes, and for the most part, all of our actions. Unfortunately with this free choice, people can choose to ruin the world. People like Hitler, Stalin, Saddam Hussein, drug dealers, murderers...have made their disastrous mark on this world. That is the down side of free choice.

Let's explore the issue of various situations. Let's look at a glass that has some water in it. We can describe that as a glass half-empty or as a glass half-full. Yes, we are accurately describing that glass of water, because either description is correct. However, if you see it as half full, then you are choosing to look at the positive side of the situation. On the other hand, if you describe the glass as half empty, then you are choosing to look at the negative side of the situa-

tion. Sometimes you have to struggle to *see* and *choose* the positive side of each situation, but it is there. (Refer to chapter 11 on "Preparation" for more information on attitude)

The following question is important for all athletes to answer. Do you want to be a thermometer or a thermostat? A thermometer allows the situation or the outside elements to control it. It goes up when it is hot and it goes down when it is cold. It really doesn't have a mind for itself. A thermostat, on the other hand, controls the environment. If it is too cold in your house, all you need to do to turn up the heat is use the thermostat.

Now let's relate this idea in athletic terms. It is raining outside and you have to compete. *Everyone* is in the same situation! One athlete chooses to be a thermometer, to be defeated by the weather, and to just become miserable. "How am I going to be able to compete today with all this rain?" Another athlete decides to be a thermostat. "Competing in the rain isn't my favorite thing to do, but we are all in the same situation. I know that I have practiced a lot in the rain, and I know what I need to do. I just need to concentrate harder and choose to be more positive." Who do you think will have a good competition and probably perform better? The next question is which athlete would you rather be with, and which one would you rather be? As you can clearly see, attitude is a choice. So it is always your choice to say, "I can do it!" no matter what the situation may be.

Positive attitude

Proverbs 16:24 *"Pleasant words are a honeycomb, sweet to the soul and healing to the bones."*

Mark 9:23 *" 'If you can'?" said Jesus. "Everything is possible for him who believes."*

Negative attitude

Proverbs 26:13 *"The sluggard says, "There is a lion in the road, a fierce lion roaming the streets!"*

Positive vs. negative attitudes

Proverbs 17:22 *"A cheerful heart is good medicine, but a crushed spirit dries up the bones."*

Proverbs 15:13 *"A happy heart makes the face cheerful, but heartache crushes the spirit."*

Thermostat Athletes	Thermometer Athletes
Focus on *solutions*	Focus on *problems*
How can I compete better?	Why is it so cold out?
How can I help others on my team?	Why can't I get warmed up?
What can I improve today?	Why can't I run as fast as….?
How can I stay positive today?	Why is this happening to me?

In other words *focus* on the *solutions*, and *don't dwell* on the *problems*.

It is all self-talk!!!!

Life is hard. Life hurts. Tough times happen! Pain is a reality in life, but misery is optional! Being miserable is your choice! Someday hard times and pain will knock on your door. If you become miserable, it is *your conscious decision* to put yourself into that mode! It can be a daily, sometimes moment-to-moment, struggle to maintain a positive attitude. But it can be done! Remember that your attitude is revealed by your actions.

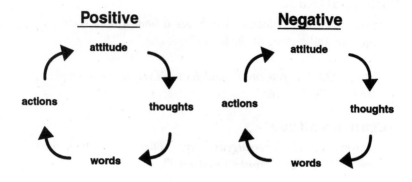

Do you have control over everything? NO! But there is one person who does have complete control, and it is God! He sees the whole picture. But you do have control over two things!

A. Your attitude
B. Your actions

So, take responsibility for yourself and don't blame everything and everyone else.

Destructive vs. encouraging statements

Notice that the statements are all about the same situation! The first one is very *negative*. The second one is *kind of positive*, because it has both positive and negative words in the statement. The last one is *totally positive*!

Sports

Negative	Kind of Positive	Totally Positive
1. I quit!	I won't quit	I will do it!
2. I can't shoot free throws today.	I'll try to shoot free throws today.	I will make 50 free throws today.
3. I am a loser.	I'll try not to be a loser.	I am a winner!

Life

Negative	Kind of Positive	Totally Positive
1. The spaghetti noodles are raw.	It's OK, we'll eat it anyway.	The sauce is great!
2. The bread is stale. I'll starve.	Put lots of peanut butter on it, it will taste O.K.	I'm thankful that I have some food and I am not starving like people in poor countries.
3. I hate school.	School is boring, but it is good for us.	I am glad that I am getting an education, because I can be what I want to be.

One day, at a soccer game, Jack's team was in a bad situation. They had only ten players, so they were always one player short. Plus they didn't have any subs to give them the rest they needed. To make matters worse, the wind was blowing incredibly hard. During the first half of the game, Jack's team played with the wind and was able to keep the game tied! The second half began and the team was still down one player. In addition, they were tired and had to play into that horrible wind. After about ten minutes they took a time-out so that they could rest. As the players were running off the field, there were many different reactions. Again, remember that all ten players were in the same situation.

1. One player said almost every swear word possible (negative).
2. Another player said, "This stinks playing into the wind, but we can do it!" (kind of positive).
3. Another player said, "This is great! Just think, by playing into the wind we will be able to get oxygen into our lungs faster" (totally positive).

This true story is a great example for all athletes.

Now write out five *Sports* and five *Life* statements using all three categories!

Sports

Negative	Kind of Positive	Totally Positive
1.		
2.		
3.		
4.		
5.		

Life

Negative	Kind of Positive	Totally Positive
1.		
2.		
3.		
4.		
5.		

Proverbs 23:17 *"Do not let your heart envy sinners, but always be zealous for the fear of the Lord."*

Proverbs 23:7 *"For as he thinks within himself, so he is."*

"You can plan your funeral or enjoy your life."
Unknown

> *"Either you control your attitude, or it controls you."*
>
> Unknown

> *"If you really want to be happy, no one can stop you."*
>
> Sister Mary Tricky

> *"I am convinced that life is 10% what happens to me and 90% how I react to it."*
>
> Chuck Swindoll

> *"People are just about as happy as they make up their minds to be."*
>
> Abraham Lincoln

Personal Notes and Ideas

1. How do I feel about my attitude?

2. Has my glass been half full or half empty? How do I want my glass to be?

3. In what ways could I allow my attitude destroy me and my team?

4. Am I a thermometer or a thermostat athlete?

5. Am I a negative, kind of positive, or a totally positive person?

6. How can I encourage my teammates to be totally positive?

7. What would Jesus do?

8. How do all the Bible verses in this chapter help me? Are there other verses that can help me be an ultimate athlete with respect to my attitude?

Worry

"Seek first the kingdom of God and all His righteousness, and all these things will be given to you as well. Therefore do not worry about tomorrow, for tomorrow will worry about itself. Each day has enough trouble of its own."

Matthew 6:33-34

According to Dorothy Galyean and a Ziggy cartoon, "Worrying is like a rocking chair. It gives you something to do, but it doesn't get you anywhere." Worrying has no benefits for anyone. Worry causes anxiety, which in return causes negative stress. Negative stress has detrimental effects on a person's mind, body, and soul. Since there is nothing good about worrying, we should do our best to not engage in this harmful emotion. Yes, it is easier said than done! However let's put worrying into perspective.

God understands and accepts the majority of our emotions. He wants us to be honest with Him. If we hurt, we need to say, "Ouch!" If we are sad, He expects us to cry. God understands when we are angry, because Jesus was angry. But God doesn't always accept or approve of every action. Being angry is OK, but to take revenge due to that anger is sin. So, God accepts almost all of our emotions. He made us emotional beings.

The one emotion that we should refrain from is worry. When we worry, we are telling God that He can't handle it! It means that we are not sure of His omnipotence. God can do absolutely anything, because He is all-powerful. But when God chooses not to give us everything we want, it doesn't mean that He isn't all-powerful. So why should we doubt Him, His wisdom, and His power. Worrying does just that! Whether you like it or not, when you worry you are telling God that He has no wisdom or power. Wow, worrying is sinning! That is a lot to think about. So when you feel like worrying, remember what you have just learned.

Faith is believing even when you can't see anything. So as people of faith, we have the choice to allow our faith to grow and trust God. On the other hand, we can sin by worrying—not giving our faith a chance to grow. It isn't easy, and at times it can be very frustrating. However when we do choose to allow our faith to grow, we are in for an incredible journey! God has given us choice. So you can trust your faith or just worry. It is your decision!

Philippians 4:6,7 *"Do not be anxious about anything, but in everything, by prayer and petition, with thanksgiving, present your requests to God. And the peace of God, which transcends all understanding, will guard your hearts and your minds in Christ Jesus."*

Psalm 55:22 *"Cast your cares on the Lord and he will sustain you; he will never let the righteous fall."*

Luke 21:14-15 *"But make up your mind to not worry beforehand how you will defend yourselves. For I will give you words and wisdom that none of your adversaries will be able to resist or contradict."*

1 Peter 5:7 *"Cast all your anxiety on Him, because He cares for you."*

Mark 5:36 *"Don't be afraid, just believe."*

"*Every morning I spend 15 minutes filling my mind full of God; and so there's no room left for worry thoughts.*"

Howard Chandler Christy

"*It is such comfort to drop the tangles of life into God's hands and leave them there.*"

Unknown

Personal Notes and Ideas

1. When have I worried about my athletics before? Did it help me at all?

2. What could I do differently the next time?

3. What situations could potentially be ruined if I worry? What is the problem?

4. What can I do to make the situation better? Write ideas and solutions (Exhaust all possibilities and create alternatives.) See chapter 48 on "Prevailing."

5. Who can help me with my situation?

6. How can the power of prayer help me not to worry?

7. How can my faith help me in my situation?

8. How can I encourage my teammates not to worry?

9. What would Jesus do?

10. How do the Bible verses in this chapter help me? Are there other verses that can help me be an ultimate athlete with respect to worrying?

Gossip

"Do not let any unwholesome talk come out of your mouths, but only what is helpful for building others up according to their needs, that it may benefit those who listen."

Ephesians 4:29

Most of us have played the game "Telephone." One person whispers a sentence to another player. Then each person takes a turn whispering this sentence to the next person in line. The last player to hear the sentence has to say it out loud. It is amazing how the final sentence is not very much like the original sentence. It is very rare to have a sentence make it around the room perfectly.

What can be learned from the game of Telephone with respect to gossip? Go to the source! Go directly to the person! Too much damage can be done if the gossip chain is allowed to continue. Many times the person hasn't done anything wrong, but the vicious gossip spreads like a contagious disease. Feelings get hurt, friendships are broken, and relationships are damaged, because of some unnecessary gossip. Yes, there are times that a person has done wrong. But instead of talking with everyone else, go to that person first. Find out the actual details, and try to come to an understanding. If you choose to start the gossip chain when there has been a problem, be assured that your original story will get distorted. The other person will be burdened with many falsehoods.

Proverbs 11:13 *"A gossip betrays a confidence, but a trustworthy man keeps a secret."*

Proverbs 16:28 *"...and a gossip separates close friends."*

Proverbs 12:18 *"Reckless words pierce like a sword, but the tongue of the wise brings healing."*

James 1:26 *"If anyone considers himself religious and yet does not keep a tight rein on his tongue, he deceives himself and his religion is worthless."*

There will be misunderstandings, because we are human and miscommunications are a fact of life. Whether you have a strong faith or not, be prepared for misunderstandings and communication problems. With respect to sports, gossip is a deadly poison that can spread like wild fire and do a huge amount of damage. Whether the problem is with another teammate, the team captain, or the coach, you need to go to the source. It is not always easy, but it is the right thing to do.

What can you do as an ultimate athlete to make a tense situation better rather than worse?

1. STOP the gossip chain! Refuse to be a part of that nonsense.
2. Go to the source. Talk to the person who is the topic of gossip.
3. Find out the true story and work toward a solution.
4. If you can't trust the person who is the topic of gossip, then schedule a meeting with a responsible third party.

Matthew 18:15-16 *"If your brother sins against you, go and show him his fault, just between the two of you. If he listens to you, you have won your brother over. But if he will not listen, take one or two others along, so that every matter may be established by the testimony of two or three witnesses."*

5. Remember that Jesus is our example in life. (Both verses refer to Jesus):

Isaiah 53:9 *"...he had done no violence nor was any deceit in his mouth."*

1 Peter 2:22 *"He committed no sin or deceit was found in his mouth."* (also refers to Isaiah 53:9)

6. Be wise and be a good example.

Psalm 15:1-3 *"Lord, who may dwell in your sanctuary? Who may live on your holy hill? He whose walk is blameless and who does what is righteous, who speaks the truth from his heart and has no slander on his tongue, who does his neighbor no wrong and casts no slur on his fellow man."*

2 Timothy 2:16 *"Avoid godless chatter, because those who indulge in it will become more and more ungodly."*

1 Peter 3:10 *"For, 'Whoever would love life and see good days must keep his tongue from evil and his lips from deceitful speech.' "*

James 4:11 *"Brothers, do not slander one another."*

"Unfortunately gossip is a big part of high school sports, because it causes many problems that are not needed."
Melissa Budde, high school volleyball MVP

"Harsh words don't break bones, but they do break hearts."
Unknown

> *"If one speaks badly of you, live so no one will believe it."*
>
> Unknown

Personal Notes and Ideas

1. What bothers me the most when people gossip?

2. How do I feel when others gossip about me?

3. How do I feel when I gossip about others?

4. Why is "going to the source" so important?

5. What can I do to stop a gossip chain on my team?

6. Who could be a responsible third party if I am having pro-lems confronting someone?

7. How can I encourage my teammates to not engage in gossip?

8. What would Jesus do?

9. How do the Bible verses in this chapter help me? Are there other verses that can help be to be an ultimate athlete with respect to gossip?

Extra verses

James 3:5-12
2 Timothy 2:14, 23, 24
Proverbs 20:19
Proverbs 18:8 (Same verse is also found in Proverbs 26:22)
James 3:3-6

Abusive Situations

"They think it is strange that you do not plunge with them into the same flood of dissipation (bad decisions), and they heap abuse on you."

1 Peter 4:4

1. Abusive situations

There are many types of abuse as there are various kinds of *pain*. Most common are sexual, physical, emotional and spiritual abuse. It is rare to experience abuse without some form of *pain* accompanying it. Abuse can have a close connection with *denial* also. One of the toughest things a person can admit is that they have been abused by a stranger or much less by a loved one. Therefore not owning up to the truth can produce a very *depressed* and *angry* person.

2. Abusers

Abusers come in all shapes and forms. Their economic level, religious background, race, gender doesn't matter—they all have one thing in common. They tend to blame, minimize, and deny so that they can *control* the other person.

A. Blame

Abusers refuse to accept the responsibility of the situation. They say that something or someone else is at fault.

Isaiah 59:4 *"No one calls for justice; no one pleads his case with integrity. They rely on empty arguments and speak lies; they conceive trouble and give birth to evil."*

Luke 14:18 *"But they all alike began to make excuses."*

B. Minimize

Abusers believe that your pain and frustrations have little to no merit. They think that you are upset over something that is no big deal. These abusers fail to see what is really happening. Many can't and won't try to see your side.

Matthew 13:13 *"This is why I speak to them in parables: 'Though seeing, they do not see; though hearing, they do not hear or understand."*

C. Deny

Abusers refuse to believe the truth about what happened or is happening.

Matt 26:25 *"Then Judas, the one who would betray him, said, 'Surely not I, Rabbi?' Jesus answered, 'Yes, it is you.'"*

Matthew 26: 74-75 *"Then he began to call down curses on himself and he swore to then, 'I don't know that man!' Immediately a rooster crowed. Then Peter remembered the word Jesus had spoken: 'Before the rooster crows, you will disown me three times...'"*

This is what God has to say about people who blame, minimize, and deny.

Romans 1:19 *"Since what may be known about God is plain to them, because God has made it plain to them. For since the creation of the world God's invisible qualities—his eternal power and divine nature—have been clearly seen, being understood from what has been made, so that men are without excuse.*

Luke 6:41:42 *"Why do you look at the speck of sawdust in your brother's eye and pay no attention to the plank in your own eye? How can you say to your brother, 'Brother, let me take the speck out of your eye,' when you yourself fail to see the plank in your own eye? You hypocrite, first take the plank out of your eye, and then you will see clearly to remove the speck from your brother's eye."*

The key to dealing with abusers is to look at their *actions,* and not their *words.*

No one deserves to be abused! No matter what! However, we are in charge of our happiness and how long we *stay* abused. Getting out of an abusive situation is not easy, but help is available. Contact:

1. NCADV (National Coalition Against Domestic Violence.) 1-800-799-7233 www.ncadv.org
2. National Domestic Violence Hotline 1-800-799-7233 or 1-800 787-3224 (TTY) www.ndvh.org

3. Types of abuse on a team
A. *Backstabbing*

When teammates talk about people behind their backs. Unfortunately this is very common among athletes.

Galatians 5:15 *"If you keep on biting and devouring each other, watch out or you will be destroyed by each other."*

B. *Envy*

When teammates are jealous of another athlete who is more talented than they are.

Galatians 5:26 *"Let us not become conceited, provoking and envying each other."*

Acts 13:45 *"When the Jews saw the crowds, they were filled with jealousy and talked abusively against what Paul was saying."*

C. Persecution

When teammates pick on other athletes or try to make their teammates' lives miserable.

Galatians 1:13,23 (The apostle Paul persecuted the church, but one teammate can do the same thing to the whole team.) *"For you have heard of my previous way of life in Judaism, how intensely I persecuted the church of God and tried to destroy it...They had only heard the report: 'The man who formerly persecuted us is now preaching the faith he once tried to destroy.'"*

Acts 14:5-6 *"There was a plot afoot among the Gentiles and Jews, together with their leaders, to mistreat them and stone them. But they found out about it and fled..."*

Acts 18:6 *"But when the Jews opposed Paul and became abusive, he shook out his clothes in protest and said to them, "Your blood be on your own heads! I am clear of my responsibility. From now on I will go to the Gentiles."*

4. Self-abuse.

What is it? Most people say that they would never self-abuse. However, most of us do choose to self-abuse. Remember the example, in chapter 24 on "Pain," about the healing process. Refer to the scratched arm and the broken leg on page 123. An example of physical self-abuse is picking at your scratched arm, or pounding your cast on the floor very hard. By doing this, neither wound will heal. Now most people would not even think of doing that, because they want their body to heal. However, it is amazing the number of people who abuse themselves emotionally by making bad choices. It can be as obvious as abusing drugs, purposely hurting your body, or habitually drinking too much alcohol. It also can be as subtle as poor eating habits, not exercising, staying in an emotionally abusive situation, and not finishing the tasks at hand. Self-abuse is detrimental to each person's quality of life. It tears away at their own self-concept, rendering many people dysfunctional.

Some teenagers are enduring incredible tragedy. They need to make sure they are taking care of themselves. Encouraging them to keep up on their studies is a good start. Sometimes they think that this is absurd considering their situation. When Paul was told, *"O.K. your Dad is abusive and is trying to ruin your life. Why should you let his craziness dominate your whole life? What do you have control of? Your grades, right? Then why destroy this part of your life? Study, graduate, and get out of the house. Then you will be able to get on with your life!"* Paul was relieved immediately, because he realized that in spite of it all, he does have some control over his destiny. Paul acknowledged that he has control over choosing friends, eating right, staying sports, and staying away from drugs and alcohol. In the past it never occurred to Paul that he should take care of himself, that he could control part of his life, and most importantly, that he had the *choice* to take that control.

a. The Arrows of Choice

Note the following diagram that depicts the quality of Paul's life. The optimum quality of life is ten points—when everything is going perfect. Note that zero represents the worst quality of life. In this level most everything is going tragically wrong. The big thick arrow shows how Paul's quality of life has been temporarily diminished due to various situations that are out of his control. Currently his quality of life has been lowered to level four.

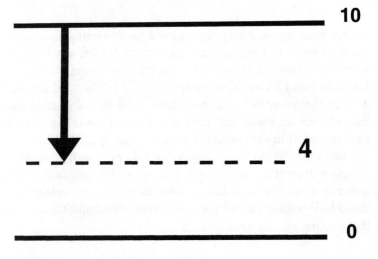

10

4

0

The next graphic shows how Paul can improve his quality of life. The thin lines represent what Paul does have under his control: drugs and alcohol, school grades, nutrition, staying in sports, and choosing friends. Notice, every little bit helps or hurts. Paul's quality of life can be improved to level 8 or ruined to level 0.

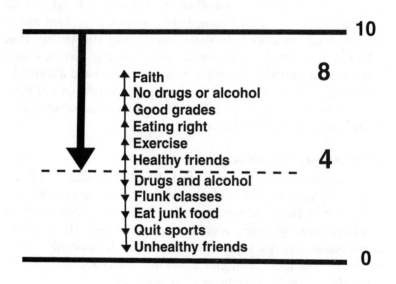

One can see that Paul does have a lot of control over his life. Granted some of his situations have made his life worse, even to level four. However, the control that Paul has is quite substantial. His choice and actions determine whether his quality of life can be as high as eight or as low as zero. This visual aid helps us all realize that various situations can have some control over our lives, but each one of us has some power to change our quality of life.

Remember, pain may happen, but misery is your choice!!

Now draw your own situation. Draw where your quality of life is due to other circumstances. Then draw where your quality of life could be if you start making good choices. Finally, list those choices that you have under your control.

————————————— 10   **What I can control:**
                    1.
                    2.
                    3.
                    4.
                    5.
————————————— 0   **6.**

Verses about self-abuse

Psalm 30:9 *"What gain is there in my destruction, in my going down into the pit? Will the dust praise you? Will it proclaim your faithfulness?"*

Psalm 57:6 *"They spread a net for my feet- I was bowed down in distress. They dug a pit in my path—but they have fallen into it themselves."*

Proverbs 22:3, 24-25 *"A prudent man sees danger and takes refuge, but the simple keep going and suffer for it. Do not make friends with a hot-tempered man, do not associate with one easily angered, or you may learn his ways and get yourself ensnared."*

Proverbs 26:27 *"If a man digs a pit, he will fall into it; if a man rolls a stone, it will roll back on him."*

5. Boundaries

We must learn the importance of boundaries and the need to reinforce them *daily!* People who continually take from you, abuse you, are called "boundary violators." Most of us are giving people, and would never think of using others. Therefore, we have a false sense of security that it won't happen to us. WRONG!!! It happens all the time! Just because we won't use people doesn't mean that other people are as conscientious as we are. BEWARE!!! What can we do when we are in an abusive situation? We need to define, and enforce our boundaries with boldness.

Let's start by taking an honest look into ourselves:

- What are people doing to you?
- Can you say no and draw the line?
- When should you draw the line?
- How do you draw the line?

There are boundary violators that come and go from our lives. We need to rethink, reprogram, and try new ideas to protect ourselves. The following is a worksheet for you. You can answer the questions generally, or you can write in names of violators and answer accordingly. For example, you may be surprised to find out that you don't have any problems with boundary violators at home, but you have friends and team members that constantly use you or vice versa. Check for patterns in this chart.

MY BOUNDARY CHART

	FAMILY	FRIENDS	WORK
My weak points.			
Do I say no?			
How can I be manipulated?			
When to draw the line?			
How to draw the line?			

The book of Esther has a story about Queen Vashti that serves as a great example of enforcing our boundaries with boldness. Esther 1:10-12 *"...when King Xerxes was in high spirits with wine, he commanded the seven eunuchs to bring before him Queen Vashti, wearing her royal crown, in order to display her beauty to the people...Queen Vashti refused to come. Then the King became furious...*" Queen Vashti said no, and put down her boundaries. She said that she would be no part of that, knowing that she would be punished. She ended up losing her title as Queen and could never see the King again. Queen Vashti chose to protect her dignity no matter what. We all need to be strong, determined, and willing to make the correct decisions like Queen Vashti.

Verses on boundaries

Psalm 104:9 "*You set a boundary they cannot cross; never again will they cover the earth.*"

Mark 6:11 "*And if any place will not welcome you or listen to you, shake the dust off your feet when you leave, as a testimony against them.*"

6. Boldness

When we need to be bold and confront people, we must be assertive, not aggressive. Being *aggressive* means that we use inappropriate means to prove our point. On the other hand, being *assertive* means that we use respectful approaches to communicate our frustrations. Assertive people will take a strong stand, but will not be intimidating or disrespectful to the other person.

a. Aggressive actions would be:
- Attacking the person verbally. "*You lazy slob, ungrateful jerk, get out of my way before I do something about it.*"
- Physically harming them.
- Spreading vicious rumors

b. Assertive actions would be:
- Confronting the person truthfully. Using "I" statements instead of "you" statements.
- Having a responsible third party help you. (Make sure they are adults and can make fair judgments)
- Looking for solutions instead of making the problem worse.

Jesus' boldest statement was in resurrection when He defied death and all evil, and became the Savior of the world. See the following verse:

Matthew 28:1-9 *"...Mary Magdalene and the other Mary went to look at the tomb. There was a violent earthquake, for an angel of the Lord came down from heaven and, going to the tomb, rolled back the stone and sat on it...The angel said to the women, 'Do not be afraid, for I know that you are looking for Jesus, who was crucified. He is not here; he has risen, just as he said. Come and see the place where he lay. Then go quickly and tell his disciples: He has risen from the dead and is going ahead of you into Galilee. There you will see him. Now I have told you.' So the women hurried away from the tomb, afraid yet filled with joy, and ran to tell his disciples. Suddenly Jesus met them. 'Greetings,' he said."*

More verses on boldness:

2 Timothy 1:7 *"For God did not give us a spirit of timidity, but a spirit of power, of love and of self-control."* (The word *self-control* means that we need to be assertive, not aggressive. We need to stand up for ourselves but not attack other people.)

Proverbs 26:4 *"Do not answer a fool according to his folly, or you will be like him yourself."*

Always remember we have *no business* doing any form of revenge!

Hebrew 10:30 *"'It is mine to avenge; I will repay,' and again, 'The Lord will judge his people.'"*

> *"First principle: never let one's self be beaten down by persons or by events."*
> Madame Marie Curie, famous scientist

> *"No one can make you feel inferior without your consent."*
> Eleanor Roosevelt

> *"Even if you have been mistreated, you are not to be defeated"*
>
> Gary Hines, Sounds of Blackness

> *"People can only ride our back if we stay bent over. The moment we decide to stand up, they fall off."*
>
> Unknown

> *"Give yourself no unnecessary pain."*
>
> Percy Bysshe Shelley

Personal Notes and Ideas

1. Who is in an abusive situation right now? Are there abusive people in my life?

2. How are these people abusing others?

   <u>Blame</u>   <u>Minimize</u>   <u>Deny</u>

3. Do I know anyone who is self-abusing? Am I self-abusing? (Refer to the arrows of choice.)

4. What have I learned about my boundaries? (Refer to your boundary chart.)

5. What can you learn from Jesus' and Queen Vashti's boldness?

6. My forgiveness strategy is: (see chapter 42 on forgiveness)

7. How can my faith help me if I, or someone else, is in an abusive situation?

8. What would Jesus do?

9. How do the Bible verses in this chapter help me? Are there other verses that can help me an ultimate athlete with respect to abusive situations?

Extra verses

Psalm 62:4
Psalm 109:1-5, 16
Titus 3:10,11
Psalm 55 Talks about abusers—especially people who used to be your friends
1 Thessalonians 1:6

Anger

> *"A fool gives full vent to his anger, but a wise man keeps himself under control."*
>
> Proverbs 29:11

eferring to chapter 1 about "Warm-Up," God made us emotional beings. Therefore we will experience all kinds of emotions while we are on earth. Jesus certainly had to deal with His emotions. He wept when His friend died. He was angry, happy, devastated, and frustrated. He was loved, honored, and betrayed. The following are some verses about Jesus' emotions:

John 11:31-36 (Jesus arrives and Lazurus is dead.) *"When Jesus saw her weeping, and the Jews who had come along with her also weeping, he was deeply moved in spirit and troubled. 'Where have you laid him?' he asked. 'Come and see, Lord,' they replied. **Jesus wept.** Then the Jews said, 'See how he loved him!'"*

Mark 14:32-34 *"They went to a place called Gethsemane, and Jesus said to his disciples, 'Sit here while I pray.' He took Peter, James and John along with him, and he began to be **deeply distressed and troubled.** 'My soul is overwhelmed* *with **sorrow to the point of death**,' he said to them. 'Stay here and keep watch.'"*

Anger can be a useful emotion. It tells us when things are going wrong. To *ignore* the emotion of anger is to set yourself up for many problems. If we inadvertently hit our knee hard against a table, we need to say, "Ouch, that hurt!" If we don't admit our feelings, we are lying and ignoring our emotions. By saying ouch, we have done nothing wrong and have been totally honest with ourselves. It is when people choose to act on their emotion of anger in an abusive way that they have crossed the line.

Revenge is not good, and will not only destroy the other person, but ourselves as well. So, what can we do when someone has done something hurtful to us. Remember the "A" words. Don't be *aggressive*, but be *assertive*! Being aggressive means that one wants to take action to hurt the other person. This action can be physically violent, or verbally hurtful through the use of demoralizing "you" statements. It could also be ignoring the person, which is another form of abandonment. Being assertive is protecting your dignity and using "I" statements. Stand up for yourself in a dignified manner and let the other person know that you don't like what is happening.

What if I am angry because of an unfortunate situation, and it really isn't anyone's fault?

1. First admit that you are angry.
2. Define what specifically has made you mad.
3. Confront your pain and get rid of your anger. Here are some ideas:

- Write a letter of frustration and rip it up.
- Hit tennis balls against a wall.
- Do your flip turns in swim practice with gusto.
- Do some slam dunks in basketball.
- Go to the golf range and send balls flying.
- Put your pillow on your bed and hit it very hard.

Remember, you don't want to do anything that will hurt you or others or damage property.

Read the following verses about Jesus when he was angry:

Mark 3:4-5 *"Then Jesus asked them, 'Which is lawful on the Sabbath: to do good or to do evil, to save life or to kill?' But they remained silent. He looked around at them in anger and, deeply distressed at their stubborn hearts, said to the man, 'Stretch out your hand.' He stretched it out, and his hand was completely restored."*

John 2:13-17 *"When it was almost time for the Jewish Passover, Jesus went up to Jerusalem. In the temple courts he found men selling cattle, sheep and doves, and others sitting at tables exchanging money. So he made a whip out of cords, and drove all from the temple area, both sheep and cattle; he scattered the coins of the money changers and overturned their tables. To those who sold doves he said, 'Get these out of here! How dare you turn my Father's house into a market!' His disciples remembered that it is written: 'Zeal for your house will consume me.'"*

Next you will find God's wisdom about anger:

Ephesians 4:26 *"'In your anger do not sin': Do not let the sun go down while you are still angry."*

Proverbs 15:1 *"A gentle answer turns away wrath, but a harsh word stirs up anger."*

Proverbs 30:33 *"...so stirring up anger produces strife."*

James 1:19-21 *" My dear brothers, take note of this: Everyone should be quick to listen, slow to speak and slow to become angry, for man's anger does not bring about the righteous life that God desires. Therefore, get rid of all moral filth and the evil that is so prevalent and humbly accept the word planted in you, which can save you."*

2 Timothy 4:5 *"But you, keep your head in all situations, endure hardship, do the work of an evangelist, discharge all the duties of your ministry."*

> *"When angry, count to ten; if very angry count to 100."*
>
> Thomas Jefferson

> *"He who angers you conquers you."*
>
> Elizabeth Kenny

> *"If you are patient in one moment of anger, you will escape a hundred days of sorrow."*
>
> Unknown

Personal Notes and Ideas

1. What things make me angry during my workouts and competitions?

2. Write down five situations that would make me angry. Then write down solutions to help me *not* burst into anger.

3. What things make me angry in life?

4. How can I be *assertive* rather than *aggressive*?

5. How can I get rid of my anger in a good way?

6. How can my faith help me when I am angry?

7. How can I encourage my teammates to deal with the anger correctly?

8. What would Jesus do?

9. How do the Bible verses in this chapter help me? Are there other verses that can help me to be an ultimate athlete with respect to my anger?

Bad Calls and
Bad Referees

*"But how is it to your credit if you receive a
beating for doing wrong and endure it? But if
you suffer for doing good and you endure it,
this is commendable before God. To this you
were called, because Christ suffered for you,
leaving you an example, that you should
follow in his steps. 'He committed no sin, and
no deceit was found in his mouth.'"*

1 Peter 2:20-23

Yes, we are all human beings and we make mistakes. Unfortunately some of our decisions and mistakes *do* affect other people. That is definitely the case with most sports. Referees, umpires, and judges determine the placing and results. It is very tough when an athlete has worked so hard and then becomes a victim of a bad call, political judging, or inaccurate timing devices. It just isn't fair! This particular problem has been a source of major frustration for many coaches and athletes over the years.

What can you do about it?

1. First and foremost, each athlete needs to be aware that when joining a team they will have to deal with this some day. It just goes with the territory.

2. No matter what happens during the competition, we need to keep our cool.

2 Timothy 4:5 *"But keep your head in all situations, endure hardship do the work of an evangelist..."*

Psalm 4:4 *"In your anger do not sin..."*

Proverbs 20:22 *"Do not say, 'I'll pay you back for this wrong!' Wait for the LORD and he will deliver you."*

3. Be able to forgive the person, no matter how bad the error was.

Proverbs 19:11 *"A man's wisdom gives him patience; it is his glory to overlook an offense."*

Ephesians 4:31-32 *"Get rid of all bitterness, rage, anger, brawling and slander, along with every form of malice. Be kind and compassionate to one another, forgiving each other, just as Christ God forgave you."*

Philippians 3:13 *"Brothers, I do not consider myself yet to have taken hold of it. But one thing I do: Forgetting what is behind and straining toward what is ahead..."*

One of the biggest judging errors in the history of ice skating took place during the 2002 Olympics ice skating pairs competition. Apparently a French judge had been bribed to place the Russian pair higher than the Canadians, allowing the Russian pair to win the gold medal. The audience, the commentators, and athletes were in shock that night. In the following days this was the topic of conversation for everyone, including all the former competitive skaters. A week later, the Olympic committee decided to give gold medals to both teams and staged another awards ceremony.

Both teams were very gracious the night of the unfortunate outcome. The Canadians, Jamie Sale and David Peltier, were doing everything they could to refrain from crying, or blaming others, as they accepted the results. It was amazing. That night David Peltier was quoted as saying, "What we can control, we did—our performance.

And no one can take that away from us. What we can't control is the judging—we can't control it. But we can walk away and move on with life." He also was honest and admitted that he wasn't happy with the situation. "I am angry. It is the toughest day of my life. I don't want to rain on anybody else's parade. We are just proud of what we did."

This is a perfect example of how an ultimate athlete would react to a situation of unfairness.

It doesn't matter if you are in a team or individual sport, because bad decisions are made by the judges, referees, and umpires. There is also politics in all level of sports, from Little League to the Olympic level. So be prepared! Don't concentrate on the score, the bad call, or the frustration—concentrate on doing your best and listen to what your coach says. Your job is to stay focused and go for a great performance.

> *"Living well is the best revenge."*
> George Herbert

Personal Notes and Ideas

1. What was the worst situation I have experienced in sports?

2. How can I stay focused on my performance, no matter what happens?

3. How can I encourage my teammates to stay focused on their performance, no matter what happens?

4. Who can help me deal with the unfairness of sports?

5. How can the power of prayer help me to persevere?

6. How can my faith help me in my situation?

7. What would Jesus do?

8. How do the Bible verses in this chapter help me? Are there other verses that can help me be an ultimate athlete with respect to bad calls?

Forgiving

"If anyone has caused grief, he has not so much grieved me as he has grieved all of you... The punishment inflicted on him by the majority is sufficient for him. Now instead, you ought to forgive and comfort him, so that he will not be overwhelmed by excessive sorrow."
2 Corinthians 2:5-7

Someone has just fouled you or played a dirty trick, your teammate made a dumb mistake, a referee made a horrible call, you just messed up... The most important thing to do is to *categorize it*. Was it a malicious, revengeful action, or was it a silly error? Now that you understand the situation, you should process it appropriately.

1. Forgiveness can begin only when we have complete awareness of the situation. We need to know what we are angry about, who made us angry, and how it affects us. If we try to forgive before we have this understanding, the forgiving will be artificial.
2. Forgiveness is a process, too. So, if you aren't ready right now to forgive, that is OK. However, strive for understanding and forgiveness. If you want to fully heal, you need to fully and sincerely forgive.

3. Learn to forgive out of *compassion* for yourself! Forgiveness allows you to change your anger from the *person* to their *action*. It is about helping yourself to let go of your anger and heal.
4. We all need forgiveness, because we all make mistakes at some time or other.
5. Forgiveness needs to be unconditional. We need to abandon our expectations that the other person will come around to our way of feeling and understanding. The fact is that person may never repent. However, do you want to spend the rest of life waiting for them to see the light? Believe it or not, humans have been given the capacity to forgive, no matter how horrendous the act is. It is a choice! It is not easy to forgive, because people generally are never ready to forgive. Do you want to take the chance of becoming bitter while you wait or would you rather get on with life?
6. We also need to learn how to forgive ourselves. That can be the most difficult thing to do, because we tend to be very hard on ourselves.

Rev. Albert Haase, a Franciscan priest based in Taiwan, wrote, "It takes a lot of emotional and psychological energy to keep a wound open, to keep a grudge alive…The longer I allow a wound to fester, the more bitterness, anger and self-pity poison my blood and eat my heart."

Matthew 6:14-15 *"But if you forgive men when they sin against you, your heavenly Father will also forgive you. But if you do not forgive men their sins, your Father will not forgive your sins."*

Ephesians 4:32 *"…forgiving each other, just as Christ God forgave you."*

Colossians 3:13 *"Bear with each other and forgive whatever grievances you may have against one another. Forgive as the Lord forgave you."*

Luke 23:34 and John 13:15 *"Jesus said, 'Father, forgive them, for they do not know what they are doing…I have set you an example that you should do as I have done for you.'"*

Always remember we have *no business* doing any form of revenge!

Hebrew 10:30 *"'It is mine to avenge; I will repay,' and again, 'The Lord will judge his people.'"*

"If you don't forgive, you become like your captors."
Corrie ten Boom (A Christian woman who helped the Jewish people during the Holocaust. She was sent to a concentration camp.)

"God has a big eraser."
Billy Zeoli

"A man must learn to forgive himself."
Arthur Davison Ficke

Personal Notes and Ideas

1. Have I forgiven anyone in the past? If so, what happened?

2. Is there someone who I still need to forgive?

3. What does this statement mean to me? Learn to forgive out of compassion for yourself.

4. What will I do if the other person refuses to apologize?

5. How can my faith help me when I need to forgive others?

6. How can I encourage my teammates to forgive others?

7. What would Jesus do?

8. How do the Bible verses in this chapter help me? Are there any other verses that can help me to be an ultimate athlete with respect to forgiveness.

Failure

*"I applied my heart to what I observed and
learned a lesson from what I saw."*

Proverbs 24:32

t is safe to say that no one wants to be a failure. This is what
people fear the most. People will do anything in order to succeed, because the thought of failing is unbearable. Some
people will resort to illegal means so that they don't have to experience being a failure. They will lie, cheat, steal, or take harmful
substances just to be a winner. What we all need to know is that
failure is a *part of life* and it is *our choice* as to how we deal with
it. Failure can destroy us, if we allow it to.

Failure can be good, if we allow it to be. We have the opportunity to learn so much about ourselves and life in general. We
can choose to become better people. Obviously failing is no fun
at all, but the future benefits can be great! We need to realize that
we are humans and we are going to make mistakes. It isn't the
mistake that is so terrible, but the failing to learn from it that can
be our demise.

> "Make a mistake once and you are a human being. To choose not to learn from your error and to continue making that mistake, makes you a fool."
>
> The Author

There are many kinds of mistakes: Defining and categorizing your mistake is crucial as to how you should deal with it.

Hurting other people

Psalm 51 is a great example of learning from mistakes. First we need to truly be sorry for what we did—especially if it caused harm to others.

Psalm 51:1-4 *"Have mercy on me O God, according to your unfailing love; according to your great compassion blot out my transgressions. Wash away all my iniquity [sin] and cleanse me from my sin. For I know my transgressions, and my sin is always before me. Against you, you only, have I sinned and done what is evil in your sight."*

Psalm 51:10-12 *"Create in me a pure heart, O God, and renew a steadfast spirit within me."*

Simple mistakes

Such as tripping over a hurdle or missing a flip turn. There is no reason to apologize or feel like a failure. Life happens and sometimes things just don't go our way.

Deliberate mistakes

Choosing to do an inappropriate action during competition or practice in order to prove a point, get revenge, or vent anger. Yes, an apology is a must, and hopefully the athlete will learn from his/her mistake.

Failure has many benefits:

1. Failure can be helpful, because it can help us from becoming conceited.

2 Corinthians 12:7-9 *"To keep me from becoming conceited because of these surpassingly great revelations, there was given me a thorn in my flesh, a messenger from Satan, to torment me. Three times I pleaded with the Lord to take it away form me. But he said to me, 'My grace is sufficient for you, for my power is made perfect in weakness...'"*

2. Failure can help us to move forward with our lives.

2 Corinthians 4:7-9 *"But we have this treasure in jars of clay to show that this all-surpassing power is from God and not from us. We are hard pressed on every side, but not crushed; perplexed, but not in despair; persecuted, but not abandoned; stuck down, but not destroyed."*

3. It can really help us to search for our inner strength and to use it. Your faith in God can be an incredible help in times like these. Remember, God loves you no matter what mistake you have made. However, He does want you to make yourself right with Him, others, and yourself.

"I've never been afraid to fail. That's something you have to deal with in reality. I think I'm strong enough as a person to accept failing. But I can't accept not trying."
NBA superstar Michael Jordan, explaining his reasons for trying out for the White Sox in 1994

"Failure is the opportunity to begin again, more intelligently."
Henry Ford

"You must do the thing you think you cannot do."
Eleanor Roosevelt

Personal Notes and Ideas

1. How do I feel about failure?

2. How could I let failure destroy me?

3. What can I learn from my mistakes?

4. How can failure help me to be a better athlete?

5. How can failure help me to be a better person?

6. Defining each failure will help me to....

7. How can I help my teammates deal with failure?

8. What would Jesus do?

9. How do all the Bible verses in this chapter help me? Are there other verses that can help me be an ultimate athlete with my failures?

Winning
and Losing

"Seek first the kingdom of God an all His righteousness, and all these things will be given to you as well."

Matthew 6:33

Winning

Catriona LeMay Doan knows all too well about winning and losing. Catriona has competed as one of the fastest sprint speed skaters in the world. In the 1984 Olympics Catriona caught an edge and and wiped out in front of millions of people. Her hopes for a medal were gone in an instant. In the 1988 Olympic games she won a gold and a bronze medal for Canada. Everyone was thrilled! *"When I meet people who are very impressed with me and my accomplishments, I just think, It's no big deal, I'm the same person...I look at life as a process, and if I took the gold medal as the top, there'd be nowhere else to go."* About competing she says, *"I've learned to not put so much pressure on myself for a certain result. God has given me a peace about my life...Whatever happens, I come off the ice saying, 'Thank you, God, for the talents and opportunities you've given me.'"*

With respect to being a gracious winner, read how an ultimate athlete would respond after winning.

1. They would be humble, because Jesus Christ was.
- They are realistic. Even though they won one day, it doesn't mean they will win the next time.

Matthew 19:30 *"So the last will be first and the first will be last."*

- They would not brag about their accomplishments. Most everyone gets tired of proud people very fast. Be humble, because gloating is not allowed.

Proverbs 24:17,18 *"Do not gloat when your enemy falls; when he stumbles, do not let your heart rejoice, for the Lord will see and disapprove…"*

An excellent example of humility is Roberto Clemente. See chapter 66 on "Fans." After winning the World Series he chose to celebrate with the fans.

2. They would be friendly and helpful.
- Take time to shake hands with the other team and be encouraging.
- Be willing to help the other athletes if they ask questions or want to talk with them.

Losing
With respect to losing, and keeping things in perspective, one needs to see the big picture. Will it really matter ten years from now that you lost this competition? If it will matter, then you will need to reexamine your priorities and reason for being here on earth. Do you have other interests in your life right now besides sports? If not, you are setting yourself up for disaster. Refer to "Spokes of Life" in chapter 79 about "Balance."

To be a good loser, read about how ultimate athletes would deal with losing.

1. They know that they did the best that they could do at that time.
Maybe it wasn't their best performance, but at that moment they tried their hardest. Therefore, they can hold their head high.

2 Timothy 4:7 *"I have fought the good fight, I have finished the race, I have kept the faith."*

2. They would maintain their emotions and keep everything together, no matter how badly they just lost.

Psalm 15:4 *"...he who keeps his oath, even when it hurts."*

3. They will look towards the future and just be more determined to do better the next time.

Philippians 3:12-14 *"Not that I have already obtained all this, or have already been made perfect, but I press on to take hold of that for which Christ Jesus took hold of me. Brothers, I do not consider myself yet to have taken hold of it. But one thing I do: Forgetting what is behind and straining toward what is ahead, I press on toward the goal to win the prize for which God has called me heavenward in Christ Jesus."*

4. They would realize that the final results don't necessarily describe the battle.

There are many times when the better team has lost due to various reasons.

Ecclesiastes 9:11 (Living Bible) *"...the swiftest does not always win the race, nor the strongest man the battle, and the wise men are often poor, and skillful men are not necessarily famous; but it is all by chance, by happening to be in the right place at the right time."*

As Christians we should be the same whether we win or lose. The outcome of the competitions shouldn't change our testimony or our outlook on life. Ecclesiastes chapter 3 says, *"There is a time for everything, and a season for every activity under heaven: a time to be born and a time to die...a time to weep, and a time to laugh."* The verse for sports would be: "There is a time to win and a time to lose."

A few years ago, at the Seattle Special Olympics, nine runners who were physically or mentally disabled gathered at the starting line for the hundred-yard dash. The race started, and they all began to run. During the race one little boy fell down, tumbled a couple of times, and began to cry. The other eight heard the boy crying and chose to slow down and look back. Then they all turned around and went back…every one of them! One girl bent down and kissed him and said, "This will make it better." Then all nine walked together arm-in-arm to the finish line. Everyone in the stadium stood, and the cheering went on for several minutes. *Helping others* is more important than *winning*.

> *"Success come in **cans**, failure comes in **can'ts**."*
> Unknown

> *"You can get yourself buying into what I call the 'athletic culture,' where winning keeps rearing its ugly head. It all starts centering around that. The winning becomes first. I think it is something you have to fight against."*
> Mike Denny, University of Nebraska wrestling coach

> *"If you approach **winning** in the wrong way, it could lead to **sinning**."*
> The Author

> *"It's not whether you get **knocked down**. It's whether you **get up again**."*
> Vince Lombardi, legendary NFL football coach

> *"No matter what, win like a champion and lose like a giant."*
> Berry Gordy, Motown's creator

> *"Winning was great. And when you lose, you tell yourself there's one more shot, one more tournament."*
>
> Zina Garrison, pro tennis player

Personal Notes and Ideas

1. How do I act as a winner?

2. How do I act as a loser?

3. What can I do to be a gracious winner?

4. What can I do to be a good loser?

5. How can I encourage my teammates to be gracious winners and good losers?

6. How can my faith help me when I win and when I lose?

7. What would Jesus do?

8. How do the Bible verses in this chapter help me? Are there other verses that can help me be an ultimate athlete with respect to winning and losing?

Missing Out

> *"Be joyful in hope, patient in affliction, faithful in prayer."*
>
> Romans12:12

It is so tough when you have worked so hard, sacrificed so much, and come so far…to just miss out by so little. It could have been half an inch, one-hundredth of a second, one free throw, one stroke…but it happened! This was your last competition, and your season is over. It might have been the state championships, national competition, Olympic trials…and you are done. There is such a sense of emptiness, frustration, sadness, disbelief, and many other emotions. How do you get over something like this?

In all kinds of challenging times, it is always good to do the following things:

Acknowledge the pain.
Admit that you hurt. Say *ouch*!

Focus on your healing.
Look for ways to process your pain and move on in life.

Trust in God.
He is always there for you. Let's look at what trust means.

Totally
Relying
Upon
Scriptural
Truth

Count your blessings!

Write down all the good things that you have in your life. Chances are the majority of athletes will have written: a house, food to eat, clothes, rides to practice, right to an education, friends and family that support me, freedom to vote, an opportunity to be in sports…If you can say most of those, then you have more than about 70 percent of the people in this world.

Turn your situation around.

Let's look at a story about Roger. He was one of the top athletes in the United States and he was at the Olympic trials. Unfortunately he injured his heel during the very last moments of his competition. Obviously he couldn't perform that well, and he just missed out on going to the Olympics. After a lot of soul searching, he knew that he couldn't train for another Olympics. So he decided to become a coach. His passion for his sport and competition helped him to become a great coach for many years.

Jesus is the Lord of compassion. He lived here on earth. He knows exactly what it is like when things don't go the way you want them to. Therefore He has an incredible amount of compassion for all of us here on earth. He is with you all the time. Allow Him to enter your life and be a part of your pain and your healing process. He cares so much for you.

Ouch verses

Psalm 62:8 *"Trust in him at all times, O people; pour out your hearts to him, for God is our refuge."*

Psalm 109:22 *"For I am poor and needy, and my heart is wounded within me."*

Psalm 55:16, 17, 22 *"But I call to God, and the Lord saves me. Evening, morning and noon I cry out in distress, and he hears my voice. Cast your cares on the Lord and he will sustain you; he will never let the righteous fall."*

Hope verses

Proverbs 24:14 *"Know also that wisdom is sweet to your soul; if you find it, there is a future hope for you, and your hope will not be cut off."*

Psalm 130:5 *"I wait for the LORD, my soul waits, and in his word I put my hope."*

Psalm 119:49-50, 76, 116 *"Remember your word to your servant, for you have given me hope. My comfort in my suffering is this: Your promise preserves my life. May your unfailing love be my comfort, according to your promise to your servant. Sustain me according to your promise, and I will live; do not let my hopes be dashed."*

Psalm 56:8 *"You have seen me tossing and turning through the night. You have collected all my tears and preserved them in your bottle! You have recorded every one in the book."* (Living Bible) (Isn't it comforting to know that God always hear us cry, and stores away our tears?)

Psalm 147:3 *"He heals the brokenhearted and binds up their wounds."*

Jesus' encouraging words

Luke 6:20-21 *"Blessed are you who are poor, for yours is the kingdom of God. Blessed are you who hunger now, for you will be satisfied. Blessed are you who weep now, for you will laugh."*

"That which hurts, also instructs."
Benjamin Franklin

"First principle: Never let one's self be beaten down by persons or by events."
Madame Marie Curie, famous scientist

One of the greatest lessons I learned as an athlete was that sometimes I will not achieve my desires. It has been important to me to have lived through unmet expectations in athletics, learned from them, and chosen to get back in the game, for life hands you the same choices."

Joel Ward, decathlete and high school coach

Personal Notes and Ideas

1. Did I miss out on some athletic competition in the past? How did I feel?

2. What did I learn from the situation?

3. How can I prepare myself for future situations?

4. What can I do to make sure that I get *better* and not *bitter*?

5. What does this statement mean to me? I have more blessings than 70 percent of the people in the world.

6. How can I take the situation and turn it around? Take a lemon and make lemonade.

7. What would Jesus do?

8. How do the Bible verses in this chapter help me? Are there other verses that can help me to be an ultimate athlete with respect to missing out?

Extra verses

Psalm 57:1
Psalm 33:20
Psalm 71:14
Psalm 34:18
Psalm 9:9-12
Proverbs 24:14

Tragedy

"Though you have made me see troubles, many and bitter, you will restore my life again."

Psalm 71:20

"And the God of all grace, who called you to his eternal glory in Christ, after you have suffered a little while, will himself restore you and make you strong, firm and steadfast."

1 Peter 5:10

Why? That is the most common question/reaction after a tragedy. *Why me? Why now? Why did it happen to her? Why?* Life is tough, and many times there are no answers to most of those questions. The one thing for certain is that tragedy is real, it exists, it is a part of life, and it affects everyone during their lifetime. As athletes we can have tragedies both on and off the athletic field. It doesn't matter how they come, or where they come from, but it does matter *how we handle ourselves* in the midst of the tragedy.

One of the most important things we can do at the onset of a tragic situation is to label it. Is it a *tragedy* or an *inconvenience*? After coming to the decision, we must confront our situation in the best way possible. Many people get confused during tough times and don't deal with the issues correctly. They label a tragedy as an inconvenience. The next thing you know is that their denial is helping them to run from reality and not process their pain. Or they label an inconvenience as a tragedy and will wallow in their pity, not moving on with their life.

All kinds of tragedy are tough, but criminal situations can be the most difficult. "Why did God allow this? Mary was such a good person..." It is hard to fathom that someone would want to kill, let alone hurt, another human being. Many people will say, "Where was God when this happened, and why didn't He stop it?" God in His omnipotent presence was there; however, He has vowed to give us all *free choice*. When we live in a world where choice is available to all, we have to live with the consequences of other people's bad choices. Of course it is not fair, but that is the way it is.

Hebrews 10:32-36 "*Remember those earlier days after you had received the light, when you **stood your ground** in a great contest in the face of suffering. Sometimes you were publicly exposed to insult and persecution; at other times you stood **side by side** with those who were so treated... So **do not throw away your confidence**; it will be richly rewarded. You need to persevere so that when you have done the will of God, you will receive what he has promised.*"

What if the tragedy is closely related to a sport or a team? Athletes have died during workouts and competitions—and off the field. Many times it is too much to bear when athletes resume practice or competitions after a funeral for a teammate. They are expecting their friend to show up at his/her locker, to be at practice, to compete in the competitions... However, their friend doesn't show up anymore. One of the best things a team can do is to dedicate every workout and competition to their friend who has passed away. The power in this is amazing, because teams tend to really unite and form a strong bond when this happens.

Becky died before her senior year in high school. Her teammates decided to dedicate the whole season to Becky. Now these athletes had always been hard workers in the past. However, that year, their commitment, intense focus, and hard work were phenomenal. This gymnastics team in the past would get a total team score of 120 points. The year that they dedicated their season to Becky, they scored 131 points. That particular year the team was weaker than other years, because some of the top gymnasts had graduated. It would have been a miracle if they had scored 120. But due to their love for Becky, they scored 131 points... See chapter 52 on "Cheerleader" and chapter 73 on "Team Spirit" for more about Becky's story.

What does the Bible say about tragedy?

2 Corinthians 1:3-5 *"Praise be to the God and Father of our Lord Jesus Christ, the Father of compassion and the God of all comfort, who comforts us in all our troubles, so that we can comfort those in any trouble with the comfort we ourselves have received from God. For just as the sufferings of Christ flow over into our lives, so also through Christ our comfort overflows."*

Psalm 34:18 *"The Lord is close to the brokenhearted and saves those who are crushed in spirit."*

2 Corinthians 4:7-11 *"But we have this treasure in jars of clay to show that this all-surpassing power is from God and not from us. We are hard pressed on every side, but not crushed; perplexed, but not in despair; persecuted, but not abandoned; struck down, but not destroyed. We always carry around in our body the death of Jesus, so that the life of Jesus may also be revealed in our body. For we who are alive are always being given over to death for Jesus' sake, so that his life may be revealed in our mortal body."*

Bible verses about hope

Hebrews 6:19 *"We have this hope as an anchor for the soul, firm and secure."*

Hebrews 10:23 *"Let us hold unswervingly to the hope we profess, for he who promised is faithful."*

Psalm 62:5 *"Find rest, O my soul, in God alone; my hope comes from him."*

Bible verses about healing

Isaiah 57:18-19 *"I have seen his ways, but I will heal him; I will guide him and restore comfort to him, creating praise on the lips of the mourners in Israel."*

Malachi 4:2 *"But for you who revere my name, the sun of righteousness will rise with healing in its wings. And you will go out and leap like calves released from the stall."*

> *"Joy is not in the absence of suffering, but the presence of God."*
>
> Unknown

> *"Don't ask God to have your problems eliminated, ask for the strength to confront them."*
>
> Majorie Espinosa, thirteen-year-old Chilean

Personal Notes and Ideas

1. What tragedies have I experienced?

2. How did I react to them?

3. What have I learned that will help me with other tragedies?

4. What tragedy am I currently experiencing? What is the problem?

5. What can I do to make the situation better? (What are some solutions? Exhaust all possibilities and create alternatives. See chapter 47 on "Prevailing.")

6. Who can help me with my tragedies?

7. How can the power of prayer help me through this tragedy?

8. How can my faith help me in my situation?

9. How can I help my teammates if they are going through a tragedy?

10. What would Jesus do?

11. How do the Bible verses in this chapter help me? Are there other verses that can help me be an ultimate athlete with respect to tragedies?

Extra verses
Romans 8:18
Hebrews 5:7-9

Perseverance

"Therefore, since we are surrounded by such a great cloud of witnesses, let us throw off everything that hinders and the sin that so easily entangles, and let us run with perseverance the race marked out for us. Let us fix our eyes on Jesus, the author and perfecter of our faith, who for the joy set before him endured the cross, scorning its shame, and sat down at the right hand of the throne of God. Consider him who endured such opposition from sinful men, so that you will not grow weary and lose heart."

Hebrews 12:1-3

There have been countless stories in the Olympics about how people have persevered under tough circumstances. For instance, in track and field, there have been many injured athletes who limped across the finish line. Many times the other competitors had finished a long time ago. Obviously these injured athletes were not trying to get a medal. They were doing what they came to do... to finish their race. It didn't matter to them that they were five minutes slower than other competitors in the sprints, or that they finished hours after all the marathon runners were done. How do most of these athletes do it? They focus their energy, emotions, and prayers on the finish line. They visualize themselves crossing that line. Therefore they can't *focus* on their pain or hardship, because they won't make it. Obviously they *acknowledge* their situation and their pain, but they *choose to focus* on their goal.

In all kinds of life's situations, we need to acknowledge what is happening to us—be honest with our problems and how they affect us. In order to persevere, we need to focus on the *solutions* that will fix our *problems*. Constantly thinking about the problem will result in a depressed person who has very little hope. Many times our problems don't vanish right away, but stay with us for a long time. So this is when perseverance comes into play. We need to keep concentrating on the solutions and our goals over—and over, and over again. We need to keep our focus positive, especially when we hurt the most.

Warning—sometimes an athlete will need to stop competing, especially if the injury is very serious. Remember to listen to your body. If it says stop, then do so, in order that you don't permanently injure yourself.

How did Jesus persevere on the cross for so long and in such pain? He kept focusing on God's promises, the solutions, and His goals. With respect to God's promises, He knew that His Father was and is the Almighty. He knew that His sacrifice would be the solution for our eternal life. He also knew His goal was to become completely obedient to God whether He liked it or not.

James 1:3-4 "*...because you know that the testing of your faith develops perseverance. Perseverance must finish its work so that you may be mature and complete, not lacking anything.*"

James 1:12 "*Blessed is the man who perseveres under trial, because when he has stood the test, he will receive the crown of life that God has promised to those who love him.*"

James 5:11 "*As you know, we consider blessed those who have persevered. You have heard of Job's perseverance and have seen what the Lord finally brought about. The Lord is full of compassion and mercy."*

1 Corinthians 13:7 "*…always trusts, always hopes, and always perseveres.*"

Special verses for hope

Romans 5:3-5 "*Not only so, but we also rejoice in our sufferings, because we know that suffering produces perseverance; perseverance, character; and character, hope. And hope does not disappoint us, because God has poured out his love into our hearts by the Holy Spirit, whom he has given us.*"

Proverbs 23:18 "*There is surely a future hope for you, and your hope will not be cut off.*"

Psalm 71:14 "*But as for me, I will always have hope; I will praise you more and more.*"

"*Tough times don't last, tough people do.*"
Unknown

"*You can keep going long after you think you can't.*"
Unknown

"*Although the world is full of suffering, it is also full of the overcoming of it.*"
Helen Keller

Personal Notes and Ideas

1. In what situations have I already persevered?

2. In what situations am I currently persevering? What is the problem?

3. What can I do to make the situation better? (Write down ideas and solutions. Exhaust all possibilities and create alternatives. See chapter 48 on "Prevailing.")

4. Who can help me persevere?

5. How can the power of prayer help me to persevere?

6. How can my faith help me in my situation?

7. How can I encourage my teammates to persevere?

8. What would Jesus do?

9. How do the Bible verses in this chapter help me? Are there other verses that can help me be an ultimate athlete with respect to perseverance?

Extra verses

Philippians 3:13-14
1 Corinthians 16:13
Galatians 6:9
Luke 13:31-33

Prevailing

"You intended to harm me, but God intended it for good to accomplish what is now being done, the saving of many lives."

Genesis 50:20

urn your situation around! Go from the defense to the offense! When people are in the midst of a problem or crisis, the majority only think about how they can survive? How can they get out? Now that is a great first step, but it isn't the end of our healing journey. We need to move forward and turn our situations around for good. Look at the lives of Martin Luther King, Jr., Gandhi, Susan B. Anthony, Harriet Tubman...They all took oppressive situations and turned them around to make society better. They not only survived their situations, but they prevailed! Therefore we can call them "prevailers." Most people were just ordinary people before they came prevailers. (By the way, Jesus Christ is the #1 prevailer of all times. This is true because He is the only person to whom all the calendars refer back to His date of birth.) What do prevailers have in common? They have the utmost desire to *exhaust all possibilities and create alternatives.* Prevailers don't take no for an answer. They keep brainstorming and trying new things until something works. The following verse serves as an example of exhausting all possibilities and creating alternatives:

Luke 13:6-8 *"A man had a fig tree, planted in his vineyard, and he went to look for fruit on it, but did not find any. So he said to the man who took care of the vineyard, 'For three years now I've been coming to look for fruit on this fig tree and haven't found any. Cut it down! Why should it use up the soil?' 'Sir,' the man replied, 'leave it alone for one more year, and I'll dig around it and fertilize it.'"*

Most people think you need to be a famous person to make a difference in this world. Contrary to popular thought, you don't have to be a V.I.P. to become a prevailer. You just need faith, and to trust in God no matter what happens. Philippians 1:12-14 *"Now I want you to know, brothers, that what has happened to me has really served to advance the gospel. As a result, it has become clear throughout the whole palace guard and to everyone else that I am in chains for Christ. Because of my chains, most of the brothers in the Lord have been encouraged to speak the word of God more courageously and fearlessly."*

The following are more prevailers in the athletic world:

John Register was a top hurdler for the United States. John felt it necessary to serve his country in war. He came back just fine and began hurdling again. One day when he was hurdling, he dislocated his knee, causing a main artery to be severed. His leg had to be amputated. "God has definitely used the loss of my limb. A lot of people thought that was going to be the end of my life, end of my career. That never really entered my mind, because I knew Christ before I had the injury. I knew that He was already preparing me for something, I was able to get through that a lot easier." Register went on with his life and became an athlete who competed in the Paralympics in swimming, and track and field.

Chicago Bears football star, Jim Branden, was injured in combat during the Vietnam war. He returned in a wheelchair because he was paralyzed. Jim hoped to get a coaching job with the Bears, but wasn't hired due to his disability. Jim was very angry and withdrew from most everyone. Due to circumstances with his nephew, Jim ended up helping out at his nephew's juvenile reformatory. He started a football team and took the toughest of tough teens and molded them in a caring, hard-working, winning team.

Roberto Clemente and Jackie Robinson were two brave baseball players that challenged racism in sports. Jackie Robinson was the first athlete of color to play professional baseball. Roberto Clemente also chose to put together some relief aid to Nicaragua after a terrible earthquake. Roberto not only changed the world of sports, but he also helped the poor.

Babe Didrickson was one of the first great female athletes that paved the way for women to compete in sports. The Associated Press voted her the "Greatest Female Athlete" for the first half of the twentieth century. In addition, the wire service gave Babe the "Female Athlete of the Year" award six times because of her track and golf accomplishments. She was the first woman to win medals in three Olympic events—two gold and one silver. She was harassed by many, but she didn't care. Some writers condemned her for not being feminine. "It would be much better if she stayed at home, got herself prettied up and waited for the phone to ring," Joe Williams wrote in the New York World-Telegram. "Babe performed at a time when female athletes were considered freakish at best, downright unacceptable at worst."

Billy Jean King, a superb tennis player, worked very hard for equal rights for women in sports. She helped to pass Title IX of the Educational Amendments Act of 1972. This law states that schools and colleges that accept federal funds need to provide athletic opportunities for women. Billie Jean was the first female athlete to win over $100,000 prize money in a single season. She spoke out for women and their right to earn the same amount as male athletes do in tennis and other sports. Billie Jean has broken many barriers by her constant lobbying and commitments to fairness. Says Olympian Willye White, "Today's young women athletes don't have a clue they're where they are because of the courage of Billie Jean King." She overcame 20/400 vision, breathing problems, and numerous knee operations. She won all of tennis's top prizes, including twenty Wimbledon titles.

Wilma Rudolph overcame childhood polio to capture three Olympic gold medals at the Rome Olympic Games and the title of fastest woman in the world. She inspired generations of girls and women to participate in track and field.

The following are verses to inspire you as you choose to make the world a better place:

Isaiah 40:31 *"...but those who hope in the Lord will renew their strength. They will soar on wings like eagles; they will run and not grow weary, they will walk and not be faint."*

Psalm 118:17 *"I will not die but live, and will proclaim what the Lord has done."*

Psalm 31:24 *"Be strong and take heart, all you who hope in the Lord."*

When you are in a tough situation, and are choosing to prevail, continue to use the *power of prayer*. Praying, praising God, and asking for the blood of Jesus for our protection will help us to prevail. (See chapter 49 on "Spiritual Warfare.")

> *"We can choose to **throw** stones, to **stumble** on them, to **climb over** them, or to **build** with them."*
>
> Unknown

> *"If the world is cold, make it your business to build fires."*
>
> Horace Tranbel

> *"Remember you can't start over in life's marathon. You often can't choose your circumstance or your situation, but you do have the privilege of choosing your attitude."*
>
> Bob Bardwell, wheelchair marathoner

Personal Notes and Ideas

1. What situations in my life need to be turned around? What is the problem?

2. What can I do to make the situation better? Write down ideas and solutions. Exhaust all possibilities and create alternatives.

3. Who can help me to be a prevailer?

4. Who is a great role model for me with respect to being a prevailer? Name at least one famous person and at least two ordinary citizens that you know personally?

5. How can the power of prayer help me turn the situation around?

6. How can my faith help me to be a prevailer?

7. How can I encourage my teammates to become prevailers?

8. What would Jesus do?

9. How do the Bible verses in this chapter help me? Are there other verses that can help me be an ultimate athlete with respect to prevailing?

Spiritual Warfare

"Be self-controlled and alert. Your enemy the devil prowls around like a roaring lion looking for someone to devour. Resist him, standing firm in the faith, because you know that your brothers throughout the world are undergoing the same kind of sufferings."

1 Peter 5:8-9

"In your anger do not sin: Do not let the sun go down while you are still angry, and do not give the devil a foothold."

Ephesians 4:26-28

Yes, unfortunately there is an evil force in this world. It would be so nice if we didn't have to deal with it and could live happily ever after here on earth. However that is not reality. We need to be prepared for everything that may come our way. No matter what others may do to us, we need to remember that our fight is not just with people here on earth. Ephesians 6:12 *"For our struggle is not against flesh and blood, but against the rulers, against the authorities, against the powers of this dark world and against the spiritual forces of evil in the heavenly realms."* The devil's nickname is the "destroyer." He will do everything in his power to try and destroy anything that is good on this earth. He goes after relationships families, friends, spouses, teammates, and your relationship with God. He doesn't stop. He is stubborn and will keep going and going. He is sneaky—posing as an angel of light. Many times he doesn't do the obvious but is very subtle. So we need to be on the lookout. We need to be ready for all of this.

> Jeremiah 6:26 *"O my people, put on sackcloth and roll in ashes; mourn with bitter wailing as for an only son, for suddenly the destroyer will come upon us."*

> Revelation 9:11 *"They had as king over them the angel of the Abyss, whose name in Hebrew is Abaddon, and in Greek, Apollyon."* (*Abaddon* and *Apollyon* mean "Destroyer.")

> Psalm 37:32 "The wicked lie in wait for the righteous, seeking their very lives."

Yes, on earth it will be a fight and a source of frustration. But remember we can be on the offense and not just the defense if we train ourselves in the way of God. Luke 21:14-15 *"But make up your mind to not worry beforehand how you will defend yourselves. For I will give you words and wisdom that none of your adversaries will be able to resist or contradict."* Think of this spiritual training exactly like your athletic endeavors. There needs to be commitment, determination, obedience, and trust in our coach, God. Therefore it is crucial that we do the following steps daily:

Step 1

Find time with God in both prayer and in reading the Bible. With respect to finding time with God, read chapter 18 on "Time-Out" and chapter 80 on "Time-Off."

Step 2

Specifically ask for protection against the evil one.

A. Ask to be covered by the blood of Jesus Christ. (See explanation below.)

B. Clothe yourself with the spiritual armor (Ephesians 6:10-18).

C. Praise God by word or by song.

Step 3

Do not fear the evil one, because God is in total control. (See explanation below.)

Explanation of Step 2

Step 2A

Unfortunately, the first sin was committed in the Garden of Eden. Eve chose to take and eat from the forbidden fruit. Therefore all of us were born into sin. Genesis 3:17 *"Cursed is the ground because of you; through painful toil you will eat of it all the days of your life."*

Back in the Old Testament, the people needed to sacrifice the blood of a lamb for protection, because the savior had not yet come. They painted the blood about their door so that God would protect them. Exodus 12:23 *"When the Lord goes through the land to strike down the Egyptians, he will see the blood on the top and sides of the doorframe and will pass over that doorway, and he will not permit the destroyer to enter your houses and strike you down."*

1 Peter 1:19 *"…but with the precious blood of Christ, a lamb without blemish or defect. "* The beauty of Christ dying for us is that we don't need to do the same thing that they did in the Old Testament. Jesus, who is called the "Lamb of God," is our final and ultimate sacrifice. Jesus suffered on the cross, and He bled and died so that we could finally be right with God. Hebrews 9:14 *"How much more, then, will the blood of Christ, who through the eternal Spirit offered himself unblemished to God, cleanse our consciences from acts that lead to death, so that we may serve the living God."* By His blood, we are saved and protected. Colossians 1:17 *"He is before all things, and in him all things hold together. And he is the head of the body, the church; he is the beginning and the firstborn from among the dead, so that in everything he might have the supremacy. For God was pleased to have all his fullness dwell in him, and through him to reconcile to himself all things, whether things on earth or things in heaven, by making peace through his blood, shed on the cross. Once you were alienated from God and were enemies in your minds because of your evil behavior. But now*

he has reconciled you by Christ's physical body through death to present you holy in his sight, without blemish and free from accusation..."

Step 2B

Ephesians 6:10-18 The armor of God *"Finally, be strong in the Lord and in his mighty power. Put on the full armor of God so that you can take your stand against the devil's schemes. For our struggle is not against flesh and blood, but against the rulers, against the authorities, against the power of this dark world and against the heavenly realms. Therefore put on the full armor of God, so that when the day of evil comes, you may be able to stand against your ground, and after you have done everything, to* **stand.** **Stand firm** *then, with the belt of truth buckled around your waist, with the breastplate of righteousness in place, and with your feet fitted with readiness that comes from the gospel of peace. In the addition to all this, take up the shield of faith, with which you can extinguish all the flaming arrows of the evil one. Take the helmet of salvation and the sword of the Spirit, which is the word of God. And pray in the Spirit on all occasions with all kinds of prayers and requests. With this in mind,* **be alert and always keep on praying** *for all the saints."*

Explanation of Step 3

Unfortunately the evil is alive and well. It is apparent when we see the condition of the world right now. However God is in *complete* control! First of all, notice that He *gave* Satan permission to do his thing here on earth. Revelation 6:4 *"Then another horse came out, a fiery red one. Its rider was* **given power** *to take peace from the earth and to make men slay each other. To him was given a large sword."* Satan didn't just go out and do it on his own strength. Second, if you read in the book of Revelation, God is all-powerful. Chapters 19 and 20 show how quickly and easily God conquers the devil and all his companions. There is no fight that goes on and on for chapters! It is over in one verse! When God decides that they need to be put away, He just does it. Therefore as powerful as Satan is, by *faith* we need to believe that God is and will be more powerful than the evil one. By faith we can choose to have no fear of the evil one.

Be on the watch…Satan will come into your life if you give him the opportunity. By choosing to sin, you are opening the door of your life to him. Be careful! Ephesians 4:26-27 *"In your anger, do not sin: Do not let the sun go down while you are still angry, And do not give the devil a foothold."*

> "Don't give satan an inch, because he will take a mile."
>
> Unknown

> "Courage is not the absence of fear. It is the presence of fear and the will to go on."
>
> Unknown

Personal Notes and Ideas

1. What have I learned about spiritual warfare with respect to:
   a. sin and the first sin?

   b. why we are not right with God?

   c. sacrificing of the lambs in the Old Testament?

   d. Why Jesus is called the "Lamb of God"?

   e. How His death, blood, and resurrection conquer sin?

2. How can I use the techniques of my athletic training to help me be ready for spiritual warfare?

3. What works the best for me so that I don't fear the evil one?

4. What does it mean to me that God is all-powerful with respect to:
   Satan being given permission?

   There being no long fight in Revelation?

5. I don't want to open the door of my life to Satan. What are my weaknesses that could be possible doors?

6. How can I effectively share this information about spiritual warfare with my teammates?

7. What would Jesus do?

8. How do the Bible verses in this chapter help me? Are there any other verses that can help me to be an ultimate athlete with respect to spiritual warfare?

God is with us, our protector, our restorer, our helper...Do not fear
Isaiah 58:9-12
Isaiah 41:10,13
Isaiah 54:16-17
Isaiah 49:15-16

Part Four
POSITIONS

Introduction to Positions

I n life we all play different roles that contribute to society. The same is true for sports. Many different roles are necessary for all athletic programs. In this chapter, we will refer to these as positions. All of these positions have their own importance and contribution to the athletic world.

1 Corinthians 12:12-26 *"The body is a unit, though it is made up of many parts; and though all its parts are many, they form one body. So it is with Christ. For we were all baptized by one Spirit into one body—whether Jews or Greeks, slave or free—and we were all given the one Spirit to drink. Now the body is not made up of one part but of many. If the foot should say, 'Because I am not a hand, I do not belong to the body,' it would not for that reason cease to be part of the body. And if the ear should say, 'Because I am not an eye, I do not belong to the body,' it would not for that reason cease to be part of the body. If the whole body were an eye, where would the sense of hearing be? If the whole body were an ear, where would the sense of smell be? But in fact God has arranged the parts in the body, every one of them, just as he wanted them to be. If they were all one part, where would the body be? As it is, there are many parts, but one body. The eye cannot say to the hand, 'I don't need you!' And the head cannot say to the feet, 'I don't need you!' On the contrary, those parts of the body that seem to be weaker are indispensable, and the parts that we think are less honorable we treat with special honor. And the parts that are unpresentable are treated with special modesty, while our presentable parts need no special treatment. But God has combined the members of the body and has given greater honor to the parts that lacked it, so that there should be no division in the body, but that its parts*

should have equal concern for each other. If one part suffers, every part suffers with it; if one part is honored, every part rejoices with it."

But in each position that we represent, we have the choice as to how we will play. Remember we may not control the *situation*, but we always have control over our *attitudes* and *actions*. History has proved time and time again that this is true. Look at the lives of people who not only survived, but prevailed and turned their situations around. There are countless examples of people who lived through the Holocaust, Apartheid, slavery, and civil rights. Many people were in the *same situation*, but there was a *variety of reactions*. Some people gave up, while others forged ahead, making the world a better place. So as athletes, no matter the position, we should do whatever we can to make our situations better and not worse.

> *"The winner is always a part of the answer/solution.*
> *The loser is always a part of the problem.*
>
> *The winner always has a program.*
> *The loser always has an excuse.*
>
> *The winner say 'Let me do it for you.'*
> *The loser says 'That's not my job.'*
>
> *The winner sees an answer for every problem.*
> *The loser sees a problem in every answer.*
>
> *Be a winner!"*
>
> Unknown

> *"Don't let what you can't do stop you from doing what you can do."*
>
> David T. Lathrop

WINNERS	LOSERS
Never quit - prevailors	Always give up - quitters
Dwell on rewards, solutions, the future...	Dwell on the problems and the past.
Encourage	Criticize, condemn, and complain.
Exhaust all possibilities and create alternatives.	Stop trying, and give up easily.
Ask **HOW** and **WHAT** statements that talk about the <u>solutions</u>: *"This is **how** I can do it!"* *"This is **what** I can do!"*	Ask **WHY** questions that talk about the <u>problem</u>: *"**Why** is this happening to me?"*
<u>Problem solvers:</u> See how they **<u>can</u>** do it with **<u>ideas</u>**!	<u>Problem creators:</u> See how they **<u>can't</u>** by using **<u>excuses</u>**.

The following chapters will talk about the various positions that belong in sports. Along with the Scripture verse and questions, a person from the Bible will be used as an example of each position.

Rookie

"Teach me to do your will, for you are my God; may your good Spirit lead me on level ground."

Psalm 143:10

Person in the Bible

The disciples gave up everything in their lives to follow Jesus. They had no idea what they were doing, or what their future would be. They knew that everything would be different, but they were willing to learn.

A. The most important attribute for a rookie is to be *willing to learn*. In order to learn, you must have the right mindset. This includes realizing that we don't know it all, we are beginners, and that we do have a lot to learn. The beauty of our situation is that we have many people who can help us. There are coaches, assistant coaches, team captains, and other teammates who can show us the way. The majority of these people will be very helpful, but some of them won't. Even if they don't have desirable personalities, they should be able to help you with the fine-tuning of your sport.

Psalm 86:11 *"Teach me your way, O Lord, and I will walk in your truth; give me a undivided heart, that I may fear your name."*

B. With respect to finding positive role models, you will have to be picky. Not every person on your team will have the same values that you do. Make sure that you're choosing to spend time with teammates who make good decisions. Some of your teammates may be very talented athletes, but their human skills and choices may be more harmful to you than helpful.

1 Corinthians 15:33 *"Do not be misled: 'Bad company corrupts good character.'"*

Ephesians 5:5-7 *"For of this we can be sure: no immoral, impure or greedy person—such a man is an idolater—has any inheritance in the kingdom of Christ and of God. Let no one deceive you with empty words, for because of such things God's wrath comes on those who are disobedient. Therefore do not be partners with them."*

1 Peter 2:1-3 *"Therefore, rid yourselves of all malice and all deceit, hypocrisy, envy, and slander of every kind. Like newborn babies, crave pure spiritual milk, so that by it you may grow up in your salvation, now that you have tasted that the Lord is good."*

Isaiah 52:11 *"Depart, depart, go out from there! Touch no unclean thing! Come out from it and be pure, you who carry the vessels of the Lord. "*

C. Don't choose to be led astray. You will find yourself falling away from what is right and true.

2 Peter 3:17 *"Therefore, dear friends, since you already know this, be on your guard so that you may not be carried away by the error of lawless men and fall from your secure position."*

Galatians 2:13 *"The other Jews joined him in his hypocrisy, so that their hypocrisy even Barnabas was lead astray."*

Galatians 5:7-10 *"You were running a good race. Who cut in on you and kept you from obeying the truth? That kind of persuasion does not come from the one who calls you. 'A little yeast works through the whole batch of dough.' I am confident in the Lord that you will take no other view. The one who is throwing you into confusion will pay the penalty, Whoever he may be."*

D. Finally be patient and confident that you will achieve your goals. Sometimes our progress in sports is hard to measure, but keep working hard each and every day. It may be weeks or months before you achieve your goal; however, it is up to you to keep a positive attitude and follow through with the good actions. The combination of hard work, a positive attitude, and a strong faith helps us to excel in sports and in life.

Philippians 1:6 *"Being confident of this, that he who began a good work in you will carry it on to completion until the day of Christ Jesus."*

"The trees that are slow to grow, bear the best fruit."
Moliere

"What counts is not necessarily the size of the dog in the fight, but the size of the fight in the dog."
President Dwight D. Eisenhower

"No matter what age you are, or what circumstances might be, you are special and still have something unique to offer. Your life, because of who you are, has meaning."
Barbara De Angelis

Personal Notes and Ideas

1. My role as a rookie is very important. What can I do to make the season a success?

2. How can I be a good teammate?

3. What can I do to help the coach?

4. Who can help me with my sport?

5. Who can help me to make good decisions on and off the court?

6. Why is it so important that I don't spend time with bad influences?

7. What can I do for God?

8. What would Jesus do?

9. How do the Bible verses in this chapter help me? Are there other verses that can help me be an ultimate rookie?

More verses

1 Corinthians 5:9-11
Romans 16:17-18
Proverbs 4:23

Benchwarmers

"Now you, brothers, like Isaac, are children of promise."

Galatians 4:28

Person in the Bible

Joseph, husband of Mary, was not the "star" of the birth of Christ. It was definitely Mary and Jesus. However Joseph played a key supportive role in the whole situation. In other words, Mary was in the starting lineup and Joseph wasn't. However, if we take time to look at the obedience and self-lessness that Joseph had, we realize that we can be important contributors even if we aren't first string. The underlined words demonstrate these great qualities of Joseph.

Matthew 1:18-25 *"This is how the birth of Jesus Christ came about: His mother Mary was pledged to be married to Joseph, but before they came together, she was found to be with child through the Holy Spirit. Because Joseph her husband was a* **righteous man and did not want to expose her to public disgrace**, *he had in mind to divorce her quietly. But after he had considered this, an angel of the Lord appeared to him in* *a dream and said, 'Joseph son of David, do not be afraid to take Mary home as your wife, because what is conceived in her is from the Holy Spirit. She will give birth to a son, and you are to give him the name Jesus, because he will save his people from their sins...' When Joseph woke up, **he did what the angel of the Lord had commanded him and took Mary home as his wife.** But he had no union with her until she gave birth to a son. And he gave him the name Jesus."*

Matthew 2:13-14 *"When they had gone, an angel of the Lord appeared to Joseph in a dream. 'Get up,' he said, 'take the child and his mother and escape to Egypt. Stay there until I tell you, for Herod is going to search for the child to kill him.' **So he got up, took the child and his mother during the night and left for Egypt...**"*

Matthew 2:19-21 *"After Herod died, an angel of the Lord appeared in a dream to Joseph in Egypt and said, 'Get up, take the child and his mother and go to the land of Israel, for those who were trying to take the child's life are dead.' **So he got up, took the child and his mother and went to the land of Israel.**"*

Yes, it is not the easiest thing to be a benchwarmer. It is tough when you practice as hard as everyone else, but get less playing time. It doesn't help your self-confidence, and can be very frustrating at times. But don't despair and jump ship. There are many things that you can do to make your situation better. First of all *patience* is a great attribute. There have been many stories of athletes who didn't do well at first. After months and years of hard work, and a positive attitude, they began to excel. Romans 8:25 "But if we hope for what we do not yet have, we wait for it patiently."

Kari began running competitively at age 14. That is considered a late start for any sport. She had a hard time keeping up in practice, and came in last for most of her races. To make matters worse, during her first high school meet, Kari had to compete against the state champion in the mile run. Kari had never competed in that event, but wanted to give it a try. Needless to say she was far behind the state champion, but she finished!

Instead of Kari being depressed and humiliated, she was thrilled that she finished her first mile race. Her second thought was, "I am going to run thirty seconds faster the next time I run!" Kari's focus for future practices and meets was not about her humiliating race, but how she could run faster. Instead of comparing herself to others, Kari chose to compare herself to Kari. Weeks and months went by and her times were getting faster and faster. Believe it or not, three years after her first race against the state champion, Kari beat that state champion. What are the lessons that can be learned here?

1. Acknowledge that we are well made!

Psalm 139:13-14 *"For you created my inmost being; you knit me together in my mother's womb. I praise you because I am fearfully and wonderfully made; your works are wonderful, I know that full well."*

Ephesians 3:17-19 *"So that Christ may dwell in your hearts through faith. And I pray that you, being rooted and established in love, may have power, together with all the saints, to grasp how wide and long and high and deep is the love of Christ, and to know this love that surpasses knowledge—that you may be filled to the measure of all the fullness of God."*

2. Patience is a great thing to have.

Proverbs 19:11 *"A man's wisdom gives him patience; it is to his glory to overlook an offense."*

3. Be patient and don't envy.

Corinthians 13:4 *"Love is patient, love is kind. It does **not envy...**"*

Galatians 5:19-21 *"The acts of the sinful nature are obvious: idolatry and witchcraft; hatred, discord, **jealousy**, fits of rage, selfish ambition, dissensions, factions and **envy**... I warn you, as I did before, that those who live like this will not inherit the kingdom of God."*

Proverbs 14:30 *"A heart at peace gives life to the body, but envy rots the bones. "*

4. Just do your best. Don't focus on others, but your own progress.

Galatians 6:4-5 *"Let everyone be sure that he is doing his very best, for then he will have the personal satisfaction of work well done, and won't need to compare himself with someone else. Each of us must bear some faults and burdens of his own. For none of us is perfect!"* (Living Bible)

5. Be confident because He'll be with you always to help you to improve all areas of your life.

Philippians 1:6 *"Being confident of this is that he who began a good work in you will carry it on to completion until the day of Christ Jesus."*

"We realize that what we are accomplishing is a drop in the ocean. But if this drop were not in the ocean, it would be missed."
Mother Teresa

"That we are alive today is proof positive that God has something for us to do today."
Anna R.B. Lindsay

Personal Notes and Ideas

1. My role as a person on the bench is important. What can I do to make the season a success?

2. How can I be a good teammate?

3. What can I do to help the coach?

4. How can I encourage my other teammates who are bench warmers?

5. What can I do for God?

6. What would Jesus do?

7. How do the Bible verses in this chapter help me? Are there other verses that can help me be an ultimate benchwarmer?

Cheerleader

"Therefore encourage one another and build each other up, just as in fact you are doing."
1 Thessalonians 5:11

Person in the Bible

Nehemiah was the great motivator. He always prayed to God and was a great organizer, constantly looking for solutions. He was in charge of rebuilding the wall of Jerusalem.

Nehemiah 2:17-20 *"Then I said to them, 'You see the trouble we are in: Jerusalem lies in ruins, and its gates have been burned with fire. Come, let us rebuild the wall of Jerusalem, and we will no longer be in disgrace.' I also told them about the gracious hand of my God upon me and what the king had said to me. They replied, 'Let us start rebuilding.' So they began this good work...they mocked and ridiculed us. 'What is this you are doing?' they asked. 'Are you rebelling against the king?' I answered them by saying, 'The God of heaven will give us success. We his servants will start rebuilding, but as for you, you have no share in Jerusalem or any claim or historic right to it.'"*

Nehemiah 4:6 *"So we rebuilt the wall till all of it reached half its height, for the people worked with all their heart."*

One of the most important positions in athletics is being a cheerleader. Yes, believe it or not! The best thing is that anyone on the team can be a cheerleader. All they need is a great attitude, a smile, an encouraging personality, and willingness to have a lot of fun. Being a good cheerleader is not necessarily being the person who can yell the loudest. It is a person who has the sheer determination to make peoples' lives better. Whether you are the top player, rookie, team manager, or injured and on the sideline, everyone can be a cheerleader. It doesn't matter if you are shy or outgoing, every athlete should make it a priority to brighten up other peoples' day.

There are many ways to do this:

- Lead cheers at the meet or on the bus.
- If you are more timid, you can create a new cheer for your team to use.
- Go to your teammates and personally encourage them before and after their event.
- Make signs and posters for the competition.
- Give a little "good luck" gift to your teammate, or share a prayer with them.

Becky was not the best gymnast on her high school team, but that didn't hinder her from trying to make the varsity team. Everyone loved Becky. No matter the situation, she always had a smile on her face and chose to give encouraging words to her teammates. She was always cheering and applauding for her friends. She was usually the first one to get up and hug her teammates after they finished a routine.

Tragically, Becky was killed in a car accident in the summer before her senior year. She died during the off-season, but all of her teammates were at the funeral. They decided to make a special award in memory of Becky and call it the Becky Blake Spirit Award. Becky will not be forgotten, and the main reason was her encouraging attitude.

What does the Bible have to say about being a cheerleader or encourager?

Proverbs 15:13 *"A happy heart makes the face cheerful, but heartache crushes the spirit."*

Proverbs 17:22 *"A cheerful heart is good medicine, but crushed spirit dries up the bones."*

Proverbs 16:24 *"Pleasant words are honeycomb, sweet to the soul and healing to the bones."*

> **"Attitude is a little thing that makes a big difference!"**
> Unknown

> **"Smile and be contagious."**
> The Author

Personal Notes and Ideas

1. My role as cheerleader is very important. What can I do to make the season a success?

2. How can I be a good encourager?

3. What are my gifts as a cheerleader? (On the front lines, or behind the scenes.)

4. How can I keep a smile on my face and encourage others when things aren't going so well?

5. How can I encourage my teammates to be cheerleaders too?

6. What can I do for God?

7. What would Jesus do?

8. How do the Bible verses in this chapter help me? Are there other verses that can help me be an ultimate cheerleader and encourager?

Captain

"In Joppa there was a disciple named Tabitha (which, when translated, is Dorcas), who was always doing good and helping the poor."

Acts 9:36

"He [Cornelius] and all his family were devout and God-fearing; he gave generously to those in need and prayed to God regularly."

Acts 10:2

Person in the Bible
Tabitha was always doing good and helping the poor.
Cornelius was a man of God and gave generously to the poor.

Each year Walter would take his team captains out to dinner at the beginning of the season. Walter wanted to treat his captains as they planned the season. Most importantly he wanted to let his captains know that they were the *main players*. Walter was convinced that the majority of the success for the season lay in the hands of his captains. Athletes look to the coaches for leadership, but many times the captains have more impact on the team. They can relate better to the athletes, because they are doing the same grueling workouts, competing with them, sharing the same goals, and are about the same age.

Captains have many roles, but the most important ones are as follows:

Shepherds

The captains need to continually look out for the best interests of their teammates. They need to be aware of what is happening with each athlete. Many times they serve as the bridge of communication for the athletes and the coaches. 1 Peter 5:2 *"Be shepherds of God's flock that is under your care, serving as overseers—not because you must, but because you are willing, as God wants you to be; not greedy for money, but eager to serve."*

a. Being a shepherd is to be a protector, and tend to the flock. John 10:11-15 *"I am the good shepherd. The good shepherd lays down his life for the sheep. The hired hand is not the shepherd who owns the sheep. So when he sees the wolf coming, he abandons the sheep and runs away. Then the wolf attacks the flock and scatters it. The man runs away because he is a hired hand and cares nothing for the sheep. 'I am the good shepherd; I know my sheep and my sheep know me—just as the Father knows me and I know the Father—and I lay down my life for the sheep.'"*

b. Being a good shepherd is to have the following qualities: 1 Corinthians 13:4-7 *"Love is patient, love is kind. It does not envy, it does not boast, it is not proud. It is not rude, it is not self-seeking, it is not easily angered, it keeps no record of wrongs. Love does not delight in evil but rejoices with the truth. It always protects, always trusts, always hopes, always perseveres."*

c. Being a shepherd is defending your flock. Proverbs 31:8-9 *"Speak up for those who cannot speak for themselves, for the rights of all who are destitute. Speak up and judge fairly; defend the rights of the poor and needy."*

Good example

    a. John 13:15 *"I have set you an example that you should do as I have done for you."*

    b. Mark 9:35 *"Sitting down, Jesus called the Twelve and said, 'If anyone wants to be first, he must be the very last, and the servant of all.'"*

    c. Romans 12:16 *"Live in harmony with one another. Do not be proud, but be willing to associate with people of low position. Do not be conceited."*

    d. Ephesians 4:29 *"Do not let any unwholesome talk come out of your mouths, but only what is helpful for building others up according to their needs, that it may benefit those who listen."*

Good listener

Psalm 10:17 *"You hear, O LORD, the desire of the afflicted; you encourage them, and you listen to their cry."* As a captain you will be working with various personalities who all have different needs. Most people who are frustrated only *need to be heard!* Sometimes there isn't a solution to the situation, but knowing that someone has heard his/her frustration is a great help. So be ready to hear almost everything. Be open and non-judgmental when you are listening to your teammates. You will have solutions for some problems, but not for all of them. Continue to remind yourself and your teammates that you are only a bridge of communication for the coaches. You don't have the power to make the final decisions. One of the best things you can do is to encourage the athlete to go and talk with the coach. They may want you to accompany them, and that is OK too.

Proverbs 17:17 *"A friend loves at all times, and a brother is born for adversity."*

Wise leader

Making good choices is crucial. Everyone is looking up to you and usually wants to follow your example. Don't do anything that you will regret later. When making decisions, remember the saying, "What would Jesus do?" Take this into consideration each time you need to make a decision. If you are still having a hard time, talk with people you esteem. They will help you. All great leaders choose to continue to get advice from others.

> Daniel 6:3-5 *"Now Daniel so distinguished himself among the administrators and the satraps by his exceptional qualities that the king planned to set him over the whole kingdom. At this, the administrators and the satraps tried to find grounds for charges against Daniel in his conduct of government affairs, but they were unable to do so.* **They could find no corruption in him, because he was trustworthy and neither corrupt nor negligent.** *Finally these men said, 'We will never find any basis for charges against this man Daniel unless it has something to do with the law of his God.'"*

Prayer Warrior

There are many ways that you can be an excellent prayer warrior. First of all, remember to pray for the team when you are in your home. Pray for the various individual needs. In addition to this you can lead an inclusive prayer time with your teammates. Remember that this prayer gathering should be optional, and no one should feel inferior if they choose not to attend. This prayer time can take place before practices, competitions, or in someone's home. Daniel 6:10 *"Now when Daniel learned that the decree had been published, he went home to his upstairs room where the windows opened toward Jerusalem. Three times a day he got down on his knees and prayed, giving thanks to his God, just as he had done before."*

More verses for captains

1 Thessalonians 2:12 *"…encouraging, comforting, and urging you to live lives worthy of God."*

1 Thessalonians 5:21-22 *"Test everything. Hold on to the good. Avoid every kind of evil."*

2 Thessalonians 3:7-9 *"For you yourselves know how you ought to follow our example. We were not idle when we were with you, nor did we eat anyone's food without paying for it. On the contrary, we worked night and day, laboring and toiling*

so that we would not be a burden to any of you. We did this, not because we do not have the right to such help, but in order to make ourselves a model for you to follow."

"No act of kindness, no matter how small, is ever wasted."

Aesop's Fables

Personal Notes and Ideas

1. My role as captain is very important. What can I do to make the season a success?

2. How can I be a good shepherd, example, and listener?

3. What choices are the most important for me to make?

4. What should I specifically pray for when I pray for the team?

5. How can I help my teammates if they are struggling with some issues?

6. What can I do for God?

7. What would Jesus do?

8. How do the Bible verses in this chapter help me? Are there other verses that can help me be an ultimate captain?

Non-captain

"Each one should use whatever gift he has received to serve others, faithfully administering God's grace in its various forms."

1 Peter 4:10

Person in the Bible

Queen Esther was married to King Xerxes. She did not have a position of power, being the queen. So Esther had to use all of her resources and talents to help the Jews. She was facing an evil man with a lot of power. His name was Haman and he was the advisor to the king. Not only did people pay honor to the king, but they also honored Haman. Queen Esther was able to outwit Haman and save the Jewish people. (Read the book of Esther in the Old Testament.)

Some people feel that you need to be chosen a leader in order to lead others. There couldn't be anything further from the truth. Many of the greatest leaders were ordinary people. They didn't become leaders because they were elected or had a gift of leading. They had a *passion* and an *unquenchable desire* to see change happen. Gandhi, Martin Luther King Jr., Susan B. Anthony, Abraham Lincoln, Mother Teresa…are examples of these kind of leaders. In the athletic arena, know that you can make a difference whether you have the title of team captain or not.

Lisa was a senior in high school and was well liked by everyone. It was apparent that she would be one of the volleyball captains. The coach decided to change the way the voting would take place. There was a lot of confusion and two other athletes became captains instead of Lisa. The coach realized her error, but it was too late to do anything. Lisa was obviously very upset, but understood what her coach was trying to do. Then to make matters worse, two weeks later Lisa broke her wrist and was out for the rest of the season. Some athletes in Lisa's situation would have felt unneeded, because they couldn't contribute to the team anymore.

However Lisa saw things differently. Instead of focusing on what she couldn't do, she focused on what she could do. Lisa went to practice every day and did her exercises. She also spent a lot of time coaching her teammates. In addition, she did everything she could to help her coach. Lisa also chose to be the team cheerleader and continue to encourage her teammates at practices and at games. She made signs, treats, and small gifts for her team. At the end-of-the-season banquet Lisa was awarded an athletic letter, even though she didn't play in one game. Her coach told the team that Lisa contributed more to the team than any other athlete and definitely deserved the letter. The whole team agreed with the coach's decision.

Acts 11:29 *"The disciples, each **according to his ability**, decided to provide help for the brothers living in Judea."*

1 Corinthians 12:27-28 *"Now you are the body of Christ, and each one of you is a part of it. And in the church God has appointed first of all apostles, second prophets, third teachers, then workers of miracles, also those having gifts of healing, those able to help others, those with gifts of administration, and those speaking in different kinds of tongues."*

Acts 4:13 *"When they saw the courage of Peter and John and realized that they were **unschooled, ordinary men**, they were astonished and they took note that these men had been* *with Jesus.*" (God uses anyone and everyone. It doesn't matter what you can or cannot do. It is a matter of being *willing* and *faithful*.)

> *"How wonderful it is that nobody need wait a single moment before starting to improve the world."*
>
> Anne Frank

> *"You cannot hope to build a better world without improving individuals."*
>
> Madame Marie Curie, famous scientists

Personal Notes and Ideas

1. My role as a non-captain is very important. What can I do to make the season a success?

2. How can I be a good teammate?

3. What can I do to help the coach?

4. What can I learn from Lisa's attitude and actions?

5. How can I encourage my teammates (who aren't captains) that we have important roles too?

6. What can I do for God?

7. What would Jesus do?

8. How do the Bible verses in this chapter help me? Are there other verses that can help me be an ultimate non-captain?

Most Valuable Player

"Don't be deceived, my dear brothers. Every good and perfect gift is from above, coming down from the Father of the heavenly lights, who does not change like shifting shadows."

James 1:16-17

Person in the Bible

Mary was chosen to be the Mother of Jesus. Luke 1:26-38 *"In the sixth month, God sent the angel Gabriel to Nazareth... 'Do not be afraid, Mary, you have found favor with God. You will be with child and give birth to a son, and you are to give him the name Jesus'... 'I am the Lord's servant,' Mary answered."*

When chosen as the MVP, give glory where glory is due. Obviously someone created you and your athletic skill. You had parents or guardians that drove you to practice, paid for the team fees, and provided many more things. You also had coaches, whether good or bad, who helped to fine-tune your talent. There were also friends, teammates, and other family members who played crucial roles in your success. So there is no need for you to boast about your accomplishments. Obviously you did sacrifice a lot to get to where you are today. However you didn't do it alone. The following are verses about pride:

Proverbs 16:18 *"Pride goes before destruction, a haughty spirit before a fall."*

Proverbs 21:4 *"Haughty eyes and a proud heart, the lamp of the wicked, are sin!"*

James 3:14-16 *"But if you harbor bitter envy and selfish ambition in your hearts, do not boast about it or deny the truth. Such 'wisdom' does not come down from heaven but is earthly, unspiritual, of the devil. For where you have envy and selfish ambition, there you find disorder and every evil practice."*

James 4:16 *"As it is, you boast and brag. All such boasting is evil."*

Todd was team captain for his high school hockey team, and had been chosen MVP for both his sophomore and junior years. He also earned his way on the All Conference Team. In his senior year he was very sick and missed half of the games. When he was able to play, he did very well. However, he needed to be in a certain number of games to be eligible for the All Conference Team. Todd's coach, Andy, pleaded extenuating circumstances and tried to get Todd on the team in spite of his missed games. The people in charge wouldn't hear of it and chose the second-best athlete on Andy's team to receive that honor. Andy was not happy about this because the other athlete was younger and had many years left to play. Andy didn't know how to break the news, but he did his best to explain to Todd what had happened. Todd's comments were, "It's OK if I didn't get 'All Conference' and my other teammate did. He has worked very hard and I have enough awards." That mature and unselfish attitude is rare these days.

This story about Todd is a perfect depiction of Philippians 2:3-8: *"Do nothing out of selfish ambition or vain conceit, but in humility consider others better than yourselves. Each of you should look not only to your own interests, but also to the interests of others. Your attitude* should be the same as that of Christ Jesus: Who, being in very nature God, did not consider equality with God something to be grasped, but made himself nothing, taking the very nature of a servant, being made in human likeness. And being found in appearance as a man, he humbled himself and became obedient to death—even death on a cross!"

As you continue your career as MVP please follow this advice:

2 Corinthians 3:4-5 "Such confidence as this is ours through Christ before God. Not that we are competent in ourselves to claim anything for ourselves, but our competence comes from God."

1 Kings 9:4 "As for you, if you walk before me in integrity of heart and uprightness, as David your father did, and do all I command and observe my decrees and laws."

Matthew 6:33 "But seek first his kingdom and his righteousness, and all these things will be given to you as well."

Romans 12:16 "Live in harmony with one another. Do not be proud, but be willing to associate with people of low position. Do not be conceited."

Isaiah 66:2 "This is the one I esteem: he who is humble and contrite in spirit, and trembles at my word."

Psalm 44:8 "In God we make our boast all day long, and we will praise your name forever. "

"It's nice to be important, but it's more important to be nice."

Sarah Hughes, 2002 Olympic gold medalist

"Talent is God-given. BE HUMBLE
Fame is man-given. BE THANKFUL.
Conceit is self-given. BE CAREFUL"

John Wooden, UCLA head basketball coach

> *"A life is not important except the impact it has on other lives."*
>
> Jackie Robinson, professional baseball player

Personal Notes and Ideas

1. My role as MVP is very important. What can I do to make the season a success?

2. How can I be a good MVP for my team?

3. What choices are the most important for me to make?

4. How can I help my teammates and my coach?

5. What can I do for God?

6. What would Jesus do?

7. How do the Bible verses in this chapter help me? Are there other verses that can help me be an ultimate MVP?

Christian

"Be imitators of God, therefore, as dearly loved children and live a life of love, just as Christ loved us and gave himself up for us as a fragrant offering and sacrifice to God."

Ephesians 5:1

Person in the Bible

Jesus was the only person who was part human and part God. He had to deal with every emotion, and at the same time His actions were always good. He did it! So if we want to be imitators of God, we need to see Jesus as our example.

In the "Explorers" chapter we talk about how the Bible is the owner's manual for our journey through life. The best way to be an imitator of anything is to study that subject. So God has given us many things to help us with our Christian journey. We have the Bible, churches, pastors, youth groups, music, Christian book stores... Make it a part of each day to learn a little bit more about Jesus. Then take it a step further and put your new knowledge into action. Live what you are learning!

We are God's ambassadors. We represent all aspects of our faith on a *moment-to-moment* basis.

2 Corinthians 5:20 *"We are therefore Christ's ambassadors, as though God were making his appeal through us. We implore you on Christ's behalf: Be reconciled to God."*

1 Peter 2:12 *"Live such good lives among the pagans that, though they accuse you of doing wrong, they may see your good deeds and glorify God on the day he visits us."*

What was Jesus like?

1. He was *gentle* and encourages us to be gentle with others. Galatians 6:1-2 *"Brothers, if someone is caught in a sin, you who are spiritual should restore him gently, But watch yourself, or you also may be tempted."* He helped the people with sin in their lives in a gentle manner. Jesus chose to draw people to Himself with a loving heart. We need to do the same with other people who are exploring their faith. Some people have been turned off to God due to some overzealous Christians. Most of these Christians mean well, but at times they do come off wrong. Romans 14:1 *"Accept him whose faith is weak, without passing judgment on disputable matters."* 1 Peter 3:15 *"But in your hearts set apart Christ as Lord. Always be prepared to give an answer to everyone who asks you to give the reason for the hope that you have. But do this with **gentleness and respect.**"*
2. He was a *man of love.* He just loved people, and spent time with them.
3. He was a *man of words,* which He always backed up with His *actions.* We need to make sure that whatever we say, we can always follow through with actions. There is a saying, "Actions speak louder than words." We need to listen carefully to this advice. It is so much more important that people *see* your faith rather than *hear* your faith. Your goal is to have people see Jesus in all that you do. This is called "Lifestyle evangelism." In other words, "Walk the talk."

Matthew 5:13-16 *"You are the salt of the earth. But if the salt loses its saltiness, how can it be made salty again? It is no longer good for anything, except to be thrown out and trampled by men. You are the light of the world. A city on a hill cannot be hidden. Neither do people light a lamp and put it under a bowl. Instead they put it on its stand, and it gives light to everyone in the house. In the same way, let your light shine before men, that they may see your good deeds and praise your Father in heaven."*

2 Corinthians 2:15 *"For we are to God the aroma of Christ among those who are being saved and those who are perishing."*

2 Thessalonians 3:7-9 *"For you yourselves know how you ought to follow our example. We were not idle when we were with you, nor did we eat anyone's food without paying for it. On the contrary, we worked night and day, laboring and toiling so that we would not be a burden to any of you. We did this, not because we do not have the right to such help, but in order to make ourselves a model for you to follow."*

2 Thessalonians 3:13 *"And as for you brothers, never tire of doing what is right."*

2 Corinthians 5:14-15 *"For Christ's love compels us, because we are convinced that one died for all, and therefore all died. And he died for all, that those who live should no longer live for themselves but for him who died for them and was raised again."*

4. He chose to *do no wrong*. Yes, He was tempted, but He chose to cling to the words of His Father, and follow through with *action*.

Romans 12:1-2 *"Therefore, I urge you, brothers, in view of God's mercy, to offer your bodies as living sacrifices, holy and pleasing to God—this is your spiritual act of worship. Do not conform any longer to the pattern of this world, but be transformed by the renewing of your mind. Then you will be able to test and approve what God's will is—his good, pleasing and perfect will."*

Galatians 6:9-10 *"Let us not become weary of doing good, for at the proper time we will reap a harvest if we do not give up. Therefore, as we have opportunity, let us do good to all people…"*

5. He was *human* and He experienced everything that we deal with here on earth. He wept (emotional), He ate and walked (physical), He prayed (spiritual), He worked (occupational), He made friends (social), and He kept learning from God (intellectual). We need to do the same. We need to continually strive in all areas of life. Some Christians choose to wear their spiritual masks. They will act as if everything is fine, because of their faith. However, they could be hurting emotionally, be in poor shape physically, be very lonely…and be too afraid to admit it. They mean well, but they aren't being real. God wants us to be honest with Him, ourselves, and others with respect to our lives.
6. Jesus was *young.* He did a tremendous amount in his short life of thirty-three years. For those of you who are younger athletes, don't feel that you need to be an adult to make a positive difference in this life. Go for it now! 1 Timothy 4:12 *"Don't let anyone look down on you because you are young, but set an example for the believers in speech, in life, in love, in faith and in purity."* Don't feel that you have nothing to contribute to society. You are a beautiful child of God and He has given you special gifts and talents to make the world a better place.
7. He was *willing.* He was willing to be led by God even if it didn't *feel* right to Him. We don't have to do it by ourselves! We can be witnesses by the power of the Holy Spirit. We just need to be willing to be led by God, Jesus, and the Holy Spirit.

Ephesians 2:10 *"For we are God's workmanship, created in Christ Jesus to do good works, which God prepared in advance for us to do."*

Acts 1:8 *"But you will receive power when the Holy Spirit comes on you; and you will be my witnesses in Jerusalem, and in all Judea and Samaria, and to the ends of the earth."*

Being a good example is crucial, according to Tom Lehman, a top professional golfer. He feels that his high school friends and coaches were very instrumental in his faith walk. "When I was a young Christian, I was surrounded by so many Christian people that it made being a Christian very easy. There were a bunch of guys on the football and basketball teams who were strong Christians...Whom I really looked up to. They were strong believers. Also, our football coach...had a big impact. Growing up, I'd think, I'd like to be like these guys. So, more than anyone else, they had a big influence on me. Meaning in life is derived from your walk with Jesus Christ. There are many people who are empty, who are looking for something beyond just the daily routine of work and whatever else. Your faith and actions can make a big difference in the lives of people. Just trust God, follow in Jesus' steps, and be *willing*."

Isaiah 6:8 *"Then I heard the voice of the Lord saying, 'Whom shall I send? And who will go for us?' And I said, 'Here am I. Send me!'"*

"Live in such a way that those who know you, but don't know God, will come to know God because they know you."

Unknown

"Holiness is the chief way by which we honor and glorify Christ in this world."

John Owen

Personal Notes and Ideas

1. My role as Christian is very important. What can I do to make the season a success athletically?

2. What can I do to help more athletes understand how they can have a personal relationship with Jesus Christ?

3. Jesus is our example. Out of the seven qualities discussed in this chapter...
   a. Which ones do I do well, and how can I make them better?

   b. Which ones do I need to improve, and how can I make them better?

4. What can I do for God?

5. What would Jesus do?

6. How do the Bible verses in this chapter help me? Are there other verses that can help me be an ultimate Christian?

"How can you believe in something that you can't see or feel?
How do you really know for sure, how do you know it's real.
So many unanswered questions, what's true and what is false?
Well I can only tell you one thing for sure, God is the bomb!

Yeah you gotta have faith,
You gotta believe,
You can not be in doubt,
You've got to figure it out,
There's only one way to heaven.

When it comes to being a Christian, it's ok to be wrong.
You don't have to be perfect, God won't strike you down.
And if you ask yourself this question, am I going up or down
How will you answer it, with a smile or a frown?
Only one thing is for sure, God is great and true.
And the only way to be with him is to hear what I'm telling you.

You gotta have faith,
You gotta believe,

You can not be in doubt,
You've got to figure it out,
Are you going to Heaven?

So many choices out there, what's right and what is wrong?
Let the Bible be your handbook, until the day you're gone.
It is the only truth, I've got the facts to back me up.
And I might sound a bit stubborn, but sometimes the truth
*   hurts.*
If Jesus is not in your heart, then you're living life all wrong.
Because if you're not living for Jesus, then what are you living
*   for?*

Do you have faith?
Do you believe?
Are you in doubt?
Or have you figured it out,
There's only one way to heaven"

Jeremy Risk
High School Student

Explorer

"God did this so that men would seek him
and perhaps reach out for him and find him,
though he is not far from each one of us. For
in him we live and move and have our
being."

Acts 17:27,28

Person in the Bible

The Bereans, Acts 17:11 "Now the Bereans were of more
noble character than the Thessalonians, for they *received the
message with great eagerness and examined the Scriptures
every day* to see if what Paul said was true."

xplorers are people who are trying to find a better life. It is
natural to want to have a better life. There are many ways
that we can improve our lives. We can always strive to
improve our lives emotionally, physically, mentally, spiritually,
socially, and occupationally. This chapter will discuss the spiritual
aspect of exploring, because this is a vital part of becoming a whole
person.

A. Frequently stated fallacies
Fallacy #1 People don't search for the meaning of life.

People who don't have faith, or question their faith, tend to search for the meaning of life. Many times they become inquisitive, and want to know more about God and people of faith. If you are in that position, continue to search for the truth. In addition, feel free to talk with a pastor or church youth leader. A great source for your uncertainty and questions is the Bible. Start by reading the Gospels in the New Testament. Begin with John, the last Gospel. Then read the other Gospels (Matthew, Mark, and Luke) after you finish John.

> *"Meaning in life is derived from your walk with Jesus Christ. There are so many people who are empty, who are looking for something beyond just the daily routine of work or whatever else."*
>
> Tom Lehman Professional Golfer

Fallacy #2 What is the big deal about the Bible? It is just filled with out-of-date information that doesn't help us right now.

This could not be further from the truth. The Scripture is very pertinent to what you are experiencing in your athletic life. Look at all the verses that have been selected for this book. The Bible is a very important tool for us and the following explains this:

Let's pause to think about a new computer. When you buy your new computer, or anything new, many things are important to you. First, you want to make sure that you are not doing anything wrong to it. The last thing that you want is to break your new toy. Second, you want to get the most out of your new computer, so that your life will be easier. Finally, when you are assembling the computer, you want to make sure the cords and cables are plugged in where they are supposed to be. So what do you do after you pull everything out of the box? You read the *owner's manual*. It has all the do's and don'ts to help you along the way.

It is the same thing with the human body. You don't want to do anything wrong to it, you want to know how to get the most out of it, and you want to make sure that it is fine-tuned. So, look at the owner's manual. It is the Bible, of course! Yes, God has provided us with our own manual to help us as we sail through life. It can help us with the ups and downs of our time here on earth.

Fallacy #3 All people who read the Bible are perfect.

We all know this isn't true. So what about the people who read the Bible and don't do what it says? What about these bad examples, these hypocritical people? Good question!

Whenever there is any doubt with respect to peoples' actions in relation to a certain faith, the best thing to do is to look at the *teaching* and not the *behavior*. What does the Bible say? Yes, there will be people who will choose to not follow the teaching and who will make bad choices. However, don't let anything, anyone, or any action rob you of the joy that you could have with your own faith in God. Romans 3:3 *"What if some did not have faith? Will their lack of faith nullify God's faithfulness?"* God is always faithful, even when we make mistakes. Living a life based on faith is not always a smooth ride, but it is worth the trip!

> *"Many people don't understand us [Christians] and think that we are trying to promote ourselves on top of this image—but that has nothing to do with it. Certainly there are some hypocrites who call themselves Christians but who are in fact are only wearing a mask. What we really want is to spread the love of God around to people, so that many people may have a personal encounter with Christ."*
>
> Jojo de Olivenca, world class professional surfer.

Fallacy #4 Others of you may say... "I have done too many terrible things in my life. God will never want me to be a part of his family."

This could not be further from the truth! Paul (who was first called Saul) is one of the well-known disciples. At first he was a horrible person and chose to persecute anyone following Jesus. He watched as Stephen, one of the disciples, was stoned to death and he gave his approval. Read in the book of Acts 7:54—8:3. Later on, Paul realized that he was wrong. Read Acts 9:1-31.

B. Facts from the Bible

Fact #1. Due to the first sin in the Garden of Eden, we were all born sinners and need forgiveness, whether we like it or not.

Romans 3:22-23 *"This righteousness from God comes through faith in Jesus Christ to all who believe. There is no difference, for all have sinned and fall short of the glory of God."*

Romans 5:12 *"Therefore, just as sin entered the world through one man, and death through sin, and in this way death came to all men, because all sinned."*

Colossians 1:13-14 *"For he has rescued us from the dominion of darkness and brought us into the kingdom of the Son he loves, in whom we have redemption, the forgiveness of sins."*

Fact #2. Jesus died for us so that we could have eternal life:

I John 5:13 *"I write these things to you who believe in the name of the Son of God so that you may know that you have eternal life."*

1 Corinthians 15:3-6 *"For what I received I passed on to you as of first importance: that Christ died for our sins according to the Scriptures, that he was buried, that he was raised on the third day according to the Scriptures, and that he appeared to Peter, and then to the Twelve. After that, he appeared to more than five hundred of the brothers at the same time…"*

1 Timothy 2:5-6 *"For there is one God and one mediator between God and men, the man Christ Jesus, who gave himself as a ransom for all men—the testimony given in its proper time."*

2 Corinthians 5:14-15 *"For Christ's love compels us, because we are convinced that one died for all, and therefore all died. And he died for all, that those who live should no longer live for themselves but for him who died for them and was raised again."*

Fact #3. We need to accept Jesus. Notice there is action on our part:

Romans 10:9-13 *"That if you **confess** with your mouth, 'Jesus is Lord,' and **believe** in your heart that God raised him from the dead, you will be saved. For it is with your heart that you **believe** and are justified, and it is with your mouth that you **confess** and are saved. As the Scripture says, 'Anyone who **trusts** in him will never be put to shame.' For there is no difference between Jew and Gentile—the same Lord is Lord of all and richly blesses all who **call on him**, for, 'Everyone who **calls** on the name of the Lord will be saved.'"*

John 1:9,12,13 *"The true light that gives light to every man was coming into the world. Yet to all who **received** him, to those who **believed** in his name, he gave the right to become children of God—children born not of natural descent, nor of human decision or a husband's will, but born of God."*

1 Peter 3:11 *"He must **turn** from evil and **do** good; he must **seek** peace and **pursue** it."*

Isaiah 55:6 *"**Seek** the Lord while he may be found; **call on him** while he is near."*

Fact #4. God loves you no matter how many bad things you have done:

(The apostle Paul is talking in the following verses.)

Corinthians 15:9-10 *"For I am the least of the apostles and do not even deserve to be called an apostle, because I persecuted the church of God. But by the grace of God I am what I am, and his grace to me was not without effect. No, I worked harder than all of them—yet not I, but the grace of God that was with me."*

1 Timothy 1:13-16 *"Even though I was once a blasphemer and a persecutor and a violent man, I was shown mercy because I acted in ignorance and unbelief. The grace of our*

Lord was poured out on me abundantly, along with the faith and love that are in Christ Jesus. Here is a trustworthy saying that deserves full acceptance: Christ Jesus came into the world to save sinners—of whom I am the worst. But for that very reason I was shown mercy so that in me, the worst of sinners, Christ Jesus might display his unlimited patience as an example for those who would believe on him and receive eternal life."

Fact #5. God loves everyone:

John 3:16 *"For God **so loved the world** that he gave his one and only Son, that whoever believes in him shall not perish but have eternal life."* (No categories are specified here. This is an inclusive statement. *All* are welcome.)

Acts 10:34-35 *"Then Peter began to speak: 'I now realize how true it is that God **does not show favoritism but accepts men from every nation** who fear him and do what is right.'"*

2 Peter 3:9 *"He is patient with you, **not wanting anyone to perish**, but **everyone** to come to repentance."*

Fact #6. We are His forever:

Romans 8:35-39 *"Who shall separate us from the love of Christ? Shall trouble or hardship or persecution or famine or nakedness or danger or sword? ...For I am convinced that neither death nor life, neither angels nor demons, neither the present nor the future, nor any powers, neither height nor depth, nor anything else in all creation, will be able to separate us from the love of God that is in Christ Jesus our Lord."*

Fact #7. We should do our best to live good lives:

1 John 5:18 *"We know that anyone born of God does not continue to sin; the one who was born of God keeps him safe, and the evil one cannot harm him."*

"God is contagious. Catch God!"

Anonymous

> *"Looking back on the 12 years I spent weightlifting, I realize that I was trying to find meaning and purpose by being involved in that sport. I finally realized that Jesus came to do what I could never do; He lived a perfect life and died in my place. Jesus asks us to make Him the ruler of our lives. He made it so clear that you're either for Him (making Him the ruler of you life), or against Him (living life your own way, without Jesus). I really believe that before forming an opinion of Jesus and what He's all about, you should read the New Testament for yourself and decide."*
>
> Adrian Keebe, world class weightlifter.

Personal Notes and Ideas

1. My role as an explorer is very important. What can I do to make the season a success?

2. Who can I talk to about my new faith or the questions I have?

3. Is there someone on the team who could help me with my faith?

4. What does this statement mean to me? "Don't let anyone, anything, or any action rob me of the joy that I can have with my faith in God."

5. What can I do for God?

6. What can I do for myself?

7. What would Jesus do?

8. How do all the Bible verses help me? Are there other verses that will help me to change positions from being an explorer to being a Christian?

Friend

"A friend loves at all times, brother for adversity."

Proverb 17:17

Person in the Bible

Joseph of Arimethea, Nicodemus, Mary Magdelene, Joanna, and Mary the mother of James are great examples of being true friends. They stood by Jesus even though it was the unpopular thing to do. Jesus had just been condemned to death because the people chose to free Barabbas instead of Him. Even Jesus' own disciple, Peter, denied him three times. Jesus was mocked and crucified on a cross. However, Joseph of Arimethea and Nicodemus gave Jesus a proper burial, while the three women followed along. Luke 23: 50-56 *"Now there was a man named Joseph...Going to Pilate, he asked for Jesus' body. Then he took it down, wrapped it in linen cloth and placed it in a tomb...The women who had come with Jesus from Galilee followed Joseph and saw the tomb and how his body was laid in it.Then they went home and prepared spices and perfumes."* Another rendition of this story is found in John 19:38-42.

There are all kinds of friends, but let's divide them into three groups. You have your *acquaintances*, your *convenient friends*, and your *"inconvenient" friends*. Acquaintances are people that you know at a distance. You say hello to them, but haven't really spent much time with them. Next are the convenient friends. These people are great for having fun, chatting about various topics, and socializing in different situations. It is nice to have friends like these, but beware…they usually aren't there for the long haul. They might be there when you need help, and they just might not.

Inconvenient friends are the ones that you would trust with all your secrets. You can bare your soul to these people. They will be with you through thick and thin. They aren't just there for the fun and when it is convenient. These people would do almost anything for you. They would drive you to the hospital at three o'clock in the morning and then go to their job that same day. They would sacrifice their sleep time to be at your side. That is why they are called inconvenient friends. They are there when it is *tough* and *inconvenient*.

Luke 22:28 *"You are those who have stood by me in my trials."*

Elena Berezhnaya and Anton Sikharulidze are great examples of an inconvenient friendship. During practice Elena was accidently hit in the head with her partner's skate and was rushed to the hospital. To make matters worse, her partner was very abusive. Anton, another skater, chose to rush to her side in the hospital. He stayed with her all the way through her recovery. He helped Elena to get her skating career off the ground again. They are now skating together and have won a gold medal at the Olympics for Russia.

Inconvenient friends are the ones who have the guts to confront us when we are making bad decisions. Listen to these people. God put these people on earth to help us with our journey in life. Proverbs 27:17 *"As iron sharpens iron, so one man sharpens another."*

As Christians we are called to love one another. Mark 12:31 *"The second is this: 'Love your neighbor as yourself.' There is no commandment greater than these."* To truly love someone is to do so *unconditionally:*

- It isn't loving them because they will do something for us, or because of who they are.

- Love isn't love when we use "ifs." I love you *if* you do this for me....
- Unconditional love is...I love you *in spite of* who you are, or what you do... I love you, period! I will be at your side even when it is inconvenient.

"A friend is someone to whom one may pour out all the contents of one's heart, chaff and grain together, knowing that the gentlest of hands will take and sift it, keep what is worth keeping and with a breath of kindness blow the rest away."

Arabic proverb

"The best mirror is a friend's eye."

Gaelic proverb

Personal Notes and Ideas

1. My role as a friend is very important. What can I do to make the season a success?

2. How can I be a good friend?

3. What does it mean to be an "inconvenient" friend?

4. Who are my "inconvenient" friends?

5. What would Jesus do?

6. How do the Bible verses in this chapter help me? Are there other verses that can help me be an ultimate friend?

Helper/Servant

"For even the Son of Man did not come to be served, but to serve, and to give his life as a ransom for many."

Mark 10:45

"Therefore I glory in Christ Jesus in my service to God."

Romans 15:17

Person in the Bible

Jesus is our perfect example of a servant. Everything He did during His life on earth was to help and serve both God and others. If He were out to serve himself, He would not have followed through with the excruciating pain of the crucifixion.

Mark 10:45 "For even the Son of Man did not come to be served, but to serve, and to give his life as a ransom for many."

Luke 22:27 "For who is greater, the one who is at the table or the one who serves? Is it not the one who is at the table? But I am among you as one who serves."

he main goal of a servant is to try and make other peoples' lives easier. Here are some great ideas for those of you who want to help:

- Help coach with the equipment. There can be a lot to do to before and after practice.
- Help your teammates in whatever they need. Fill their water bottles for them, carry their cleats if their arms are full…
- Help your team managers with their jobs.
- Help the opposing team get situated during the competition.
- Write down more ideas….

Doing various chores always helps other people and continues to keep us humble. By practicing humility, we will be appreciative of others and of what we have.

1 Timothy 3:13 *"Those who have served well gain an excellent standing and great assurance in their faith in Christ Jesus."*

I Timothy 1:12 *"I thank Christ Jesus our Lord, who has given me strength, that he considered me faithful, appointing me to his service."*

"Service is rent due for living on this planet."
Salimah Majeed

"It's my job, my responsibility as a human being…to give back."
Herman Edwards, NY Jets head coach

"Everyone can be great, because everyone can serve."
Martin Luther King, Jr.

> *"Serving the Lord is the central point of everything I do."*
> David Robinson, professional basketball player and NBA MVP

Personal Notes and Ideas

1. My role as a servant is very important. What can I do to make the season a success?

2. How can I be a good servant to my teammates?

3. What can I do to help the coach?

4. How can I encourage my teammates to be good servants?

5. What can I do for God?

6. What would Jesus do?

7. How do the Bible verses in this chapter help me? Are there other verses that can help me be an ultimate helper/servant?

Extra verses

John 13:3-17
Matt 19:30
Galatians 5:13

Student

"Teach me **knowledge** and **good judgment,**
for I believe in your commands."

Psalm 119:66

 n this verse:
Knowledge represents learning
Good judgement represents good decisions and actions

Person in the Bible
Apollos was very teachable and followed through with what he learned.

Acts 18:24-28 *"Meanwhile a Jew named Apollos, a native of Alexandria, came to Ephesus. He was a learned man, with a thorough knowledge of the Scriptures. He had been instructed in the way of the Lord, and he spoke with great fervor and taught about Jesus accurately, though he knew only the baptism of John. He began to speak boldly in the synagogue. When Priscilla and Aquila heard him, they invited him to their home and explained to him the way of God more adequately. When*

*Apollos wanted to go to Achaia, the brothers encouraged him and wrote to the disciples there to welcome him. On arriving, he was a great help to those who by grace had believed. For he **vigorously refuted** the Jews in public debate, proving from the Scriptures that Jesus was the Christ."*

What can we do to be good students in school and with God's word?

1. Listen in order to be wise.
Proverbs 19:20 *"**Listen** to advice and **accept** instruction, and in the end you will be wise."*

Psalm 78:1 *"O my people, hear my teaching; **listen** to the words of my mouth."*

Proverbs 1:5, 8 *"Let the wise **listen** and add to their learning, and let the discerning get guidance. **Listen**, my son, to your father's instruction and do **not forsake** your mother's teaching."*

2. It takes action on your part to learn. (Notice all these verses use action words)
Proverbs 2:1-4 *"My son, if you **accept** my words and **store** up my commands within you, **turning** your ear to wisdom and **applying** your heart to understanding, and if you **call out** for insight and **cry aloud** for understanding, and if you **look for it** as for silver and **search** for it as for hidden treasure."*

Psalm 51:12 *"Restore to me the joy of your salvation and grant me a **willing spirit**, to sustain me."*

3. It also takes action to keep your learning alive and functioning.
Proverbs 4:13 *"**Hold on** to instruction, **do not let it go**; **guard** it well, for it is your life."*

Psalm 78:4, 6 *"We will not hide them from their children; we will **tell** the next generation the praiseworthy deeds of the Lord, his power, and the wonders he has done. So the next* *generation would know them, even the children yet to be born, and they in turn would **tell** their children."*

4. Use your learning to be wise and to not make bad decisions. Proverbs 1:15 *"My son, **do not go** along with them, **do not set foot** on their paths."*

Proverbs 4:14-15 *"**Do not set foot** on the path of the wicked or walk in the way of evil men. **Avoid it, do not travel** on it; **turn** from it and **go** on your way."*

Paul was on a four-year scholarship for basketball at one university, but he wasn't being challenged enough academically. So after his freshman year he gave up his scholarship to go to a different university for a better education. He continued playing basketball at the new college and graduated with honors. The most amazing part of this story was that Paul was no longer on scholarship and had to pay for his schooling. The new college was a private one and it cost a lot of money. However, Paul was serious about his academics and was willing to go the extra mile.

Most athletes live and breathe for their sport. However it is imperative that each student/athlete strive to get good grades. For most athletes, the *occupational* part of their multidimensional life is their education. Refer to chapter 79, "Balance," about the "Spokes of Life." Remember that everyone needs to have a balanced life. You never know with sports, and there are no guarantees in life. You could get injured, experience burnout, or get too old to compete. Plan for life after sports and get a degree!

Venus Williams was born June 17, 1980 and turned pro on Oct 31, 1994 when she was fourteen years old. Her father chose to limit her appearances on the WTA tour. She continued her studies for high school and got her diploma in 1997. Her father told both of his daughters, "Education is power, not chasing around some tennis ball." When Venus was at the top of her game, she decided to ease off her tennis a little and concentrate more on her studies for college.

Colossians 3:16 *"Let the word of Christ dwell in you richly as you teach and admonish one another with all wisdom, and as*

*you sing psalms, hymns and spiritual songs with gratitude in
your hearts to God."*

> *"I just want to keep up with my schoolwork.
> My next goal is to get in the high 1,500's on
> my SATs."*
> Sarah Hughes, after winning the Olympic gold at age sixteen.
> (Sarah takes all honors classes and has won the Presidential Award for
> Academic Excellence. She will graduate on time and with honors.)

Personal Notes and Ideas

1. My role as a student/athlete is very important. What can I do to make the season a success athletically and academically.

2. How can I organize my time so that I can excel in both school and sports?

3. How can I encourage my teammates to get good grades also?

4. What can I learn from Paul's situation?

5. How can I be a good student of God's word?

6. How can being a good student of God's word help me with life?

7. What would Jesus do?

8. How do the Bible verses in this chapter help me? Are there other verses that can help me be an ultimate student/athlete?

Professional Athlete

"No one can serve two masters. Either he will hate the one and love the other, or he will be devoted to the one and despise the other. You cannot serve both God and money."

Matthew 6:24

Person in the Bible

Bad example: Judas sold his soul for money. Matthew 26:14-16 *"Then one of the Twelve—the one called Judas Iscariot—went to the chief priests and asked, 'What are you willing to give me if I hand him over to you?' So they counted out for him thirty silver coins. From then on Judas watched for an opportunity to hand him over."*

Good example: Zacchaeus, a chief tax collector. Luke 19:8 *"But Zacchaeus stood up and said to the Lord, 'Look, Lord! Here and now I give half of my possessions to the poor, and if I have cheated anybody out of anything, I will pay back four times the amount.'"*

"You need to play for God and God alone. Whatever else comes along is nice, but it doesn't really mean as much as having God say 'well done.' I think of myself as a Christian who plays golf, not a golfer who is a Christian. At the beginning of my pro career, I put so much emphasis on money and in being successful that all of the things I felt from age fifteen to age twenty-two were shot down by the things I saw all around me. I went from doing things for God's glory and trying to be His kind of guy to trying to make money and be successful, just for myself. I took my being knocked way down to realize that God wanted me to be His man."

Tom Lehman

Proverbs 23:4 *"Do not wear yourself out to get rich; have the wisdom to show restraint."*

Proverbs 27:24 *"For riches do not endure forever, and a crown is not secure for all generations."*

1 Timothy 6:10 *"For the love of money is a root of all kinds of evil. Some people, eager for money, have wandered from the faith and pierced themselves with many griefs."*

Ecclesiastes 5:10 *"Whoever loves money never has money enough; whoever loves wealth is never satisfied with his income. This too is meaningless."*

Hebrews 13:5 *"Keep your lives free from the love of money and be content with what you have."*

Popular thought is that pro athletes have the perfect life. Rosalyn Summers, who was the 1984 silver medalist in figure skating and now professional skater, has this to say: "Many professional athletes look like they have everything—

money, popularity, excitement, and security. What people don't understand is that athletes often experience deep internal struggles...But even in the midst of the glamour...I've found that money and fame don't give me the security and sense of purpose I long for. It's hard to explain this, even to your closest friends because people don't feel sorry for you when they see how much money you've made...Though I will always wrestle with various trials and times of loneliness in life, I have found a friend in Christ who is with me wherever I travel and whenever I need him."

Many pro athletes are bad role models. Countless times in the news we have heard of drinking and driving, spousal abuse, drug problems, and so on. However, there are many pro athletes who choose to use their status as a platform for sharing their faith. They want to be positive role models. Michael Chang, the youngest player to win a Grand Slam tennis event publicly thanked Jesus Christ after winning the French Open. He said, "Without him, I'm nothing." Chang's reason for praising God in public is because, "I've just received so much joy, so much love, and so many blessings from the Lord. When something good happens to you, you want to share it with people!"

John 5:30 *"By myself I can do nothing; I judge only as I hear, and my judgment is just, for I seek not to please myself but him who sent me."* You are a human being first, and tons of people depend on you whether you like it or not. Be good and do good. Never forget, actions speak louder than words!

"Take the responsibility of being a role model seriously, regardless if you want young people to look up to you. We've come to inherit this position of being a role model. It's our responsibility—our privilege—to take it seriously and provide young people with the information they need to reach their dreams."
Adrienne Johnson, professional basketball player for the Orlando Magic

"It's better to have a good name than all the riches in the world."

Herman Edwards, NY Jets head coach, referring to Proverbs 22:1
"A good name is more desirable than great riches;
or to be esteemed is better than silver or gold."
For athletes, substitute money for silver and gold for medals.

*"From what we get, we can make a living;
what we give, however makes a life.*

Arthur Ashe, pro tennis player

Personal Notes and Ideas

1. What pro athlete is a great role model for me and why?

2. What pro athlete is a poor role model for me and why?

3. When I am a pro athlete I will make sure that I...

4. How can I encourage my teammates to choose positive role models?

5. What can I do for God?

6. What would Jesus do?

7. How do the Bible verses in this chapter help me? Are there other verses that can help me be an ultimate professional athlete?

Extra Verses

Psalm 49:16-20
James 1:10-11

Role Model

1. Bad role models

"I do not sit with deceitful men, nor do I consort with hypocrites."

Psalm 26:4

Person in the Bible

Pharoah Ramses was a man obsessed with his power. He wouldn't listen to his own brother, Moses. Exodus chapters 7-12 shows how Ramses repeatedly hardened his heart and wouldn't listen. He chose to make it very difficult for the Israelites, if not unbearable.

Description of a bad role model:

Psalm 52:7 *"Here now is the man who did not make God his stronghold but trusted in his great wealth and grew strong by destroying others!"*

God's opinion about bad role models:

Psalm 101:3-8 *"I will set before my eyes no vile thing. The deeds of faithless men I hate; they will not cling to me. Men of perverse heart shall be far from me; I will have nothing to do with evil. Whoever slanders his neighbor in secret, him will I put to silence; whoever has haughty eyes and a proud heart,* **him will I not endure.** *My eyes will be on the faithful in the land, that they may dwell with me; he whose walk is blameless will minister to me. No one who practices deceit will dwell in my house; no one who speaks falsely will stand in my presence. Every morning I will put to silence all the wicked in the land; I will cut off every evildoer from the city of the Lord."*

Advice:

Proverbs 20:12 *"Ears that hear and eyes that see—the Lord has made them both."* (Be attentive, listen to yourself, and see what you are doing with your life!)

Unfortunately there are many poor role models in the world of sports, who have a profound affect on many people. "This topic is very deserving of our attention because the fact of the matter is observational learning is one of the primary means in which children learn," reports William Gayton, Ph.D. and sports psychologist. According to Tina Hoff, director of Kaiser's Public Health Information, "Some of this bad behavior we're seeing in professional sports is filtering down to local school yards and gyms around the country." As athletes we need to be proactive about being good sports. The best thing is to take a lemon and make lemonade. Learn from these bad examples, and vow that you will be different.

Will good triumph over evil? We are in tough times right now and it looks like evil is winning. There is proof that GOOD will overcome any evil in this world:

1. God promises it! Look in the book of Revelation. Jesus easily puts Satan away for good.
2. Let's turn off all the lights in the room and light a small match. Light *always* overtakes darkness! No matter how big the room is, and how tiny the light is, the light will always be seen. John 1:5 *"The light shines in the darkness, but the darkness has not understood it."*
3. Look at the funerals in history. People gather by the multitudes, and there is worldwide mourning for the good people. Many times the world stops when these wonderful people

die. Look at Gandhi, Martin Luther King, Mother Teresa, Princess Diana, John F. Kennedy, just to name a few. Now let's take a look at the bad people. Did many people show up and mourn the death of Hitler or Stalin? Will there be world-wide mourning for bad dictators or all the terrorists? Some people will show up, but there will *not* be worldwide mourning. The majority of the people want good in this world!

> *"The quality and character of a person come out in their disappointments. They can demonstrate their **true** character in those really disappointing and down times"*
> Mike Denny, University of Nebraska wrestling coach

> *"If you can't be a good example, then you'll just have to be a horrible warning."*
> Catherine Aird

2. Good role models

> *"Therefore, prepare your minds for action; be self-controlled; set your hope fully on the grace to be given you when Jesus Christ is revealed. As obedient children, do not conform to the evil desires you had when you lived in ignorance. But just as he who called you is holy, so be holy in all you do; for it is written: 'Be holy, because I am holy.'"*
> 1 Peter 1:13-16

Person in the Bible

Moses was humble when he was called by God to lead the Israelites to freedom. Exodus 3:8-12 *"The Lord said, 'I have indeed seen the misery of my people in Egypt. I have heard them crying out because of their slave drivers, and I am concerned about their suffering. So I have come down to rescue them... So now, go. I am sending you to Pharaoh to bring my people the Israelites out of Egypt.' But Moses said to God, 'Who am I, that I* should go to Pharaoh and bring the Israelites out of Egypt?' And God said, 'I will be with you.'"

There was a big problem with the Pairs Skating at the 2002 Olympics. See chapter 41, "Bad Calls and Bad Referees," for more information. David Peltier was interviewed and he said, "We are athletes and we will go on. We controlled what we could, our skating. We couldn't control the judging or the outcome. But nobody can take away how we feel about how we did. *We were all a good example for the youth of today.*" Referring to all four of them (David Peltier, Jamie Sale, Elena Berezhnaya, and Anton Sikharulidze) What makes an ultimate role model?

- Knowing that you need to make good decisions when you are on and off the field.
- Taking care of the beginner athlete, helping the unfortunate people, volunteering, etc.
- Saying no to drugs, alcohol, and smoking.
- Keeping your emotions under control during the competition.
- Being humble and thankful during media interviews.
- Add to the list

1 Corinthians 13:4-7 *"Love is patient, love is kind. It does not envy, it does not boast, it is not proud. It is not rude, it is not self-seeking, it is not easily angered, it keeps no record of wrongs. Love does not delight in evil but rejoices with the truth. It always protects, always trusts, always hopes, always perseveres."*

Acts 5:42 *"Day after day, in the temple courts and from house to house, they never stopped teaching and proclaiming the good news that Jesus is the Christ.*

"It's great to have this medal and everything right now. But there's a lot of responsibility that comes with it. I have a responsibility to represent my country well and a responsibility to represent the skating community well."
Sarah Hughes, Olympic gold medalist, when interviewed about her newfound fame

"My life is a message."

Mahatma Gandhi

"Sports do not build character, they reveal it."

Haywood Hale Brown

To Any Athlete

"There are little eyes upon you, and they're watching night and day.

There are little ears that quickly take in every word you say.

There are little hands all eager to do anything you do.

And little children who are dreaming of the day they'll be like you.

You're the children's idol, you're the wisest of the wise.

In their minds about you no suspicions ever rise.

They believe in you devoutly. They hold all that you say and do.

They will say and do in your way, when grown up like you.

There's a wide–eyed little youngster who believes you're always right.

And their ears are always open and they watch both day and night.

You are setting an example every day in all you do.

For the children who are waiting to grow up to be like you."

Anonymous

Personal Notes and Ideas

1. How can I be a great role model?

2. What are my weak points? In other words, how can I blow it?

3. What are ideas and solutions to help me so that I don't blow it?

4. What are my strong points that make me a great role model?

5. How can I encourage my teammates to be great role models?

6. Name some athletes who are good role models.

7. What would Jesus do?

8. How do the Bible verses in this chapter help me? Are there other verses that can help me be an ultimate role model?

Part Five
PEOPLE

Introduction to People

I f you want to be an athlete, be ready to enter into a people profession. Whether you are a beginner or a professional athlete, you will be interacting with many people on a daily basis. Some of these people will be your best friends and others may be a challenge to your patience. Either way, athletes need to know that they are in the people business. Athletes must choose to not become self-centered, egotistical, or proud. Ultimate athletes are very others-centered, kind, giving, and willing to help at a moments' notice.

The following chapters will discuss the various types of people that you may encounter during your athletic career. These chapters will give you some advice about maintaining a a positive relationship with all of these people. Remember you can't control other peoples' attitudes and actions. However you are responsible for the way *you think and act!* Granted, you will encounter some tough personalities, but you can learn how to respond appropriately to them.

Advice from God:
We should control our actions for God.
Nehemiah 5:15-16 *"But out of reverence for God I did not act like that."*

Go to the source!
Nehemiah 5:7 *"I pondered them in my mind and then accused the nobles and officials. I told them, 'You are exacting usury from your own countrymen!' So I called together a large meeting to deal with them."*

Be a person who is kind to others.
Ephesians 4:29 *"Do not let any unwholesome talk come out of your mouths, but only what is helpful for building others*

up according to their needs, that it may benefit those who listen."

Be inclusive of others, God is!

Galatians 3:28 *"There is neither Jew nor Greek, slave nor free, male nor female, for you are all one in Christ Jesus."*

Coaches

"Obey your leaders and submit to their authority. They keep watch over you as men who must give an account. Obey them so that their work will be a joy, not a burden, for that would be of no advantage to you."

Hebrews 13:17

Person in the Bible

Moses not only led many people to freedom, but he also spent time coaching Joshua. Moses knew that he would need someone to take over for him. Joshua was teachable and obedient to whatever Moses wanted.

Numbers 11:28 *"Joshua son of Nun, who had been Moses' aide since youth..."* They had spent a lot of time together, and in the end, Moses was not able to lead his people to the chosen land.

Deuteronomy 31:7-8 *"Then Moses summoned Joshua and said to him in the presence of all Israel, 'Be strong and courageous, for you must go with this people into the land that the*

LORD swore to their forefathers to give them, and you must divide it among them as their inheritance. The LORD himself goes before you and will be with you; he will never leave you nor forsake you. Do not be afraid; do not be discouraged.' "

Joshua 1:1-5 *"After the death of Moses the servant of the LORD, the LORD said to Joshua son of Nun, Moses' aide: 'Moses my servant is dead. Now then, you and all these people, get ready to cross the Jordan River into the land I am about to give to them—to the Israelites. I will give you every place where you set your foot, as I promised Moses…As I was with Moses, so I will be with you; I will never leave you nor forsake you.'"*

Take some time to read Acts 27:1-28:1, when Paul and other prisoners were put on a ship to go to Italy. During the trip, Paul realized they were all in danger, and the following happened in verses 27:10-11: *"So Paul warned them, 'Men, I can see that our voyage is going to be disastrous and bring great loss to ship and cargo and our own lives also.' But the centurion, instead of listening to what Paul said, followed the advice of the pilot and the owner of the ship."* Sure enough a storm came, and in verse 27:21, *"Paul said, 'Men you should have taken my advice not to sail from Crete; then you would have spared yourselves this damage and loss.'"*

Don't be a know-it-all, even if you do know more about your sport than your coach. Be helpful to your coaches and act as a resource for them. Many coaches are volunteers and just want to help. Some coaches may welcome your help and others may not. However it is your choice if you make the situation better or worse. Be *willing* and *teachable*. Many things can be learned from others, both older and younger. Don't be like hard clay. Choose to be soft, moldable clay. Always strive to better yourself.

Do your best to see the *whole picture*. Most importantly, *choose* to see the best in your situation. There are many ways to describe a situation. Look at a glass of water that is filled half way. You could describe this glass as "half full" or "half empty." You are accurately describing the glass of water no matter which description you choose. However, if you see the glass as half full, then you are choosing to see the good rather than the bad. You are an optimist! If you see the glass as half empty, you are choosing to focus on the negative part. If you continue to do so, and be a pessimist, then you are setting yourself up for one unhappy life. See more about this in Chapter 36 about "Attitude."

With respect to our coaches, we should have positive attitudes:

1. Be teachable.

Psalm 25:4 *"Show me your ways, O Lord , teach me your paths."*

Proverbs 16:20 *"Whoever gives heed to instruction prospers, and blessed is he who trusts in the Lord."*

Proverbs 2:2-5 ***"Turning*** *your ear to wisdom and* ***applying*** *your heart to understanding, and if you* ***call out*** *for insight and* ***cry aloud*** *for understanding, and if you* ***look*** *for it as for silver and* ***search*** *for it as for hidden treasure, then you will understand the fear of the Lord and find the knowledge of God."* (Notice all the action words. We need to have a good attitude when we are learning, and also follow through with good actions.)

Proverbs 19:20 *"Listen to advice and accept instruction, and in the end you will be wise."*

2. Don't argue or complain, but accept discipline from your coaches.

Philippians 2:14 *"Do everything without complaining or arguing."*

Proverbs 15:22 *"Plans fail for lack of counsel, but with many advisers they succeed."*

Proverbs 12:1 *"Whoever loves discipline loves knowledge, but he who hates correction is stupid."*

3. Submit to and obey your coaches.

Ephesians 6:5-6 *"Slaves, obey your earthly masters with respect and fear, and with sincerity of heart, just as you would obey Christ. Obey them not only to win their favor when their eye is on you, but like slaves of Christ, doing the will of God from your heart."*

Colossians 3:22 *"Slaves, obey your earthly masters in everything; and do it, not only when their eye is on you and to win their favor, but with sincerity of heart and reverence for the Lord."*

Romans 13:1-2 *"Everyone must submit himself to the governing authorities, for there is no authority except that which God has established. The authorities that exist have been established by God. Consequently, he who rebels against the authority is rebelling against what God has instituted, and those who do so will bring judgment on themselves."*

Even if you don't like your coach's personality, it is in your best interest to listen to instructions and obey them. Most coaches have been around longer in the athletics world than you have. They also tend to see the whole picture when many athletes aren't able to do so. We need to respect others in almost every situation, and this includes the coaches that aren't that good. In doing so, you will make many lives much easier, including your own.

"For peace of mind, resign as general manager of the universe."
Larry Eisenberg

"Don't bother to give God instructions; just report for duty."
Corrie ten boom, Holocaust survivor and prevailer

"I treat my coaches as though they are my parents. During the season I would see my coach more often than my parents."
Melissa Budde, high school volleyball MVP

Personal Notes and Ideas

1. How can I help my coaches?

2. How can I encourage my teammates to help our coaches?

3. What can I do to be teachable/coachable?

4. How can I encourage my teammates to be teachable/coachable?

5. What can I do to refrain from arguing or complaining?

6. What would Jesus do?

7. How do the Bible verses in this chapter help me to relate to my coaches? Are there other verses that can help me be an ultimate athlete to my coaches?

Bad
Coaches

"For God did not give us a spirit of timidity, but a spirit of power, of love, and of self-discipline."

2 Timothy 1:7

Person in the Bible

King Ahab represents a bad coach. I Kings 16:30-33 *"Ahab son of Omri did more evil in the eyes of the Lord than any of those before him. He not only considered it trivial to commit the sins...began to serve Baal and worship him. He set up an altar for Baal...did more to provoke the Lord, the God of Israel, to anger than did all the kings of Israel before him."*

An example of a person in the Bible who defied a bad coach is Daniel. Daniel respectfully stood up for himself and his faith. Let's assume that Daniel is the athlete and the administrators are the bad coaches. King Darius represents the good coach.

Daniel 6:3-6 *"Now Daniel so distinguished himself among the administrators and the satraps by his exceptional qualities that the king planned to set him over the whole kingdom. At this, the administrators and the satraps tried to find grounds for charges against Daniel in his conduct of government affairs, but they were unable to do so. They could find no corruption in him, because he was trustworthy and neither corrupt nor negligent. Finally these men said, 'We will never find any basis for charges against this man Daniel unless it has something to do with the law of his God.'"*

The administrators asked King Darius to make a new law. A person praying to any god or man, instead of the king, would be thrown into the lions' den. When Daniel heard about this, he continued to pray three times a day as he always did before. The men found Daniel praying. They told King Darius and forced the king to follow through.

Daniel 6:14-24 *"When the king heard this, he was greatly distressed; he was determined to rescue Daniel and made every effort until sundown to save him… So the king gave the order, and they brought Daniel and threw him into the lions' den. The king said to Daniel, 'May your God, whom you serve continually, rescue you'…At the first light of dawn, the king got up and hurried to the lions' den. When he came near the den, he called to Daniel in an anguished voice, 'Daniel, servant of the living God, has your God, whom you serve continually, been able to rescue you from the lions?' Daniel answered, 'O king, live forever! My God sent his angel, and he shut the mouths of the lions. They have not hurt me, because I was found innocent in his sight. Nor have I ever done any wrong before you, O king'… At the king's command, the men who had falsely accused Daniel were brought in and thrown into the lions' den, along with their wives and children."*

Dealing with a bad coach is not easy. First, you must define what the coach does that you consider inappropriate. Then categorize this fault, and act accordingly. If your coach is sloppy, lazy, arrives late, only works with the talented people, has favorites, isn't always fair…it is normal to be frustrated. You don't have to agree with his or her actions, but treating them with respect is crucial. You might have personal differences, and sometimes those need to be put aside. Your coach may be good at teaching technique, writing workouts, creating lineups... This particular coach may be able to physically fine-tune you for your sport, but obviously not socially, emotionally, or spiritually. There should be other people on your team who can help you in those areas.

If your coach is cruel, obnoxious, says things that are personally degrading, touches athletes incorrectly, cheats...then something *must* be said. This person is not an appropriate role model for athletes, even if he or she teaches good physical technique.

As an athlete in a tough situation, it is important to turn your situation around. In other words take a lemon and make some lemonade. Joe had both good and bad coaches. One of his bad coaches would drink so much alcohol on away trips that he had a hard time getting to finals the next day. Another coach would always punish their team if they lost, even if the athletes had performed their best. Other coaches would cheat, be grouchy with everyone except their favorites, or ignore the others.

After competing for years in tennis, Joe decided that he wanted to be a coach. As he was pondering his philosophy of coaching, he decided to *not* do what his bad coaches had done. So as he started his coaching career, he made sure that he didn't make any of those mistakes. After five years of coaching, an athlete asked Joe which one of his coaches was his example for his coaching style. This athlete really liked how Joe coached. Joe thought about it first and then said, "I didn't have many good coaches, but I just make sure that I don't coach like all of the bad ones that I have had." This is a great example of turning a lemon into lemonade.

Joe's story teaches us how one can benefit from bad coaching in the long run. What about the present situation? Ask God for advice! James 1:5 *"If any of you lacks wisdom, he should ask God, who gives generously to all without finding fault, and it will be given to him."*

If you have a coach who doesn't really know your sport, you and the other athletes can coach and help each other. Don't be obvious or rude to your coaches, because they may be trying very hard. They may be volunteer parents who are filling in due to lack of qualified coaches. 1 Timothy 4:12 *"Don't let anyone look down on you because you are young, but set an example for the believers in speech, in life, in love, in faith and in purity."*

Your coach may have favorites, and it is very obvious. Maybe your coach is very negative and no one does anything right. Then it will be up to the athletes to build each others' self-concepts and be encouraging.

If your coach is possessed with winning, then reassure each other that winning is not the only thing. Be proud of yourselves for trying to do your best, even if you lose.

If you have a coach who is very abusive and tends to say awful things to the athletes, document everything and write down the inappropriate behavior. Make sure that you write the date and specifically what happened. Don't start a gossip ring and attempt a military coup. Go to the source! Ask the team captains, or some parents, to go with you and talk to the coach. This may be scary, but it is the *right* thing to do! If your coach doesn't attempt to improve his/her behavior, then go to their bosses. This coach may be asked to leave. Make sure that your intentions are good ones. This can *not* be a personal vendetta against a coach that you don't like. This coach has to have done things wrong, and you need to have it documented. Then follow through in a respectful manner. Here are examples of setting boundaries:

Psalm 1:1 *"Blessed is the man who does not walk in the counsel of the wicked or stand in the way of sinners or sit in the seat of mockers."*

Psalm 18:26 *"To the pure you show yourself pure, but to the crooked you show yourself shrewd."*

1 Corinthians 5:11-13 *"But now I am writing you that you must not associate with anyone who calls himself a brother but is sexually immoral or greedy, an idolater or a slanderer, a drunkard or a swindler. With such a man do not even eat...God will judge those outside. Expel the wicked man from among you."*

No one is perfect, and we need to look at the good side as well as the bad side of each person. No coach will ever be perfect—coaches are human beings too. Unfortunately some athletes forget that, and do a lot of damage to the team. Be willing to overlook some character flaws and look at the whole picture.

Be a positive force on your team. Romans 12:18 *"If it is possible, as far as it depends on you, live at peace with everyone."* Romans 14:19 *"Let us therefore make every effort to do what leads to peace and to mutual edification."* (Edification means building each other up.)

It is a delicate balance between enforcing your boundaries and loving your enemies. You may need to have strict boundaries, but we are also called to love others. Make sure that you love *them*, but dislike their *actions*. Luke 6:27-29 *"But I tell you who hear me: Love your enemies, do good to those who hate you, bless those who curse you, pray for those who mistreat you. If someone strikes you on one cheek, turn to him the other also. If someone takes your cloak, do not stop him from taking your tunic. Love your enemies…"*

If the coach is abusive, then you need to take the correct steps in finding a new coach. John12:35-36 *"The man who walks in darkness does not know where he is going. Put your trust in the light while you have it, so that you may become sons of light."*

Matthew 24:13 *"But he who stands firm to the end will be saved."*

You will also need to forgive them. Matthew 18:21-22 *"Then Peter came to Jesus and asked, 'Lord, how many times shall I forgive my brother when he sins against me? Up to seven times?' Jesus answered, 'I tell you, not seven times, but seventy-seven times.'"*

> *"Learn from the mistakes of others…you can't live long enough to make them all yourself."*
> Unknown

> *"Forgive out of compassion for yourself."*
> The Author

> *"It takes a lot of emotional and psychological energy to keep a wound open and keep a grudge alive...The longer I allow the wound to fester, the more bitterness, anger, and self-pity poison my blood and eat my heart."*
>
> Rev. Albert Haase

Personal Notes and Ideas

1. What can I do so that I can maintain a relationship with a coach I don't like?

2. How can I turn a lemon into lemonade?

3. How can I encourage my teammates to make the best out of a situation when a coach is bad?

4. What bothers me about my coach, and how can I positively deal with my frustrations?

5. What can I learn from Joe's story?

6. What would Jesus do?

7. How do the Bible verses in this chapter help me deal with bad coaches? Are there any other verses that can help me to be an ultimate athlete with respect to bad coaches?

More verses on this subject are found in:

Proverbs 15:32
Proverbs 15:5
1 Thessalonians 5:12-13
John 14:15-16
1 Peter 2:18-21
1 Peter 2:13-14
Hebrews 12:5-11
Proverbs 23:12

Teammates

"Then make my joy complete by being like-minded, having the same love, being one in spirit and purpose. Do nothing out of selfish ambition of vain conceit, but in humility consider others better than yourselves. Each of you should look not only to your own interests, but also to the interests of others. ...Do everything without complaining or arguing, so that you may become blameless and pure, children of God..."

Philippians 2:2-4, 14

Person in the Bible

The disciples are an excellent example of how a group of men from various backgrounds, possessing different talents and having diverse personalities, can come together for one cause.

I. We are all diverse, but we need each other here on earth.

1 Corinthians 12:12-26 *"The body is a unit, though it is made up of many parts; and though all its parts are many, they form*

one body... And if the ear should say, 'Because I am not an eye, I do not belong to the body,' it would not for that reason cease to be part of the body. If the whole body were an eye, where would the sense of hearing be? If the whole body were an ear, where would the sense of smell be? But in fact God has arranged the parts in the body, every one of them, just as he wanted them to be. If they were all one part, where would the body be? As it is, there are many parts, but one body. The eye cannot say to the hand, 'I don't need you!' And the head cannot say to the feet, 'I don't need you!' On the contrary, those parts of the body that seem to be weaker are indispensable, and the parts that we think are less honorable we treat with special honor. And the parts that are unpresentable are treated with special modesty, while our presentable parts need no special treatment. But God has combined the members of the body and has given greater honor to the parts that lacked it, so that there should be no division in the body, but that its parts should have equal concern for each other. If one part suffers, every part suffers with it; if one part is honored, every part rejoices with it."

Genesis 2:18 "*The Lord God said, 'It is not good for the man to be alone. I will make a helper suitable for him.'*" (God decided to give us other people to help us with our journey of life on earth.)

Ecclesiastes 4:9-10 "*Two are better than one, because they have a good return for their work: If one falls down, his friend can help him up...*" So if two are better than one, we can get more done if we choose to combine our energies.

Matthew 18:20 "*For where two or three come together in my name, there am I with them.*" He was expecting us to work together in groups.

2. Communication is the key, even if you compete in an individual sport.

 a. Be an encourager, not a destroyer. Don't be picky and tear down your teammates. Constructively help each other and

321

always point out good things. Ninety-nine percent of the time, everyone on your team is trying to do their best, and no one is trying to sabotage the game. Think positive, believe in your teammates, and communicate positively.

Matthew 7:1-5 *"Do not judge, or you too will be judged. For in the same way you judge others, you will be judged, and with the measure you use, it will be measured to you. Why do you look at the speck of sawdust in your brother's eye and pay no attention to the plank in your own eye? How can you say to your brother, 'Let me take the speck out of your eye,' when all the time there is a plank in your own eye? You hypocrite, first take the plank out of your own eye, and then you will see clearly to remove the speck from your brother's eye."*

b. Accept that you have made an error. Many athletes will say "my bad" to show that they accept the fact that they made a mistake. But let's take it one step further. Let's use words that are more positive. For instance you can say "I will" or "will do." This stands for "I will do better." Many team sports need code words. Keep them positive!

3. We can be the nuclear glue to keep the team together when we model the love of Christ.

1 Corinthians 13:4-7 is great advice to help any type of team work together, enjoy each other's company, and accomplish something. It talks about all the qualities that love can offer us. If we choose to abide by these, we will have a much better team in many different ways. There should be less antagonism and fewer fights on *our* part. We cannot control the actions of others, but by our good actions and attitude we can encourage others to do the same. Hopefully our good character will become contagious to others on the team.

1 Corinthians 13:4-7 *"Love is patient, love is kind. It does not envy, it does not boast, it is not proud. It is not rude, it is not self-seeking, it is not easily angered, it keeps no record of wrongs. Love does not delight in evil but rejoices with the truth. It always protects, always trusts, always hopes, always perseveres."*

Romans 12:10,16 *"Be devoted to one another in brotherly love. Honor one another above yourselves… Live in harmony with one another. Do not be proud, but be willing to associate with people of low position. Do not be conceited."*

2 Corinthians 2:15 *"For we are to God the aroma of Christ among those who are being saved and those who are perishing."*

4. Handling the negative teammates.

What about those antagonistic teammates—those teammates who are really a challenge to love? They continue to be self-centered, act destructively, say mean things, and have a negative attitude. We need to love them, but not necessarily agree with their actions. Refer to chapter 39 about "Abusive Situations" for more information.

> *"In spite of everything, I still believe that people are really good at heart."*
> Anne Frank, diary entry, 1944

> *"We must learn to live together as brothers or perish together as fools."*
> Martin Luther King, Jr.

> *"Teammates are very important, because if your team gets along and has common goals, you will achieve more."*
> Melissa Budde, high school volleyball MVP

Personal Notes and Ideas

1. How can I be a good teammate?

2. How can I continue to communicate with my teammates?
   A. At practice

B. At meets

C. Off the field

3. What are some positive code words for my team and sport?

4. How can I maintain a relationship with a teammate I don't respect?

5. How can I be a good ambassador and example for Jesus Christ?

6. How can I encourage my teammates to also be good teammates?

7. What would Jesus do?

8. How do the Bible verses in this chapter help me? Are there any other verses that help me be an ultimate teammate?

Team Managers

"Love is patient, love is kind. It does not envy, it does not boast, it is not proud."

1 Corinthians 13:4

Person in the Bible

Peter really stepped up to the plate after Jesus' death. He started speaking in front of crowds of people so that Jesus' ministry would prevail. Acts 1:5 *"In those days Peter stood up among the believers (a group numbering about a hundred and twenty)"* Acts 2:14 *"Then Peter stood up with the Eleven, raised his voice and addressed the crowd:'Fellow Jews and all of you who live in Jerusalem, let me explain this to you; listen carefully to what I say.'"*

Team managers are vital to the success of an athletic season. Record keeping, statistics, paper work, and odd jobs all need to be done. Coaches can be buried in this work—giving them less time to do active coaching. Team managers take up the slack for the coaches and athletes. They are a very important part of the team. Just as important as the top athlete! They need to be included in all team activities, cheers, and meetings. They need to be respected as a team member and not just a slave who caters to everyone's needs.

Many times athletes tend to use managers to get what they need. Remember there is no letter "I" in the word TEAM. Therefore as athletes we need to think about what *we* can do to help the managers. Help them put away the equipment, take statistics, and do other odd jobs. We need to make them feel that they are an important part of the team. Relationships are like bank accounts. If you keep withdrawing money from your account, without depositing any money, you will become bankrupt. It is the same with relationships. If you keep taking and not giving to others, your friendship account will also become empty.

1 Peter 2:17 *"Show proper respect to everyone."*

1 Thessalonians 5:12 *"Now we ask you, brothers, to respect those who work hard among you."*

> *"Let every man be respected as an individual and no man idolized."*
>
> Albert Einstein

Personal Notes and Ideas

1. How can I help my team manager?

2. How can I encourage my teammates to help make our manager feel like a part of the team?

3. What does this statement mean to me? "There is no letter 'I' in the word TEAM."

4. What would our team be like if we didn't have a manager?

5. What would Jesus do?

6. How do the Bible verses in this chapter help me to relate to my team manager? Are there other verses that can help me be an ultimate athlete to my team manager?

Fans

"For who makes you different from anyone else? What do you have that you did not receive? And if you did receive it, why do you boast as though you did not?"

1 Corinthians 4:7 (This is a message for all athletes.)

Person in the Bible
Followers of Jesus. Crowds of people were always following Jesus. One time, He used five loaves of bread and two fish to feed five thousand people.

We are all human beings! God loves each one of us. There is no such thing as a super human being. Yes, there are people who will make better choices in life. However, the truth remains that we are all human beings. Therefore, "Do unto others as you would have them do unto you." Respect is of utmost importance if we are to coexist peacefully on this earth. Having said that, athletes are not better than non-athletes. Athletes choose to use their time differently and that is all.

So all of us in the athletic community should be respectful to everyone. This can be done if each athlete practices true humility. Being humble is imperative if we want to be more like Jesus.

327

Proverbs. 27:1-2 *"Do not boast about tomorrow, for you do not know what a day may bring forth. Let another praise you, and not your own mouth; someone else, and not your own lips."*

James 3:13-14 *"Who is wise and understanding among you? Let him show it by his good life, by deeds done in the humility that comes from wisdom. But if you harbor bitter envy and selfish ambition in your hearts, do not boast about it or deny the truth."*

So when our fans surround us or want to talk with us, we need to be sincerely humble. Jesus treated his fans with compassion. He took time and listened to them. He never thought that He was too good to talk to anyone. If Jesus were an athlete today, He would:

• Take time to talk with fans, and find out about them.
• Sign an autograph with a good attitude.
• Wave to the fans, and make them feel appreciated.
• Thank the fans whenever being interviewed or speaking publicly.
• No matter the situation, always give the glory to God in heaven. Without our Maker in life, we would not be here.
• Be compassionate.

As human beings, we will be held accountable for every word we say. Matt 12:36-37 *"But I tell you that men will have to give account on the day of judgment for every careless word they have spoken. For by your words you will be acquitted, and by your words you will be condemned."* This holds true for athletes too. Athletes do not have any special permission from God to say things that boost their egos or to tear down another person.

A great athlete and humanitarian, Roberto Clemente, spent his time celebrating in the streets with fans after he won his first World Series in professional baseball. He didn't go to the locker room, because he felt that he needed to be with his loyal fans and thank them. Roberto was an incredible role model for athletes. Among his list of achievements, he helped fight racism in professional sports, paid for many poor childrens' surgeries, and led a delegation of disaster relief to Nicaragua after a devastating earthquake.

> *"Remember that your fans are watching you. Your reaction after a great competition or a struggling moment reflect your relationship with God."*
>
> Joe Thiel, collegiate athlete and coach

Personal Notes and Ideas

1. How can I show respect for the fans?

2. How can I encourage my teammates to treat the fans with respect?

3. What can I do to genuinely stay humble?

4. What can I learn from the way Jesus would treat His fans?

5. What can I do to be a great humanitarian like Roberto Clemente?

6. What would Jesus do?

7. How do the Bible verses in this chapter help me? Are there other verses that can help me be an ultimate athlete with the fans?

Media

"For who makes you different from anyone else? What do you have that you did not receive? And if you did receive it, why do you boast as though you did not?"

1 Corinthians 4:7

Person in the Bible

The Pharisees were people who chose to continually find fault in many people. They chose to torment Jesus with their righteous attitudes.

Luke 15:2 *"But the Pharisees and the teachers of the law muttered, 'This man welcomes sinners and eats with them.'"*

Luke 11:53-54. *"When Jesus left there, the Pharisees and the teachers of the law began to oppose him fiercely and to besiege him with questions, waiting to catch him in something he might say."*

he media can be your best friend or your worst enemy. The presence of the media is a fact of life, whether we like it or not. Be very careful what you do and say. With our technology today, anything can be recorded and then replayed, and replayed. It can certainly come back to haunt you. Athletes live in a fish bowl, because everything can be seen and heard by all. It isn't necessarily fair, but it comes with the territory. One bad action or word can cause an athlete a lot of damage, because the media is there to record it. Think before you talk, and don't let your emotions get the best of you. Yes, we are humans and we make mistakes, but be aware that your every move is being watched.

For important events, a reporter will be right there after the race, game, event, or competition. This can be frustrating if the athlete has just made a huge mistake. After performing terribly, most people don't want to talk to anyone, especially the media. However, the media will be right there asking you tons of questions. Some times the questions are out of line and ridiculous. However, you are in control of your *attitudes* and *actions*. So be prepared for times like this. Practice responding to the media in all situations. Have some answers ready. During times like these, you will need to use your intellect instead of your emotions.

Another important factor is that you not just representing yourself. It could be your nation, school, team, or God. Use this time to let people know that you are striving to become an ultimate athlete. Athletes that are well-rounded have their lives in perspective, and know there is more to life than just athletics. This is your time to shine! Don't be fake or false, because that will hurt you in the long run, too. Be honest, talk in a straightforward manner, be polite, and do the best that you can. Those of you who have made a commitment to Christ can use this time to show people that your faith is helping you to deal with all the situations in life. 2 Corinthians 3:5 *"Such confidence as this is ours through Christ before God. Not that we are competent in ourselves to claim anything for ourselves, but our competence comes from God."*

For the most part, your audience or fans don't really know you. Use these media opportunities to let the general public know who you are and what you stand for. Just remember you can talk all you want, but *actions speak louder than words!*

1 Corinthians 13:4 *"Love is patient, love is kind. It does not envy, it does not boast, it is not proud."*

1 Peter 5:5-6 *"Young men, in the same way be submissive to those who are older. All of you, clothe yourselves with humility toward one another, because, 'God opposes the proud but gives grace to the humble.' Humble yourselves, therefore, under God's mighty hand, that he may lift you up in due time."*

Proverbs 25:27 *"It is not good to eat too much honey, nor is it honorable to seek one's own honor."*

Philippians 2:3-8 *"Do nothing out of selfish ambition or vain conceit, but in humility consider others better than yourselves. Each of you should look not only to your own interests, but also to the interests of others. Your attitude should be the same as that of Christ Jesus: Who, being in very nature God, did not consider equality with God something to be grasped, but made himself nothing, taking the very nature of a servant, being made in human likeness. And being found in appearance as a man, he humbled himself and became obedient to death—even death on a cross!"*

"My obligation is to do the right thing. The rest is in God's hands."
Martin Luther King, Jr.

"Be confident, but not boastful. Talk more about your teammates. Whenever you receive recognition, someone gave you the opportunity."
Glen Mason, head football coach, University of Minnesota

Personal Notes and Ideas

1. What must I do so that the media is helpful to me and not hurtful?

2. How can I prepare myself for interviews by the media.
after a great competition

after performing poorly

3. How can I encourage my teammates to speak appropriately to the media?

4. How can I share my faith through the media?

5. What would Jesus do?

6. How do the Bible verses in this chapter help me? Are there any other verses that help me be an ultimate athlete with regard to the media?

Recruiters

"But I tell you that men will have to give account on the day of judgment for every careless word they have spoken. For by your words you will be acquitted, and by your words you will be condemned."

Matthew 12:36-37

Person in the Bible

John the Baptist was the man who prepared the way for Jesus. He was definitely hoping to recruit more people to come to know, love, and accept Jesus as their savior. Let's see what Jesus had to say about him. Luke 7:27-28 *"I will send my messenger ahead of you, who will prepare your way before you. I tell you, among those born of women there is no one greater than John; yet the one who is least in the kingdom of God is greater than he."* For more information about John the Baptist, read the third chapter of Matthew.

ecruiters are another fact of life in sports. It is exciting to know that someone wants you to compete for them. It makes you feel good, because you know that all of your hard work has paid off. The most important thing that you can do is to *be yourself*. Don't try to be like anyone else, and make sure that you promote yourself correctly. Yes, there is stress with recruiters. Some athletes really depend on a scholarship to pay for their college expenses. Other athletes have dreams of playing with the pros and will do almost anything to achieve that goal. If you choose to exaggerate, you will need to live up to all of those falsehoods. That is very tough to do, if not impossible.

Matthew 23:12 *"For whoever exalts himself will be humbled, and whoever humbles himself will be exalted."*

Proverbs 11:2 *"When pride comes, then comes disgrace, but with humility comes wisdom."*

Proverbs 16:18 *"Pride goes before destruction, a haughty spirit before a fall."*

Be humble and allow God to take care of business. God loves you and has a plan for you. He will show you what to do for your future. All you need to do is to trust Him. Matthew 6:33 *"But seek first his kingdom and his righteousness, and all these things will be given to you as well."* Remember when God closes a door, He always opens another window. Refer to the following verses about humility.

Acts 10:25-26 *"As Peter entered the house, Cornelius met him and fell at his feet in reverence. But Peter made him get up. 'Stand up,' he said, 'I am only a man myself.'"*

1 Corinthians 13:4 *"Love is patient, love is kind. It does not envy, it does not boast, it is not proud."*

James 3:13-14 *"Who is wise and understanding among you? Let him show it by his good life, by deeds done in the humility that comes from wisdom. But if you harbor bitter envy and selfish ambition in your hearts, do not boast about it or deny the truth."*

1 Peter 5:5-6 *"Young men, in the same way be submissive to those who are older. All of you, clothe yourselves with humility*

toward one another, because, 'God opposes the proud but gives grace to the humble.' Humble yourselves, therefore, under God's mighty hand, that he may lift you up in due time."

Let your recruiters know about other important issues in your life. If you are talking to a college recruiter, make sure that you emphasize your studies and find out what the college can do for you academically. With respect to professional sports, make sure that you find out about the team's program and not just focus on the money issue. After finding out the practical issues of the prospective team, take it a step further and proclaim your faith. In a kind and gentle manner, let your recruiters know where you stand. If there is any boasting to do, we should boast about what the Lord has done in our lives. 2 Corinthians 1:12 *"Now this is our boast: Our conscience testifies that we have conducted ourselves in the world, and especially in our relations with you, in the holiness and sincerity that are from God. We have done so not according to worldly wisdom but according to God's grace."*

Finally be careful with recruiters. They will paint a beautiful picture so that they can get you to come and compete for their team. Make sure that they are genuine. Do your homework on the prospective team. Talk with other people who are currently playing on the team. What are the *real* conditions? Talk with your coaches, your parents, and your pastor. Make sure that you have a chance to see the college, the town, the living accommodations, and the sports facility before you make any decisions. Make sure that you pray about your decision and listen carefully to what God has to say.

> *"People who lie will need to have a good memory."*
>
> Unknown

> *"It is unwise to be too sure of one's own wisdom. It is healthy to be reminded that the strongest might weaken and the wisest might err."*
>
> Gandhi

> "It is far more impressive when others discover your good qualities without your help."
>
> Miss Manners

> "It was pride that changed angels into devils; it is humility that makes men as angels."
>
> Saint Augustine

Personal Notes and Ideas

1. How can I show respect to my recruiters?

2. Why is boasting about my accomplishments not the best thing to do?

3. Humility is important to God—why should it be important to me?

4. How can I encourage my teammates to be humble with recruiters?

5. What non-sports issues are important to me that I should ask the recruiter?

6. What can I do to if I get too much pressure from a recruiter?

7. Who can give me great advice about my upcoming decision?

8. What would Jesus do?

9. How do the Bible verses in this chapter help me? Are there other verses that can help me be an ultimate athlete with respect to recruiters?

Parents

"Children, obey your parents in the Lord, for this is right. 'Honor your father and mother'— which is the first commandment with a promise—'that it may go well with you and that you may enjoy long life on the earth.' Fathers, do not exasperate your children; instead, bring them up in the training and instruction of the Lord."

Ephesians 6:1-4

his chapter will be divided into two parts. The first part talks about how to be a parent of an athlete. The second part is about how athletes should relate to their parents.

1. For parents

Person in the Bible

Elizabeth and Zechariah were two people who really respected what family was all about. They needed to wait a long time until they were able to have their own son, John the Baptist. Go to the first chapter of Luke to read about their story.

1 Timothy 3:4-5 *"He must manage his own family well and see that his children obey him with proper respect, (If anyone does not know how to manage his own family, how can he take care of God's church?)"*

Psalm 127:3-5 *"Sons are a heritage from the Lord, children a reward from him. Like arrows in the hands of a warrior are sons born in one's youth. Blessed is the man whose quiver is full of them."*

Proverbs 23:25 *"May your father and mother be glad; may she who gave you birth rejoice!"*

First and foremost, all parents need to remember that their children are precious gifts from God. It doesn't matter if they are misbehaving or acting appropriately. They are all incredible human beings that should always be treated fairly and with respect. God has given parents the wonderful opportunity of raising children to become contributors to society. It takes a lot of patience, wisdom, forgiveness, faith, and love to be a good parent. It is definitely a very frustrating but most rewarding job. *Positive* discipline is a must!

Proverbs 6:23 *"For these commands are a lamp, this teaching is a light, and the corrections of discipline are the way to life."*

Proverbs 13:24 *"He who spares the rod hates his son, but he who loves him is careful to discipline him."*

Proverbs 19:18 *"Discipline your son, for in that there is hope; do not be a willing party to his death."*

Proverbs 29:17 *"Discipline your son, and he will give you peace; he will bring delight to your soul."*

We all need guidance, but many times the children need more guidance and discipline to keep them on the right track. Positive discipline is telling our children the boundaries, rules, and consequences up front. If their attitudes and actions are opposite to your rules, then they have *chosen* their consequence. In essence, you are not disciplining, because they have chosen their new situation or experience—for example, being sent to the bedroom.

All parents need to be aware that raising athletes can be complicated. Parents want their children to succeed and they will do almost anything to help them. Most parents have good intentions, but they can do more harm than good. Parents need to be parents, and not change roles on their children. Let's look at the CAP triangle. (Coach/Athlete/Parent) The triangle approach is the best way to visualize this idea. The athletes are on top with the coaches and parents supporting them.

Referring to the diagram:

1. The coaches are in charge of coaching the athletes.
   (Designing the workouts, correcting the strokes, choosing
   the team lineup....) The coaches are also responsible for

communicating to the parents how their children are progressing.

2. The parents get the fun task of praising their children for what they have accomplished, and being patient and positive with the whole process. The P for parents stands for *Praise, Patience,* and *Positiveness.* Coaches need to realize that the parents are the experts on their children, and can give the coaches a wealth of pertinent information about their children. (Such as: my child broke his arm last January, my daughter had a very scary experience in the water at age two, my son is dealing with an Attention Deficit Disability, my daughter just witnessed her friend get hit and killed by a driver....) This information is vital for the coaches.

3. The athletes receive praise, coaching techniques, and constructive criticism from the coaches. They should receive praise, patience, and positiveness from the parents.

Young athletes are bombarded daily with peer pressure. It is imperative that parents spend time with their children teaching them how to make the correct decisions in life. At first, the parents set the boundaries for their children. Next, the parents need to take it a step further. They need to train the children how to draw the line. All children will need to learn how to set up their own wise boundaries and follow through with them.

Psalm 78:2-7 *"I will open my mouth in parables, I will utter hidden things, things from of old—what we have heard and known, what our fathers have told us. We will not hide them from their children; we will tell the next generation the praiseworthy deeds of the Lord, his power, and the wonders he has done... which he commanded our forefathers to teach their children, so the next generation would know them, even the children yet to be born, and they in turn would tell their children. Then they would put their trust in God and would not forget his deeds but would keep his commands."*

2. For the children

Person in the Bible
Joseph, son of Jacob. When you read in Genesis 37, you will find out how special Joseph was as a child. He continued to obey his father, even when his brothers didn't. Genesis 37:2 *"Joseph, a young man of seventeen, was tending the flocks with his brothers…and he brought their father a bad report about them."*

Athletes need to realize that their parents have been around a lot longer than they have. Therefore the golden rule is to respect, obey, and recognize that they aren't perfect either. Parents might not know everything, but chances are they do know more than you on most subjects.

1 Peter 5:5-6 *"Young men, in the same way be submissive to those who are older. All of you, clothe yourselves with humility toward one another, because God opposes the proud but gives grace to the humble. Humble yourselves, therefore, under God's mighty hand, that he may lift you up in due time."*

Ephesians 6:1 *"Children, obey your parents in the Lord, for this is right."*

Colossians 3:20 *"Children, obey your parents in everything, for this pleases the Lord."*

Proverbs 15:10 *"Stern discipline awaits him who leaves the path; he who hates correction will die."*

Proverbs 19:27 *"Stop listening to instruction, my son, and you will stray from the words of knowledge."*

Some of you may have overbearing parents, but the majority of the time they mean well. They only want the best for you. Sometimes they can get caught up in the moment and get carried away. There are many reasons for overactive parents. Some parents did not have success in sports when they are younger, so they choose to live through the success of their children. Other parents were sports stars and want their children to follow in their footsteps. Some just want their children to be happy and will do anything so that their child will succeed. The most important thing is to keep all communication open with your parents. Let them know, in a kind manner, if they are becoming overbearing. Let them know that you appreciate their support, and couldn't do it without them. However, they need to let go and leave the coaching up to your coaches.

If parents are abusive, this is a completely different story. Refer to chapter 39 about "Abusive Situations" to learn how to deal with these kind of people.

> *"My parents mean a lot to me, because they are always there to support me in all my sports. They make sure that I know that they are always so proud of my accomplishments."*
> Melissa Budde, high school volleyball MVP

Personal Notes and Ideas

1. How can I help and respect my parents?

2. How can I encourage my teammates to help and respect their parents?

3. How can I prepare myself to be ready if my parents are:
   Pressuring me to perform

   Coaching me

   Reacting negatively to my performance

4. As a parent or a child, what does the CAP triangle mean to me?

5. What would Jesus do?

6. How do the Bible verses help me in this chapter? Are there any other verses that can help me be an ultimate athlete for my parents and God?

Siblings/Family

"Bear with each other and forgive whatever grievances you may have against one another. Forgive as the Lord forgave you."

Colossians 3:13

"Finally, all of you, live in harmony with one another; be sympathetic, love as brothers, be compassionate and humble. Do not repay evil with evil or insult with insult, but with blessing, because to this you were called so that you may inherit a blessing."

1 Peter 3:8-9

Person in the Bible

Jacob's family. The following is a short version of what happened to Jacob's family from Genesis 37 through Genesis 47. Jacob had many sons; however, he favored Joseph because he was born from his once-barren wife. Jacob gave Joseph an amazing coat with many different colors. Obviously the other brothers became very jealous.

1. The jealous brothers tried to kill Joseph, but ended up selling him as a slave.
2. After many hard times, Joseph became governor of the land.
3. There was a big famine and Joseph's brothers went to Egypt to get some grain. They had no idea that Joseph was the governor, nor did they recognize him.
4. When Joseph saw his brothers for the first time he chose to teach them a lesson.
5. The brothers realized that they sinned.
6. The second time, Joseph confronted them and told them the truth about who he was.
7. They reconciled and Joseph chose to take care of his family.

This story shows that families *can* work through problems, personality differences, or betrayal. It is also a story of reconciliation. No family is perfect, and each family is bound to have their struggles. However the moral to the story is to do your best, and to not give up. Work through the issues, and strive to forgive each other. Come to the point where you can take care of each other no matter what happens. Romans 12:16 *"Live in harmony with one another. Do not be proud, but be willing to associate with people of low position. Do not be conceited."*

What are some tips?

Proverbs 15:1 *"A gentle answer turns away wrath, but a harsh word stirs up anger."*

James 5:9 *"Don't grumble against each other, brothers, or you will be judged. The Judge is standing at the door!"*

Ephesians 4:31-32 *"Get rid of all bitterness, rage and anger, brawling and slander, along with every form of malice. Be kind and compassionate to one another, forgiving each other, just as in Christ God forgave you."*

1 Timothy 5:8 *"If anyone does not provide for his relatives, and especially for his immediate family, he has denied the faith and is worse than an unbeliever."*

Satan is the destroyer and always is trying to break up good relationships. Be aware of this. Revelation 9:11 *"They had as king over them the angel of the Abyss, whose name in Hebrew is Abaddon, and in Greek, Apollyon."* (*Abaddon* and *Apollyon* mean "destroyer.")

Athletic families can have more obstacles and challenges in creating a good family environment.

1. One sibling can be better than the other siblings. When the younger ones do better, it can cause jealousy among the older siblings. On the other hand, if the older ones are more talented, then the younger siblings have to live up to their legacy.
2. Schedules are hectic due to practice and competition schedules. Many times it is tough to have a sit-down family dinner.
3. Finances can be tough because of the cost of sports. Parents may need to work more hours, or multiple jobs, to pay for everything.
4. Tragedies and injuries happen all the time in athletics. These situations can tear a family apart, or make them more unified.

Be aware of these potential conflicts!

> *"There are much more important things than sports—family, friends and a life centered on God."*
>
> Jaime Woudstra, student athlete

> *"I believe in the three F's: family, friends and faith."*
>
> John Wooden, UCLA basketball coach, when asked about the key to his success

> *"The bond that links your true family is not one of blood, but of respect and joy in each other's life."*
>
> Richard David Bach, author of *Jonathan Livingston Seagull*

Personal Notes and Ideas

1. How can I be a good family member?

2. How can I continue to help and encourage family unity?

3. What kind of challenges does my family have?

4. How can I be a positive contributor to those family challenges?

5. How can I encourage my teammates to be good family members?

6. What would Jesus do?

7. How do the Bible verses in this chapter relate to my family? Are there other verses that can help me to be an ultimate family member?

Opposing Teams

"But I tell you who hear me: Love your enemies, do good to those who hate you, bless those who curse you, pray for those who mistreat you. If someone strikes you on one cheek, turn to him the other also. If someone takes your cloak, do not stop him from taking your tunic. Give to everyone who asks you, and if anyone takes what belongs to you, do not demand it back. Do to others as you would have them do to you."

Luke 6:27-31

"Show proper respect to everyone: Love the brotherhood of believers, fear God, honor the king."

1 Peter 2:17

Person in the Bible

When Paul was named Saul he did as much destruction to Jesus' ministry as possible. Saul was the number one enemy. However, God stopped him one day and challenged him to change. Saul chose to follow God and this is when

348

his name was changed to Paul. He is responsible for writing most of the New Testament. The disciples had a hard time accepting Paul and believing that he had truly changed. Acts 9:26 *"When he came to Jerusalem, he tried to join the disciples, but they were all afraid of him, not believing that he really was a disciple."*

irst of all, we really need to do our best to be at peace with our enemies. This can be very tough to do, and it takes a lot of patience and forgiveness. Who really are our enemies? They are the people trying to destroy our lives. In wars…there will be enemies. What does God say about enemies? We should be at peace with them and feed them. We need to do our best so that we don't make the situation worse. (However there are times that we need to fight back for self-preservation or freedom. We will also need to use our boundaries with abusive people. See chapter 39) But for the most part, it is our choice whether we make the situation *work* or make it *worse.*

Proverbs 25:21 *"If your enemy is hungry, give him food to eat; if he is thirsty, give him water to drink."*

Proverbs 16:7 *"When a man's ways are pleasing to the Lord, he makes even his enemies live at peace with him."*

Let's put our sports into perspective. The opposing team should not be referred to as our enemies. They are not trying to kill us or take away our freedom. They are here to give us competition and to win the game. Yes, some other teams and coaches cheat, play dirty, or are very horrible. However, we need to look at the other team as a chance for us to compete. If we didn't have other teams, we would not have meets, games, or matches. Could you actually imagine training all year long without one competition? You would have to go to the play-offs without any competition experience. Sure you have practiced, lifted, and stretched, but competing is another mentality.

There are many things that you can do to create a friendly environment during competition. For instance, when you are hosting the competition you can make welcome signs, greet the other team as they arrive, and show them to the locker rooms. For all competitions, whether you are hosting or not, you can shake hands when you arrive, wish them good luck, shake hands at the end, and give the other team a friendly cheer.

Here are some Bible verses:

A. If you are afraid of the other team, because they are the best in the league:

Psalm 118:6 *"The Lord is with me; I will not be afraid. What can man do to me?"*

Psalm 56:3,4,10,11 *"When I am afraid, I will trust in you. In God, whose word I praise, in God I trust; I will not be afraid. What can mortal man do to me? In God, whose word I praise, in the Lord, whose word I praise—in God I trust; I will not be afraid. What can man do to me?"*

B. At the end of the game, be gracious winners and good losers.

Proverbs 24:17,18 *"Do not gloat when your enemy falls; when he stumbles, do not let your heart rejoice, or the Lord will see and disapprove..."*

> *"You can make it work, or you can make it worse."*
>
> The Author

> *"Nothing in life is to be feared. It is only to be understood."*
>
> Madame Marie Curie

Personal Notes and Ideas

1. How can I show respect for the opposing team and coaches?

2. How can I encourage my teammates to treat the other team with respect?

3. What can I do to help the other team if my team is hosting the competition?

4. What can I do if I get fearful because the other team is very powerful?

5. What can I do to be a gracious winner and a good loser?

6. What would Jesus do?

7. How do the Bible verses in this chapter help me? Are there other verses that can help me be an ultimate athlete to the opposing team?

Team Spirit, Sacrifice, and Unity

eam spirit, sacrifice, and unity are the keys to success. All athletes need to be selfless and put others first! It is a real shame when a team has a ton of talent, but doesn't know how to work together as a team. This happens because there are too many egos that get in the way. According to Dot Richards, who won a gold medal in 1996 with the women's softball team, "I know because of my faith in God that everything happens for a reason. There is a destiny for each of us. In life's journey, how many lives can we affect in a positive way? Life isn't about one person—me, or you—it's about all of us and how we can learn to lift other people up. That's what really makes life worth living and what gives us purpose on earth. I hope when my days are done that people can look and say that I have made a difference in the lives of many people."

Let's look into these three important team issues:

1. Team spirit

1 Thessalonians. 5:11 *"Therefore encourage one another and build each other up, just as in fact you are doing."*

Person in the Bible

Timothy was known as the encourager. The following verses are from a letter from Paul to the Philippians. Philippians 2:19-22 *"I hope in the Lord Jesus to send Timothy to you soon, that I also may be cheered when I receive news about you. I have no one else like him, who takes a genuine interest in your welfare. For everyone looks out for his own interests, not those of Jesus Christ. But you know that Timothy has proved himself, because as a son with his father he has served with me in the work of the gospel."*

It is imperative that we choose to build people up, rather than tear them down. This is not only true for our athletics, but for every aspect of life. We are human beings and we don't always perform perfectly. As we live our lives, we make bad decisions and mistakes, or hurt each other. Most of the time these mistakes are unintentional or happen from lack of experience. However, each and every day we need to react to these mistakes whether it is our fault or not. We can be vengeful and cruel, or we can try to be supportive of everyone involved. By *choosing* to be supportive, we can all learn from our mistakes and move on with life. We all need encouragement on a daily basis.

1 Corinthians 13:5 *"It is not rude, it is not self-seeking, it is not easily angered, it keeps no record of wrongs."*

Living Bible Translation—Proverbs 16:15 *"When a king's face brightens, it means life; his favor is like a rain cloud in spring."* (A smile goes a long way and has much benefit. Author's translation.)

Ephesians 4:29 *"Do not let any unwholesome talk come out of your mouths, but only what is helpful for building each others up according to their needs, and that it may benefit those who listen."*

Romans 12:8 *"If it is encouraging, let him encourage; if it is contributing to the needs of others, let him give generously; if it is leadership, let him govern diligently; if it is showing mercy, let him do it cheerfully."*

Romans 15:2 *"Each of us should please his neighbor for his good, to build him up."*

> *"I can live two months on a good compliment."*
> Mark Twain

> *"Our job is not to straighten each other out but to help each other up."*
> Neva Coyle

Extra verses
2 Corinthians 10:8
Hebrew 10:24,25
Proverbs 15:1
Luke 6:37-38

2. Team sacrifice

1 John 3:16 *"This is how we know what love is: Jesus Christ laid down his life for us. And we ought to lay down our lives for our brothers."*

Person in the Bible
Jesus sacrificed his life, for our sins. He made no mistakes but He gave up His chance to live a full life on this earth. John 15:13 *"Greater love has no one than this, that he lay down his life for his friends."*

As human beings, and especially as athletes, we have a hard time seeing the big picture. We get frustrated if we get less playing time, have to play a different position, or have to compete in our least favorite event. There is no letter "I" in the word TEAM! Our individual goals have to take second place to the team goals. Therefore the competition lineup may be different. Coaches need to do what is best for the team. They also try hard to satisfy the athletes, but the team comes first. Sometimes coaches need to make some tough decisions! However you are in control of *your* attitude and actions. Even though the decision might not be in your favor, it is your choice to help or hurt the team. Pouting, arguing, and complaining have no place in the athletic field. Working together, encouraging and supporting one another is crucial for a team to survive and thrive.

A. Good example

Philippians 2:2-4,11 *"Then make my joy complete by being like-minded, having the same love, being one in spirit and purpose. Do nothing out of selfish ambition or vain conceit, but in humility consider others better than yourselves. Each of you should not look only into your own interests, but also the interests of others... Do everything without complaining or arguing."*

B. Bad example

Mark 9:33-34 *"They came to Capernaum. When he was in the house, he asked them, 'What were you arguing about on the road?' But they kept quiet because on the way they had argued about who was the greatest."*

2 Corinthians 12:20 *"For I am afraid that when I come I may not find you as I want you to be, and you may not find me as you want me to be. I fear that there may be quarreling, jealousy, outbursts of anger, factions, slander, gossip, arrogance and disorder."*

The beauty of being on a team is that we are all unique and can offer our different talents to make the team better. Some of us are faster, more flexible, more outgoing, or more understanding. Whatever your gift may be, you need to share it with your teammates. Romans 12:4-5 *"Just as each of us has one body with many members, and these members do not all have the same function, so in*

Christ we who are many form one body, and each member belongs to all the others. "

But even though we are different we can be one team with one purpose. Read Nehemiah, chapter 3, in the Old Testament. The Jerusalem wall needed to be rebuilt, and everyone contributed in a different way to finish the wall. Everyone used their own talents and strengths to make a part of the wall.

Acts 4:32 *"All the believers were one in heart and mind. No one claimed that any of his possessions was his own, but they shared everything they had."*

Ephesians 4:11-13 *"It was he who gave some to be apostles, some to be prophets, some to be evangelists, and some to be pastors and teachers, to prepare God's people for works of service, so that the body of Christ may be built up until we all reach unity in the faith and in the knowledge of Son of God and become mature..."*

1 Corinthians 10:24 *"Nobody should seek his own good, but the good of others."*

> *"It means being not just willing but **eager** to sacrifice personal interest or glory for the welfare of all."*
>
> John Wooden, UCLA basketball coach

> *"If you want to be a team player, there are sacrifices to make. By no means am I comparing my sacrifice that Christ made for us, but that's just a small picture of pretty much the same thing. I have to make sacrifices day in and day out for the betterment of the team, as He made sacrifices for the betterment of the world—for those who want to follow him."*
>
> Howard Griffith, NFL fullback

3. Team Unity

Ephesians 4:1-6,15,16,25 *"As a prisoner for the Lord, then, I urge you to live a life worthy of the calling you have received. Be completely humble and gentle; be patient, bearing with one another in love. Make every effort to keep the unity of the Spirit through the bond of peace. There is one body and one Spirit—just as you were called to one hope when you were called—one Lord, one faith, one baptism; one God and Father of all, who is over all and through all and in all. Instead, speaking the truth in love, we will in all things grow up into him who is the Head, that is, Christ. From him the whole body, joined and held together by every supporting ligament, grows and builds itself up in love, as each part does its work. Therefore each of you must put off falsehood and speak truthfully to his neighbor, for we are all members of one body."*

Person in the Bible

Mary Magdelene, Joanna, and Mary the mother of James stayed unified through everything. Even in the death of Jesus, they stood together and cared for Jesus' body.

"There is no letter 'I' in the word TEAM." Most athletes have heard this saying before, but let's really look into this idea. We are all different and have our own needs. However we need to put our needs second to the needs of the team.

Let's see what it says in the Bible:

Proverbs 25:27 *"It is not good to eat too much honey, nor is it honorable to seek one's own honor."*

2 Thessalonians 5:12-15 *"Now we ask you, brothers, to respect those who work hard among you, who are over you in the Lord and who admonish you. Hold them in the highest regard in love because of their work. Live in peace with each other. And we urge you, brothers, warn those who are idle, encourage the timid, help the weak, be patient with everyone. Make sure that nobody pays back wrong for wrong, but always try to be kind to each other and to everyone else."*

1 Corinthians 1:10 *"I appeal to you, brothers, in the name of our Lord Jesus Christ, that all of you agree with one another so that there may be no divisions among you and that you may be perfectly united in mind and thought."*

James 4:1-3 *"What causes fights and quarrels among you? Don't they come from your desires that battle within you? You want something but don't get it. You kill and covet, but you cannot have what you want. You quarrel and fight. You do not have, because you do not ask God. When you ask, you do not receive, because you ask with wrong motives, that you may spend what you get on your pleasures."*

So how do all these verses relate to team spirit, sacrifice, and unity within the athletic community? The following is a rewording of the previous Bible verses and how we can apply them to our athletic lives. These ideas go for both team sports and individual sports...because we all represent a team of some sort.

1. Have the same goals, being one in spirit and purpose, don't be selfish, be humble and consider each other's needs.
2. Respect each other, live in peace, remind those who are slacking off, be patient, and don't go for revenge.
3. We all have different roles, and each team needs people with various specialties to build each other up and to be unified. Be inclusive and accept diversity. Set aside differences and work toward the goal and what is best for the team.
4. No negative statements against each other; use only positive words to build each other up.
5. It is so much better when we are working together and not fighting.
6. When someone makes a mistake, don't judge or condemn him or her. If it is a mistake during a competition, just forgive them and move on. If they do something against you personally, then assertively confront them. Next, sort through the issue, forgive them, and move on.

> *"Snowflakes are one of nature's most fragile things, but just look what they can do when they stick together."*
>
> Vesta M. Kelly

> *"We could learn a lot from crayons: Some are sharp, some are pretty, some are dull and some have weird names and all are different colors...but they all have to learn to live in the same box."*

Personal Notes and Ideas

1. How can I be encouraging to others in all kinds of situations?

2. How can I help my teammates to be supportive of each other?

3. What are some sacrifices that I may need to make for my team?

4. What can I do to prepare myself, and my teammates, for possible last-minute sacrifices for the team?

5. How can I be a major player with respect to our team unity?

6. What does the following statement mean to me? "There is no letter 'I' in the word TEAM."

7. How can I be like-minded if I don't agree with some of my teammates' attitudes and actions?

8. How can I prepare myself to react appropriately if:
   • Someone makes me very mad?

   • There is a major team problem?

9. What would Jesus do?

10. How do the Bible verses in this chapter help me with respect to team spirit sacrifice, and unity? Are there other verses that can help me be an ultimate athlete with respect to these team issues?

Part Six
MISCELLANEOUS

Introduction to Miscellaneous

The following chapters are about various themes, but all are important to athletes. The athletic world is comprehensive and at times it can be complicated. These final chapters should help you tie together the loose ends of your athletics. There may not be chapters in this book about some of the issues that are important to you. So feel free to write your own chapters about those concerns. You can do it! You have had enough practice at learning how to become an ultimate athlete. Just transfer all that knowledge to any situation, issue, problem, or opportunity that may come your way.

Mark 9:23 *"'If you can'? said Jesus. 'Everything is possible for him who believes.'"*

Philippians 1:27 *"Whatever happens, **conduct yourselves in a manner worthy of the gospel of Christ.** Then, whether I come and see you or only hear about you in my absence, I will know that you stand firm in one spirit, contending as one man for the faith of the gospel."*

Nutrition

"Do you not know that your body is a temple of the Holy Spirit, who is in you, whom you have received from God? You are not your own; you were bought at a price. Therefore honor God with your body."

I Corinthians 6:19,20

God is the great creator, who continues to amaze us with His creation. Just look at the Rocky Mountains, a breathtaking rainbow, a beautiful red rose…God has done a phenomenal job! However, His greatest creation is the human being. Take the time to ponder how magnificently we were made. Our bodies are complex and need a lot of tender loving care. With respect to nutrition, we can compare our bodies to automobiles. If you put the wrong kind of fuel in a car, the car will not perform very well. As a matter of fact, you could even cause damage to the car. It is the same with our bodies, because God designed us to thrive when we eat the correct food. We have the capacity to *help* or *harm* our bodies by what we eat and drink.

As athletes we should be very picky about what we eat. A simple way to remember what we eat is as follows. The following is a list: (Notice: The foods are listed by numbers so that they correlate with each other.)

Food that is good for me	Food that is not so healthy
1. Unprocessed food	1. Processed food
2. Low-fat foods (nothing fried)	2. Foods high in fat
3. Little sugar. (If any at all.)	3. Lots of sugar—A sugar rush is very harmful to your performance.
4. Complex carbohydrates: fruit, whole wheat bagels, potatoes, noodles…	4. Processed carbohydrates
5. Protein (not high in fat)	5. Protein (with lots of fat)
6. Low-fat milk, 100% fruit juice, water…	6. Caffeine, pop, sugar drinks…

Take special care to eat correctly the last two to three weeks before a big competition. Eat well-balanced and healthy meals. During the 48 hours before a competition, start being very vigilant with your nutrition. Absolutely no sugar, pop, caffeine, or fried foods. During the 3 to 4 hours before you compete, keep foods that are slow to digest at a minimum. These foods include dairy products and meat. Plan ahead and take your food to the competition site. You can't always count on the host site to provide the food that you need. Remember your body is like a car, and it needs the right fuel to perform at its best.

Bible verses:

Romans 12:1 *"Therefore, I urge you, brothers, in view of God's mercy, to offer your bodies as living sacrifices, holy and pleasing to God—this is your spiritual act of worship."*

Proverbs 23:20-21 *"Do not join those who drink too much wine or gorge themselves on meat, for drunkards and gluttons become poor, and drowsiness clothes them in rags."*

Phillippians 3:17-21 *"Join with others in following my example, brothers, and take note of those who live according to the pattern we gave you. For, as I have often told you before and now say again even with tears, many live as enemies of the cross of Christ. Their destiny is destruction, their god is their stomach, and their glory is in their shame. Their mind is on earthly things. But our citizenship is in heaven. And we eagerly await a Savior from there, the Lord Jesus Christ, who, by the power that enables him to bring everything under his control, will transform our lowly bodies so that they will be like his glorious body."*

"Take care of your body and eat good foods so that you will have more energy and power when you compete."

The Author

Personal Notes and Ideas

1. What good foods do I already eat?

2. What are the bad foods that I eat?

3. What can I specifically do to improve my eating habits?

4. How does poor nutrition hurt an athlete's body and its performance?

5. What does God have to say about eating, drinking, and taking care of our bodies?

6. My favorite healthy foods on competition day are:

7. How can my faith help me eat correctly?

8. What would Jesus do?

9. How do the Bible verses in this chapter help me? Are there any other verses that can help me be an ultimate athlete with respect to nutrition?

Goals

"Love the Lord your God with all your heart and with all your soul and with all your mind and with all your strength."

Mark 12:30

One thing that all athletes have in common is that they all have goals. Some of these goals can be short term and others can be for years into the future. What happens when you don't achieve an athletic goal? How does an ultimate athlete handle a situation like this? Let's look at Ricky's story.

Ricky wanted to break 10 seconds in his 100-yard dash. He had come so close many times, and even broke 10 seconds in a relay. But Ricky wanted to do it on his own. He was team captain and this would be the last race of his career at state finals for his university. Ricky was a talented athlete, but he was chosen to be the team captain because of his great leadership qualities. Ricky was also a Christian and his teammates knew it too. They esteemed him for his values and for how caring he was with everyone on the team.

Ricky had qualified for the final championships, and everyone was cheering for him. He raced with all of his heart and he finished knowing that he had given it his all. After crossing the finish line he looked up and saw that his time was a 10.01. Ricky had missed it by one-hundredth of a second. This was his last race of his career. He bowed his head in total amazement at how close he had come. Ricky thought to himself, "Yes this was my big goal, and I didn't get it. However God is more important to me than beating 10 seconds. People look up to me, and I need to show by my actions that God is number one to me." So he prayed a quick prayer, "God this is disappointing, but help me to hold my chin up and encourage other teammates because the meet is not over."

As he walked back to his team, all the teammates came to console him. But Ricky said, "I'm OK because I did my best—my best time is 10.01. Sure I wanted to break 10 seconds, but we have more races to run. Let's get psyched up!" His teammates were so impressed with his attitude. Days later, Ricky was very happy with his reaction at the meet. Obviously he was frustrated, because he didn't break 10 seconds. However, when he thought about his faith and going to Heaven, it really didn't hurt that much.

Here are some great goals to strive for:

Romans 12:2 *"Do not conform any longer to the pattern of this world, but be transformed by the renewing of your mind. Then you will be able to test and approve what God's will is— his good, pleasing and perfect will."*

Psalm 26:1 *"Vindicate me, O Lord, for I have led a blameless life; I have trusted in the Lord without wavering."*

Psalm 37:3 *"Trust in the Lord and do good; dwell in the land and enjoy safe pasture."*

Psalm 40:8 *"I desire to do your will, O my God; your law is within my heart."*

Psalm 61:8 *"Then will I ever sing praise to your name and fulfill my vows day after day."*

Being holy is a great goal:

1 Peter 1:13-16 *"Therefore, prepare your minds for action; be self-controlled; set your hope fully on the grace to be given you*

when *Jesus Christ is revealed. As obedient children, do not conform to the evil desires you had when you lived in ignorance. But just as he who called you is holy, so be holy in all you do; for it is written: "Be holy, because I am holy."*

Leviticus 19:2 *"Speak to the entire assembly of Israel and say to them: 'Be holy because I, the Lord your God, am holy.'"*

2 Timothy 1:9 *"...who has saved us and called us to a holy life—not because of anything we have done but because of his own purpose and grace. This grace was given us in Christ Jesus before the beginning of time."*

Proverbs 20:9 *"Who can say, 'I have kept my heart pure; I am clean and without sin'?"*

Words we want to hear from God:

Luke 19:17 *"'Well done, my good servant!' his master replied. 'Because you have been trustworthy in a very small matter, take charge of ten cities.'"*

Luke 3:22 *"...and the Holy Spirit descended on him in bodily form like a dove. And a voice came from heaven: 'You are my Son, whom I love; with you I am well pleased.'"*

*"My goal is: not to be **liked** by others, not to **be** like others, but to **be like** Jesus."*
Ana Maria Germanson

"I'd rather shoot for the stars and miss than shoot for nothing and get hit."
Unknown

"There is but one thing in the world really worth pursuing—the knowledge of God."
R.H. Benson

> *"I read my goals every day. I believed them,
> prayed them, slept them, and dreamt them."*
> Mike Singletary, Chicago Bears NFL Hall of Fame

Personal Notes and Ideas

1. What are my top five goals in life?

2. What are my top five goals in athletics?

3. Out of the ten goals listed above, which ones are the most important?

4. How can I encourage my teammates to strive for good goals?

5. How can my faith help me when I do or don't achieve an important goal?

6. What would Jesus do?

7. How do the Bible verses in this chapter help me? Are there other verses that can help me be an ultimate athlete with respect to goals?

Obedience

"Remind the people to be subject to rulers and authorities, to be obedient, to be ready to do whatever is good."

Titus 3:1

Person in the Bible

The following verse shows us Philip's allegiance to God. Philip didn't hesitate or ask many questions when he was told to do something. One time he actually ran to do his deed. Acts 8:26-30 "Now an angel of the Lord said to Philip, 'Go south to the road—the desert road—that goes down from Jerusalem to Gaza.' So he started out...On his way home...the Spirit told Philip, 'Go to that chariot and stay near it.' Then Philip *ran* up to the chariot..."

Obeying is not such a bad thing! Unfortunately the word *obedience* has a bad rap and bad connotation. It sounds like something that is all drudgery and very boring. Nothing could be further from the truth. If we as learners can choose to obey our wise teachers, we are in for a thrilling life. There are many ways that we are learners in this life: parent/child, teacher/student, doctor/patient, coach/athlete, pastor/church member, police and firefighters/citizens... and the list goes on. By not obeying these various wise teachers, we will find ourselves in trouble, with problems, possibly in danger, and hurt in many ways. We can become hurt emotionally, physically, spiritually, mentally, socially, and occupationally. The reason parents tell children not to touch a hot stove is because they don't want their little ones getting burned. There are many ways in life that you can get burned, and the best prevention is to just do what you are told. Rules and procedures are made for your benefit, not to hurt you! Be to practice on time, get to bed early before meets, don't do drugs and alcohol—all are there to help you become an ultimate athlete and person!

> Ephesians 6:5,6 *"Slaves, obey your earthly masters with respect and fear, and with sincerity of heart, just as you would obey Christ. Obey them not only to win their favor when their eye is on you, but like slaves of Christ, doing the will of God from your heart."*

> Hebrews 13:17 *"Obey your leaders and submit to their authority. They keep watch over you as men who must give an account. Obey them so that their work will be a joy, not a burden, for that would be of no advantage to you."*

> Ephesians 6:1-4 *"Children, obey your parents in the Lord, for this is right. 'Honor you father and mother'—which is the first commandment with a promise—'that it may go well with you and that you may enjoy long life on the earth.' Fathers, do not exasperate your children; instead, bring them up in the training and instruction of the Lord."*

Peer pressure can be hard to withstand. If a friend or teammate wants you to do something that is disobedient, then they aren't really your friend. True friends don't jeopardize and ruin your life. They may say that they are your friends, but they really aren't. (Look at chapter 58 about convenient and inconvenient friends) Real friends will go out of their way to help you become a *better* person.

Don't compare yourself with other people your age and say, "At least I am not as bad as that person. So please give me a break." You should only be comparing yourself to Jesus Christ, and asking yourself, "What would Jesus do?" Jesus is our role model and gauge as to whether we are truly being obedient. If we choose to follow Jesus then we must be obedient just like He was. 1 John 2:6 *"Whoever claims to live in him must walk as Jesus did."* He was obedient all the way to the cross. He was crying to His Father, and even sweating blood, when He prayed in the Garden of Gethsemane. Obviously He wasn't in the mood to die, but He did it!

In the Garden of Gethsemane:

Mark 14:36 *"'Abba, Father,' he said, 'everything is possible for you. Take this cup from me. Yet not what I will, but what you will.'"*

Matthew 26:39 *"Going a little farther, he fell with his face to the ground and prayed, 'My Father, if it is possible, may this cup be taken from me. Yet not as I will, but as you will.'"*

Obey because we love God:

John 14:23 *"Jesus replied, 'If anyone loves me, he will obey my teaching. My Father will love him, and we will come to him and make our home with him.'"*

1 John 5:3 *"This is love for God: to obey his commands. And his commands are not burdensome."*

Love one another:

1 John 3:23,24 *"And this is his command: to believe in the name of his Son, Jesus Christ, and to love one another as he commanded us. Those who obey his commands live in him, and he in them. And this is how we know that he lives in us: We know it by the Spirit he gave us."*

2 John 1:6 *"And this is love: that we walk in obedience to his commands. As you have heard from the beginning, his command is that you walk in love."*

Consequences when we don't obey:

Ephesians 5:6 *"Let no one deceive you with empty words, for because of such things God's wrath comes on those who are disobedient."*

As athletes, let's take it a step further, and not just obey when the coaches are looking. Ephesians 6:6 *"Obey them not only to win their favor when their eye is on you, but like slaves of Christ, doing the will of God from your heart."* Being obedient makes your life easier and safer. You should have less hassles, because of your cooperation with others. When you do things your own way, and choose to not follow the directions, expect to have more problems and frustrations.

Yes, sometimes in your life you will have teachers, adults, role models, or coaches who aren't the best examples. As a matter of fact they can be downright horrible. See chapters 39 and 64 on "Abusive Situations" and "Bad Coaches" for more information on how to deal with people like that.

> *"Obedience to God is when someone does what is right even though it is the unpopular thing to do."*
>
> The Author

Oliver Christopher heard a call from God to defend the poor. He chose to obey God and fight for the rights of the less fortunate. Oliver realized that this was a great way to show his faith in Christ.

> *"The more I prayed about injustice the more I felt Jesus wanted me to be involved. I could have walked away from the challenge, but I didn't."*
>
> Oliver Christopher, karate champion

Personal Notes and Ideas

1. What does obedience mean to me?

2. How can I benefit from being obedient to my wise teachers?

3. What are some possible consequences if I choose to disobey?

4. How does Jesus' obedience impact my life?

5. How can I encourage my other teammates to be obedient too?

6. What would Jesus do?

7. How do the Bible verses in this chapter help me? Are there any other verses that can help me to be more obedient?

Integrity/Dignity

*"So I strive always to keep my conscience
clear before God and man."*

Acts 24:16

Integrity is staying true to your principles, no matter what happens. It is choosing to take a stand for what you believe in without compromising. According to Webster's dictionary, integrity is:

"1 : firm adherence to a code of especially moral or artistic values :
    INCORRUPTIBILITY
2 : an unimpaired condition : SOUNDNESS
3 : the quality or state of being complete or undivided :
    COMPLETENESS synonym see HONESTY"

Another word that is similar to integrity is *dignity*. Each one of you has their own God-given dignity. God has created us and has made us in his image. Therefore we should not tarnish this precious image. According to Webster's dictionary, dignity is:

"the quality or state of being worthy, honored, or esteemed."

It is imperative that we choose to live a life of integrity and dignity. Keeping our integrity and God-given dignity pure is more important than winning.

We have all heard the following sayings:

- "Win at all costs."
- "Don't settle for second best."
- "Losing isn't an option."
- "Do whatever it takes..."
- "Fight to win."

These sayings have been used to psych us up to do our best. However, they can also have a negative effect. Some athletes will revert to bad choices in order to win. So, let's change these sayings to:

- "Keep your integrity at all costs."
- "Don't settle for losing your integrity."
- "Losing your integrity is not an option."
- "Don't do whatever it takes, because you might lose your integrity."
- "Fight to keep your integrity."

Proverbs 11:3 *"The integrity of the upright guides them, but the unfaithful are destroyed by their duplicity."*

The following are opposites of integrity and God-given dignity:

Lying

Proverbs 14:5 *"A truthful witness does not deceive, but a false witness pours out lies."*

Cheating

Proverbs 1:19 *"Such is the end of all who go after ill-gotten gain; it takes away the lives of those who get it."*

Stealing

Proverbs 10:2 *"Ill-gotten treasures are of no value, but righteousness delivers from death."*

Jeremiah was ridiculed and persecuted for his faith in God. However Jeremiah would not, and could not, allow his enemies to rule over his life. He chose to keep his integrity intact and do what was right. He continued being faithful to God in the midst of some extreme circumstances. Instead of listening to his enemies, Jeremiah chose to trust in God. Read the following verses in Jeremiah 20:8-11:

> *"Whenever I speak, I cry out proclaiming violence and destruction. So the word of the LORD has brought me insult and reproach all day long. But if I say, 'I will not mention him or speak any more in his name,' his word is in my heart like a fire, a fire shut up in my bones. I am weary of holding it in; indeed, I cannot. I hear many whispering, 'Terror on every side! Report him! Let's report him!' All my friends are waiting for me to slip, saying, 'Perhaps he will be deceived; then we will prevail over him and take our revenge on him.' But the LORD is with me like a mighty warrior; so my persecutors will stumble and not prevail. They will fail and be thoroughly disgraced; their dishonor will never be forgotten."*

Rueben Gonzalez was playing racquetball in the finals of his first professional tournament. It appeared that he had won the match point with an amazing shot. Even the judges ruled that his shot was good. But he saw the ball bounce wrong and told the officials. To the amazement of all, Rueben immediately disqualified himself. He was quoted later as saying, "It was the only thing I could do to maintain my integrity." This is a beautiful example proving that winning *isn't* the most important thing in sports.

Everyone knows the famous Nike logo, "Just do it." This is a fantastic saying for everyone, whether they are athletes or not. Let's take this great slogan and make it even better by adding one word. Just do it *right*! Adding the extra word can help us to keep our integrity and dignity pure.

During a very close meet against the conference champions, it all came down to the last relay. This makes for an exciting meet! Katie's assistant coach told her that, by mistake, a runner competed in the last relay. It was his fifth event of the meet, which was illegal. No one else knew except for Katie and her assistant coach. The one runner was too young to know all the rules. Katie knew that if she disqualified her relay, they would lose the meet. Katie felt badly for her team, because they put their heart and their soul into this meet. She also knew that her athlete volunteered to help out by running in the last relay. He had no idea that he was hurting the team.

Knowing that she would have sad athletes she said, "There is only one thing to do, and it is to tell the truth." Katie told the officials, and disqualified her last relay. Her team lost by a couple of points. Instead of being upset, Katie chose to use this as a teachable moment. She told every detail to her team. She asked them if they would rather win with a cheating coach, or to lose with an honest coach. They all said that they wanted an honest coach. Amazingly, no one was really upset about the loss!

Are you familiar with the book of Job in the Old Testament? Job was a man of many tragedies. However God gave Satan permission to torment Job. No matter what Job had to suffer, he never cursed God.

Job 2:3 *"Then the Lord said to Satan, 'Have you considered my servant Job? There is no one on earth like him; he is blameless and upright, a man who fears God and shuns evil. And he still maintains his integrity, though you incited me against him to ruin him without any reason.'"*

After all Job's tragedy, his wife tells him to give up. Job 2:9 *"His wife said to him, 'Are you still holding on to your integrity? Curse God and die!'"*

Job 27:5 *"I will never admit you are in the right; till I die, I will not deny my integrity."*

Job 31:6 *"Let God weigh me in honest scales and he will know that I am blameless."*

Here are more verses about integrity:

1 Kings 9:4 *"As for you, if you walk before me in **integrity** of heart and uprightness, as David your father did, and do all I command and observe my decrees and laws."*

Romans 9:1 *"Speak the truth in Christ—I am not lying, my conscience confirms it in the Holy Spirit."*

Titus 2:7 *"**In everything** set them an example by doing what is good. In your teaching show **integrity**..."*

Isaiah 59:4 *"No one calls for justice; no one pleads his case with integrity. They rely on empty arguments and speak lies; they conceive trouble and give birth to evil."*

*"Courage is when you **do** what you **know** is right, even if you cannot convince your best friend to do the same."*

Gandhi

*"The way to **lead** is to follow your **conscience**."*

U.S. Senator Paul D. Wellstone

Personal Notes and Ideas

1. What does *integrity* mean to me?

2. What does *God-given dignity* mean to me?

3. Is it more important to win or to maintain my integrity/dignity?

4. Would I be able to do what Rueben or Katie did?

5. How can I encourage my teammates to put integrity/dignity over winning?

6. What would Jesus do?

7. How do the Bible verses in this chapter help me? Are there any other verses that can help me with my integrity/dignity?

The "C" Word

*"I can do everything through him who gives
me strength."*

Philippians 4:13 is a great verse. It really helps us to stay positive and focused on our goals. However we cannot abuse this verse and think that we can do everything that *we* want. The things we desire are not necessarily what God wants. He knows better than we do about *everything*. So make sure that you remember that you can do all things…*that God wants you to do*…because He will give you strength.

The "C" word means *can't*. There was a coach who didn't allow her athletes to use the word *can't*. The coach even refused to say the word in front of her athletes. So she said that she never wanted to hear the "C" word.

Emily was an athlete who had a minor disability. She participated in sports so that she could get some exercise and become stronger. Her coach, Vicky, was aware of Emily's bad leg and made her workouts different from the other athletes. Vicky challenged Emily every day, but she never made the workouts too hard. Emily always felt successful after each practice. One day Vicky decided to have her try a new exercise. She knew it would be hard, but she was sure that Emily would be able to do it. Vicky told Emily about the new exercise, and explained how to do it. Emily immediately said, "What are you talking about? That is impossible!"

Vicky pulled Emily aside and assigned her a new task. Emily needed to interview the assistant coach, Jenny, as to why the word *impossible* was not in her dictionary. Then she had to write a report and hand it into her coach. Vicky gave Emily a piece of paper and a pencil. Emily went over to Jenny and started to interview her. Jenny was a former athlete, but due to a skiing accident, she became paralyzed. Jenny chose to continue her athletic career by being a coach rather than an athlete. All of Emily's teammates saw her interviewing Jenny and writing up a report. After practice, the athletes asked Emily what she was doing, and why she had to do it. Emily's comment was, "Never say the word *impossible* around Vicky!" Everyone, including Vicky, broke out into laughter. Yes, Emily had learned her lesson!

If you want to be an ultimate athlete you need to make sure that you never use the words *impossible* or *can't*. If you choose to say those words, then you are going against God's Word, because with Him, *all things are possible!* In addition, these words are very contagious, and if said in practice or competitions, they can spread around very fast. No matter what happens, we *can* and we *need* to stay positive. See chapter 36 on "Attitude." Take time to reread chapter 48 on "Prevailing." It talks about exhausting all possibilities and creating alternatives.

Psalm 18:29 "*With your help I can advance against a troop**; with my God I can scale a wall.*" (**Or can run through a barricade*)

"*Success come in cans, failure comes in can'ts.*"
Unknown

Personal Notes and Ideas

1. What is the big deal about saying the words *impossible* and *can't*?

2. What can I do so that I don't use those words at practice, competition and in life?

3. How can I encourage my teammates to not say the words *impossible* and *can't?*

4. How can my faith help me when I feel like using negative words?

5. What would Jesus do?

6. How do the Bible verses in this chapter help me? Are there other verses that can help me be an ultimate athlete with respect to using the "C" word?

Balance

"Jesus answered, 'It is written: Man does not live by bread alone, but on every word that comes from the mouth of God.'"

Matthew 4:4

"...rather train yourself to be godly. For physical training is of some value, but godliness has value to all things, holding promise for both the present life and the life to come."

1 Timothy 4:7-8

God is an incredible creator! He created the heavens and the universe. Take time to think about how magnificent everything is. From the tiny little snowflake to a colorful butterfly, to a beautiful palm tree, to a breathtaking mountain range...your amazement will never cease. God also did a fantastic job in creating human beings. We can walk, talk, feel, think, eat, hear, believe, love... Wow! Even the best computer in the world can not do as many things as a human being. God has made us as multidimensional human beings. The six dimensions of man are emotional, mental/intellectual, occupational, physical, social, and spiritual. It is very important that we strive to be strong in all areas of our lives. God desires that we live life to the fullest. Ignoring one or more dimensions is not the way God intended for us to live.

If you aim at nothing, you get just that! Nothing! So as we strive to keep all of our dimensions healthy and strong, we need to know what to do. What can we do to reach our goal of healthy balance in all areas of our lives? One of the best activities is to draw our Spokes of Life.

Imagine your life as a bicycle wheel with six spokes. Each spoke represents a different dimension. The first thing that you do is to draw the midpoint to serve as the axle. Then draw every spoke from the inside out. If you have a short spoke, then that particular dimension of your life is not doing very well. If the spoke is long, or touches the rim, then that part of your life is going great.

Let's look at Billy's spokes. One year Billy's family had to move to a new state, he had a broken leg, and he wasn't doing well in school. Therefore, spokes five, two, and six are very short. Emotionally, Billy was a basket case due to all of his misfortune, so spoke one is almost nonexistent. He was doing fine mentally and spiritually, so spokes four and three are much longer. Yet none of the spokes reach the rim of the wheel. When we look at the spokes within the circle, we see which areas Billy needs to work on so his ride can be smoother.

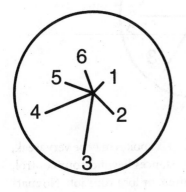

1. Emotional
2. Physical
3. Spiritual
4. Mental/Intellectual
5. Occupational
6. Social

When we make a rim that connects with the ends of the spokes (illustration below), we see how rough Billy's ride is. This illustration shows us that we should all strive to balance our lives.

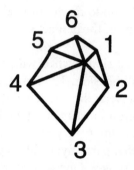

Billy drew his spokes a year later. It is amazing how they had changed. Billy was able to fix his life because he knew specifically what he needed to work on.

Many times the conditions of your six spokes may be very weak, but it is not your fault. Due to circumstances beyond your control, you move to a different state, get injured, or lose your job. No matter the reason, it is *your* choice to do something about it.

Now you can draw a circle, mark the midpoint to serve as the axle, and draw each spoke as it represents your life today. Does it look like a smooth or a bumpy ride?

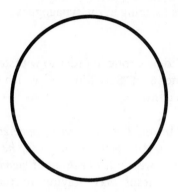

After an honest look at each dimension of your life, you can develop a plan of action to make your life more balanced. Remember, balance is the key to health.

Please don't feel down if you have a short spoke. That is called life. The road of life does give us some twists and turns along the way. If you have a short spoke, it means that you are experiencing a tough part of life. You are still a person of much value and very loved. Give yourself some time and that spoke will get longer.

Jesus was multidimensional.
Emotional

John 11:35 *"Jesus wept."*

Mental/intellectual

Jesus needed to stay mentally sharp to be able to confront the Pharisees...

Luke 2:52 *"And Jesus grew in wisdom and stature, and in favor with God and men."*

Occupational

Jesus worked as a carpenter.

Mark 6:3 *"Isn't this the carpenter? Isn't this Mary's son and the brother of James, Joseph, Judas and Simon?"* (Referring to when Jesus was teaching in the synagogues.)

Physical

1. Jesus needed to be strong in order to withstand all the pain. Refer to chapter 6 on "Sore Muscles," which explains how a crucifixion is done.

Luke 22: 43 *"An angel from heaven appeared to him and strengthened him. And being in anguish, he prayed more earnestly, and his sweat was like drops of blood falling to the ground."* (When Jesus was praying in the Garden of Gethsemane before His death.)

Luke 23:44 *"It was now about the sixth hour, and darkness came over the whole land until the ninth hour, for the sun stopped shining. And the curtain of the temple was torn in two. Jesus called out with a loud voice, 'Father, into your hands I commit my spirit.' When he had said this, he breathed his last."* (Jesus withstood many hours on the cross until His body finally stopped.)

2. He also understood the importance of the physical aspect, because he healed the sick.

Matthew 15:30 *"Great crowds came to him, bringing the lame, the blind, the crippled, the mute and many others, and laid them at his feet; and he healed them."*

Matthew 14:14 *"When Jesus landed and saw a large crowd, he had compassion on them and healed their sick."*

Social

Jesus spent time with many people. So we need to meet together. We shouldn't be lone rangers.

Mark 4:1 *"Again Jesus began to teach by the lake. The crowd that gathered around him was so large that he got into a boat and sat in it out on the lake, while all the people were along the shore at the water's edge."*

Hebrews 10:24-25 *"And let us consider how we may spur one another on toward love and good deeds. Let us not give up meeting together, as some are in the habit of doing, but let us encourage one another—and all the more as you see the Day approaching."*

Spiritual

Jesus spent time in prayer with His Father.

Mark 1:35 *"Very early in the morning, while it was still dark, Jesus got up, left the house and went off to a solitary place, where he prayed."*

> *"But the championship is temporary. Your fulfillment and joy definitely comes from Jesus and your family. Who you're becoming, the chararcter you're developing, that's what is going to last."*
> Kris Korver, NAIA Men's Coach of the Year

> *"If you have to spend your whole life looking for this thrill of victory, how disappointed you will be. Because it just wasn't that thrilling. Relationships are what give meaning to life. A relationship with God is wonderful. He loves us unconditionally. And we need to love the people around us—hopefully the same way. And that's much more meaningful and lasts a lot longer than any success on the golf course."*
> Tom Lehman, professional golfer

Personal Notes and Ideas

1. What areas of my life are strong right now? What can I do to maintain or improve those spokes?

2. What areas of my life are weak right now? What can I do to improve those areas?

3. Why is it so important to have balance in my life?

4. How can I help my other teammates to have balance in their lives?

5. What would Jesus do?

6. How do the Bible verses in this chapter help me? Are there other verses that can help me be an ultimate athlete with respect to balance?

Time
Off

"Devote yourselves to prayer, being watchful and thankful..."

Colossians 4:2

According to chapter 18, a "time-out" is having quiet time with Bible and studying God's word. In this chapter, "time off" represents our time in prayer with God. It is our time to communicate with Him. There are many ways to communicate with God, and they will be discussed in this chapter. In sports we all need to take some time off and get away from the pressures of our athletic lives. After finishing a season, it is important to take some days off before starting your training regimen again. Your body, mind, and emotions all need a rest. Jesus is a great example for us. He was always busy and in high demand. However, He always took time away from His hectic life to be in communication with His Father.

Where and when:

Luke 5:16 *"But Jesus often withdrew to lonely places and prayed."*

Luke 4:42 *"At daybreak Jesus went out to a solitary place. The people were looking for him and when they came to where he was, they tried to keep him from leaving them."*

1 Thessalonians 5:17 *"...pray continually."*

Psalm 5:3 *"Each morning I will look to you in heaven and lay my requests before you, praying earnestly."* (Living Bible)

Why:

Genesis 2:2 *"By the seventh day God had finished the work he had been doing; so on the seventh day he rested from all his work."*

Philippians 4: 6,7 *"Do not be anxious about anything, but in everything, by prayer and petition, with thanksgiving, present your requests to God. And the peace of God, which transcends all understanding, will guard your hearts and your minds in Christ Jesus."*

How:

A great way to learn how to pray is to say the "Our Father". See Matthew 6:9-13

James 4:3 *"When you ask, you do not receive, because you ask with wrong motives, that you may spend what you get on your pleasures."*

1 John 5:14,15 *"This is the confidence we have in approaching God: that if we ask anything according to his will, he hears us. And if we know that he hears us—whatever we ask—we know that we have what we asked of him."*

Who:

Jesus is our example.

Luke 22:44 *"And being in anguish, he prayed more earnestly, and his sweat was like drops of blood falling to the ground."*

Mark 14:36 *"Abba, Father he said, everything is possible for you. Take this cup from me. Yet not what I will, but what you will."*

What:

It is a conversation with God. During this time you should take time to:

- Listen to what He has to tell you. Remember a conversation involves two-way communication.
- Tell God your innermost feelings… a great way to pray is to remember the word ACTS. Your prayers can go in the following order:

> **A**doration
> **C**onfession
> **T**hanks
> **S**upplication (Prayer Requests)

- Be still—quiet your heart, soul, and mind and rest in Him.

Dixie Grace, psychologist, feels that we must have a certain focus when we begin our prayer time. We should reflect on how much we *have*, rather than how much we *need*. By thinking about what we need, we are being more task oriented by building a list for God. If our focus is on what we have, we will be communication oriented and building a *relationship*. This way we will be *visiting* with God and not treating Him like a vending machine. Dixie feels that it is very important that we don't hog the whole conversation, but truly engage in two-way communication. We need to listen to God and find out what His will is in our lives.

> *"In order that God can work His miracles, God doesn't need us taking over all of the time. All that we need to do is to pray, obey, and get out of the way!" "There is great happiness in not wanting, in not being somewhere, in not going somewhere."*
>
> J. Krishnamurti

Personal Notes and Ideas

1. Where can I pray?

2. What is the best time for me to pray?

3. Why is it important for me to pray?

4. What do the following verses mean to me? 1 John 5:14-15 and Mark 14:36. (You can find them in this chapter.)

5. How can I encourage my teammates to pray?

6. How can praying help my faith?

7. What can I learn from Jesus' example?

8. What would Jesus do?

9. How do the Bible verses in this chapter help me? Are there other verses that can help me be an ultimate athlete with respect to taking time off/praying?

Extra verses

James 5:13-16
Mark 1:35
Deuteronomy 8:3
Matthew 6:9-13

Postgame Show

"...to love the Lord your God, to walk in all his ways, to obey his commands, to hold fast to him and to serve him with all your heart and all your soul."

Joshua 22:5

A. The rollercoaster of athletics

Many people think that their athletic career will be full of great times and successes. This can be true for part of their sporting life. However being an athlete is not always easy. The rollercoaster of the sports world can be exhilarating and also downright depressing. It is a long winding journey with many ups and downs. All athletes are in for a long haul. An athletic career cannot be compared to a 100-yard dash. It is more like a 26-mile marathon with hurdles. It is up to each athlete to make their athletic career *work* or make it *worse!*

This powerful truth is evident in the life of Jim Morris. When Jim was a boy, he wanted more than anything to play in a professional baseball game. For many reasons he was not able to until he became thirty-five years old. Finally in 1999, when he was a high school teacher and baseball coach, he accepted a dare from his athletes. If they won the district championship, he had to try out for the major leagues. Beating all the odds, he ended up pitching his first game for Tampa Bay on Saturday September 18 against the Texas Rangers. To learn more about his amazing story, watch the movie *The Rookie.* Jim is quoted as saying, "Reach out! Put a dream or goal just past where you can touch it at that moment. Then, once you do touch it, you've gotta reach a little higher. And a little bit higher. And a little bit higher. That's how you get better, no matter what you do in life."

1 Thessalonians 1:3 *"We continually remember before our God and Father your work produced by faith, your labor prompted by love, and your endurance inspired by hope in our Lord Jesus Christ."*

Philippians 1:6 *"Being confident of this, that he who began a good work in you will carry it on to completion until the day of Christ Jesus."*

"It is important for you to know that your ideals are often tested more in defeat than in victory. To know that this is not the end, but the beginning of what you can do."
Vice President Walter Mondale

B. Step up to the plate.

We need to step up to the plate in more ways than one. As athletes, human beings, and children of God, we need to do our best to make this world a better place to live both on and off the field.

1 Corinthians 15:58-59 *"Therefore, my dear brothers, stand firm. Let nothing move you. Always give yourselves fully to the work of the Lord, because you know that your labor in the Lord is not in vain."*

"We must be the change we seek in this world."
Gandhi

> *"We all do better, when we all do better."*
> Paul D. Wellstone

C. God is faithful.

Athletics give us no automatic promises for our future, but our faith in God does. God is always there! He is faithful and never changes.

Hebrews 13:8 *"Jesus Christ is the same yesterday and today and forever."*

1 Corinthians 1:9 *"God, who has called you into fellowship with his Son Jesus Christ our Lord, is faithful."*

Psalm 73:25-26 *"Whom have I in heaven but you? And earth has nothing I desire besides you. My flesh and my heart may fail, but God is the strength of my heart and my portion forever."*

D. God always has a plan.

Jeremiah 29:11-13 *"For I know the plans I have for you, declares the LORD , plans to prosper you and not to harm you, plans to give you hope and a future. Then you will call upon me and come and pray to me, and I will listen to you. You will seek me and find me when you seek me with all your heart."*

Isaiah 58:11 *"The Lord will guide you always; he will satisfy your needs in a sun-scorched land and will strengthen your frame. You will be like a well-watered garden, like a spring whose waters never fail."*

John 16:13 *"But when he, the Spirit of truth, comes, he will guide you into all truth. He will not speak on his own; he will speak only what he hears, and he will tell you what is yet to come."*

E. Let your light shine.

As children of God, we should do our best to let our light shine for others to see. This light should not be obtrusive and forceful.

The illumination from our lives must be welcoming, inspirational, and motivational to others.

> Psalm 118:17 *"I will not die but live, and will proclaim what the Lord has done."*

> *"Live your life by design, not by accident."*
>
> Unknown

> *"You miss 100 percent of the shots never taken."*
>
> Wayne Gretzky, pro hockey player

The following verse is for you, from the author:

> Numbers 6:24-26 *"The LORD bless you and keep you; the LORD make his face shine upon you and be gracious to you; the LORD turn his face toward you and give you peace."*

You Can Be the Ultimate Athlete
Order Form

Postal orders: Susan Germanson
10035 Russell Ave. N.
Brooklyn Park, MN 55444

Telephone orders: (763) 424-2565

E-mail orders: ouchsg@comcast.net

Please send *You Can Be the Ultimate Athlete* to:

Name: _____

Address: _____

City: _____ State: _____

Zip: _____

Telephone: (_____) _____

Book Price: $19.95

Shipping: $3.00 for the first book and $1.00 for each additional book to cover shipping and handling within US, Canada, and Mexico. International orders add $6.00 for the first book and $2.00 for each additional book.

Or order from:
ACW Press
85334 Lorane Hwy
Eugene, OR 97405

(800) 931-BOOK

or contact your local bookstore